## GUERILLA WARFARE

*RESTRICTED*

# CONTENTS

| | Page |
|---|---|
| FOREWORD | vii |
| PREFACE | ix |
| CHAPTER 1. INTRODUCTION TO GUERILLA WARFARE | 1 |
| (a) Its meaning and scope | 1 |
| (b) Examples, 1800–1939 | 5 |
| (c) Arab Operations 1916–1918 | 12 |
| CHAPTER 2. JUGOSLAVIA: SECOND WORLD WAR | 21 |
| (a) The Guerilla Campaign | 21 |
| (b) Politics, Liaison and Support | 42 |
| CHAPTER 3. GREECE: SECOND WORLD WAR | 65 |
| CHAPTER 4. FURTHER EUROPEAN CAMPAIGNS: SECOND WORLD WAR | 91 |
| (a) Albania | 91 |
| (b) Italy | 100 |
| (c) France | 106 |
| (d) Other European Countries | 117 |
| (e) Soviet Guerilla Operations | 120 |
| CHAPTER 5. FAR EAST: SECOND WORLD WAR | 131 |
| (a) Outline of Guerilla Warfare, South East Asia | 131 |
| (b) Malaya, 1941–45 | 133 |
| (c) Burma, 1942–45 | 147 |
| (d) S.O.E. Organisation in India by 1945 | 156 |
| CHAPTER 6. MALAYA: POST 1945 | 163 |
| CHAPTER 7. SUMMARY OF GUERILLA WARFARE | 173 |
| BIBLIOGRAPHY | 197 |

# MAPS AND DIAGRAMS

Map 1. Boer Operations 1899–1902

Map 2. Arab Operations 1916–1918

Map 3. Jugoslavia

Map 4. Jugoslavia: the Fourth Offensive

Map 5. Jugoslavia: Operation 'BEARSKIN'

Map 6. Jugoslavia: Operation 'RATWEEK'

Map 7. Greece

Map 8. Albania

Map 9. Italy

Map 10. France

Map 11. Malaya

Map 12. Burma


| | |
|---|---:|
| Table 1. Greek Resistance Movements . . . . | 67 |
| Table 2. Albanian Resistance Movements . . . . | 92 |
| Table 3. Malayan Communist Guerilla Organisation . . | 137 |
| Table 4. S.O.E. Base Organisation (S.E.A.C.) . . . | 157 |

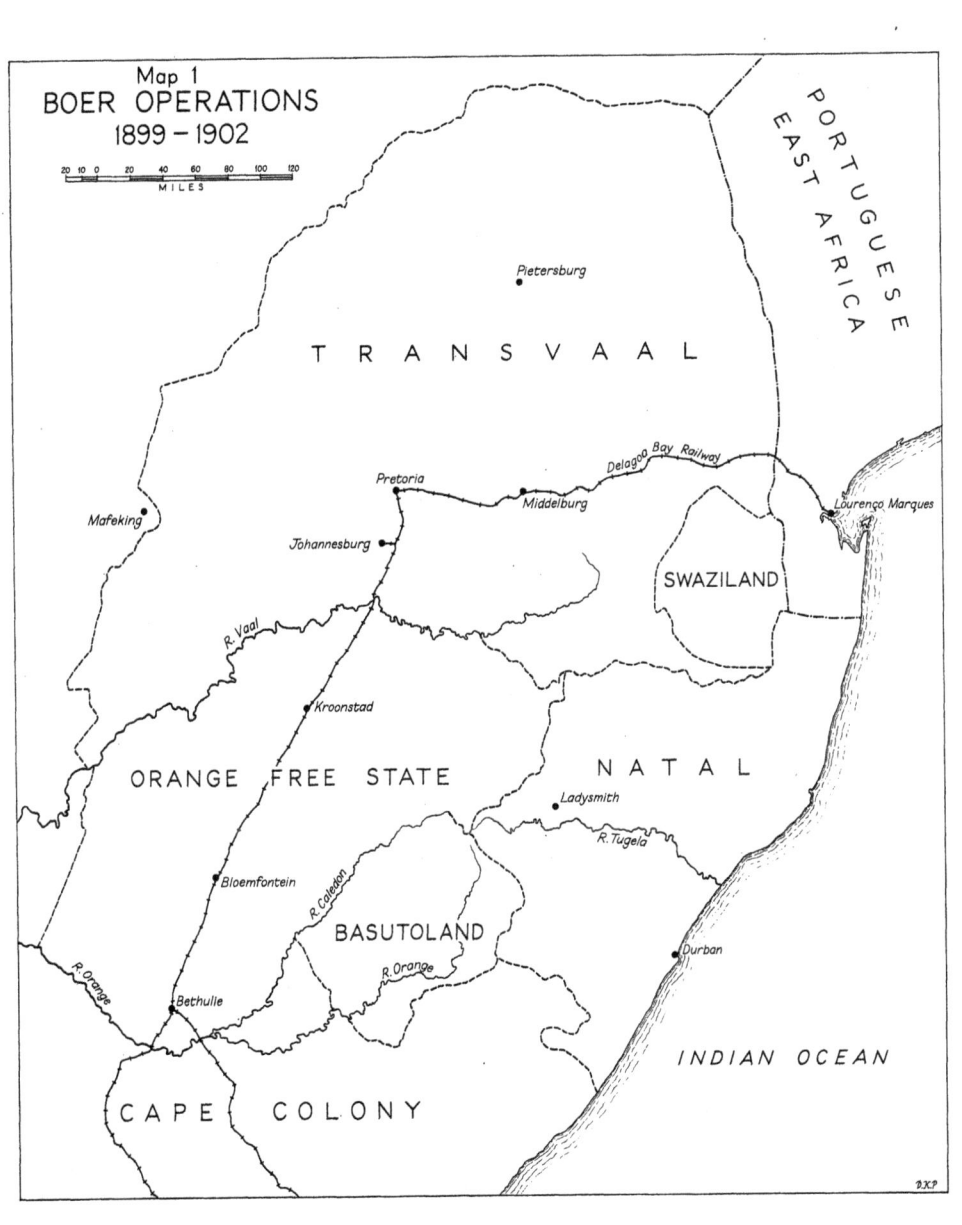

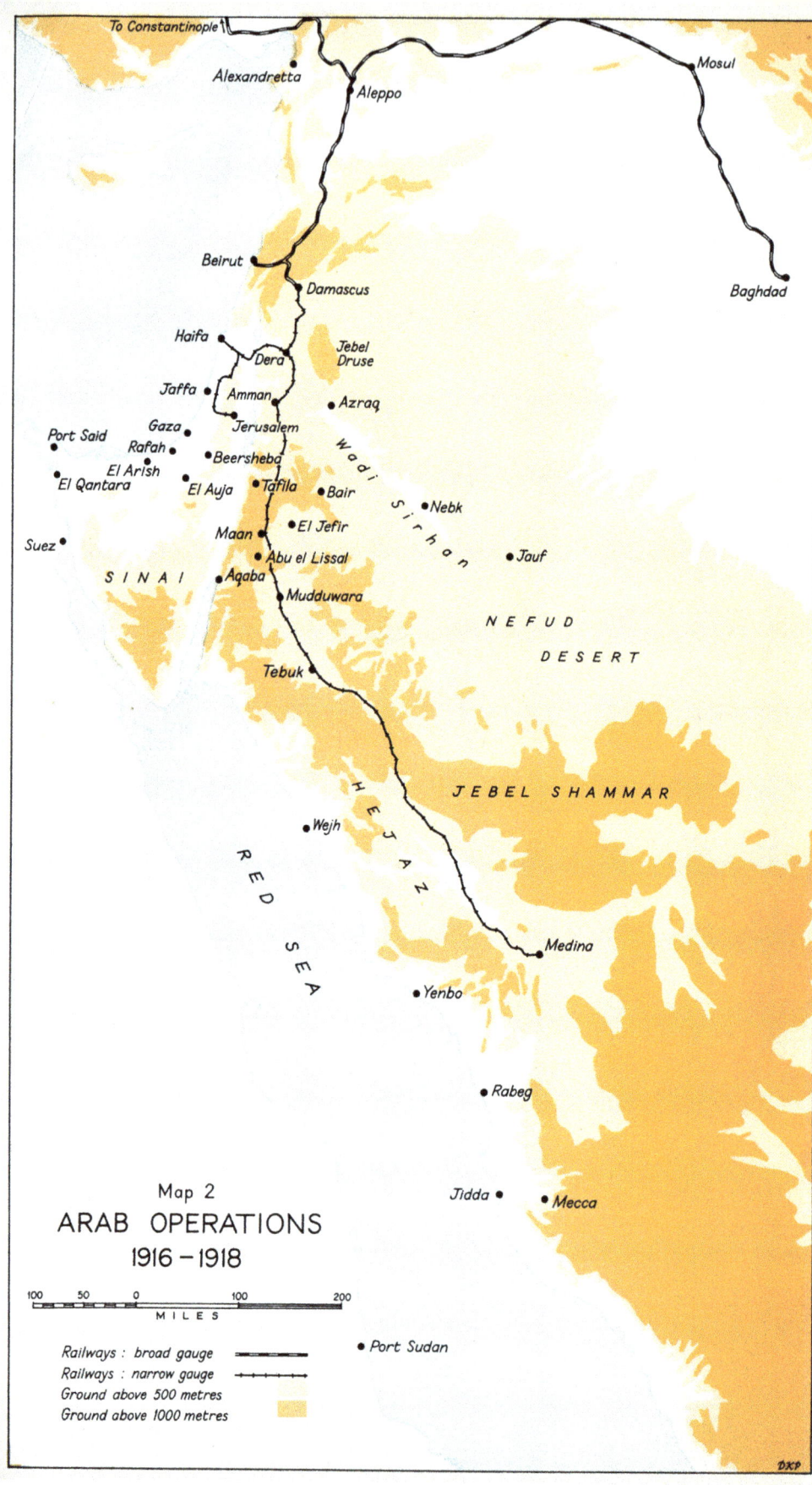

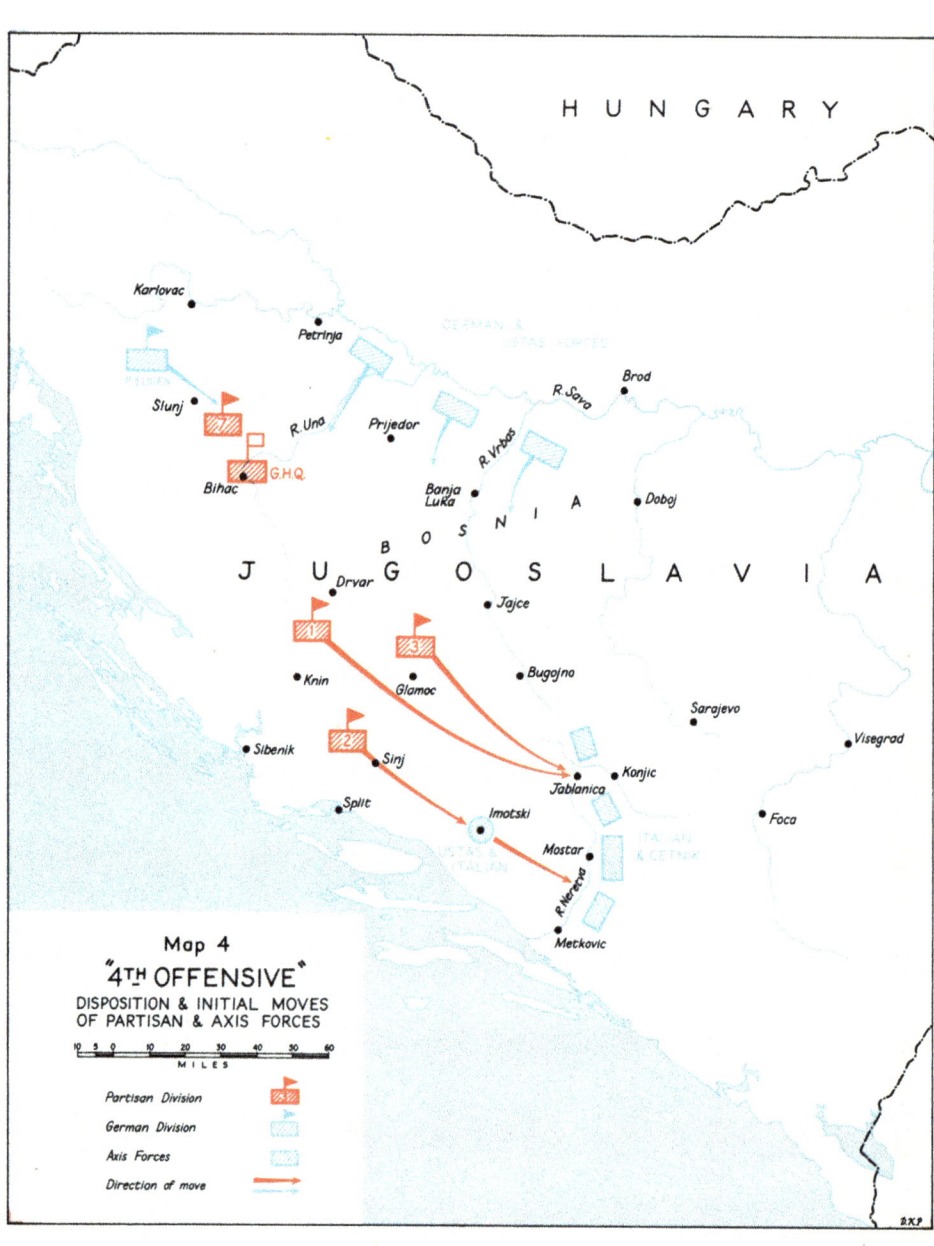

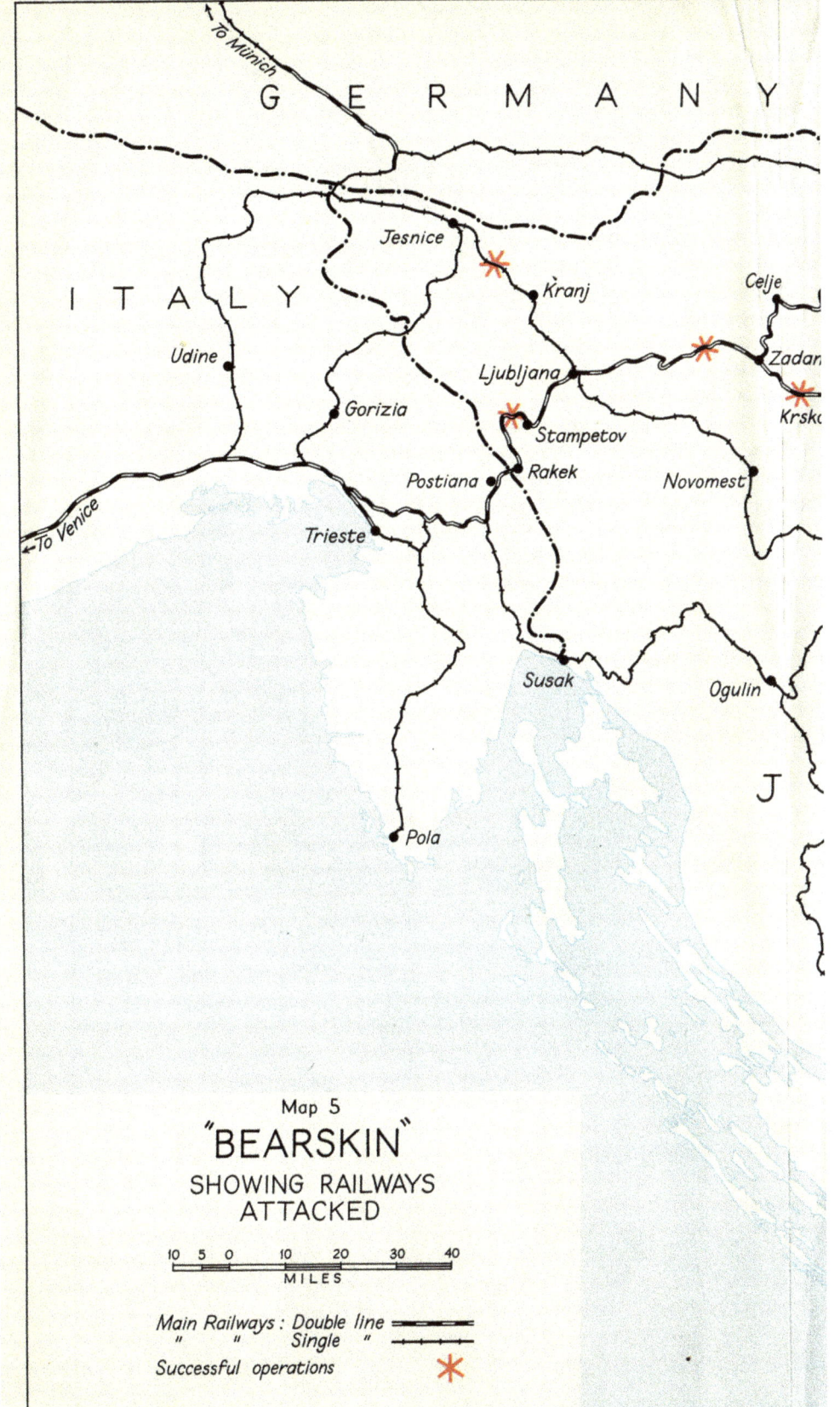

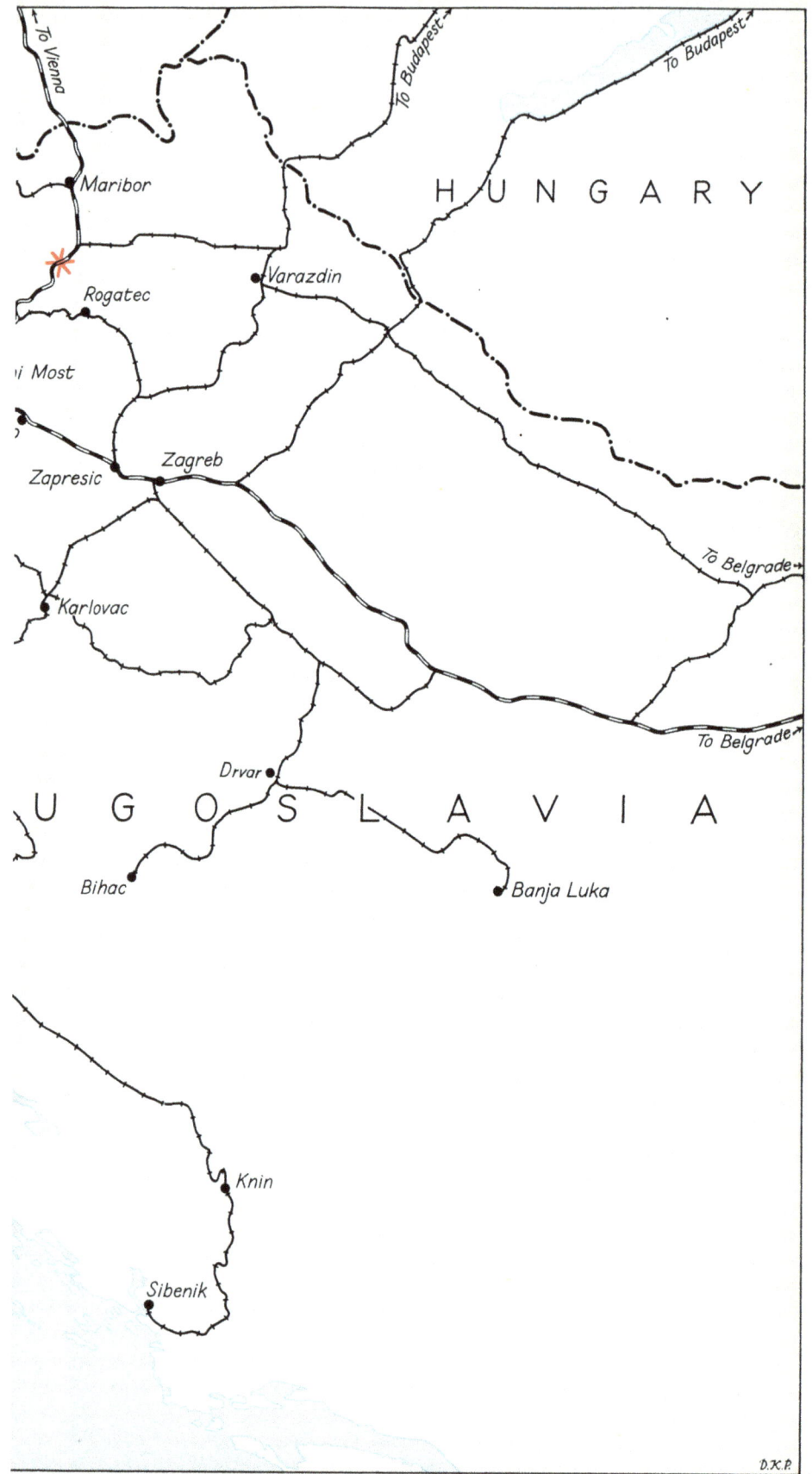

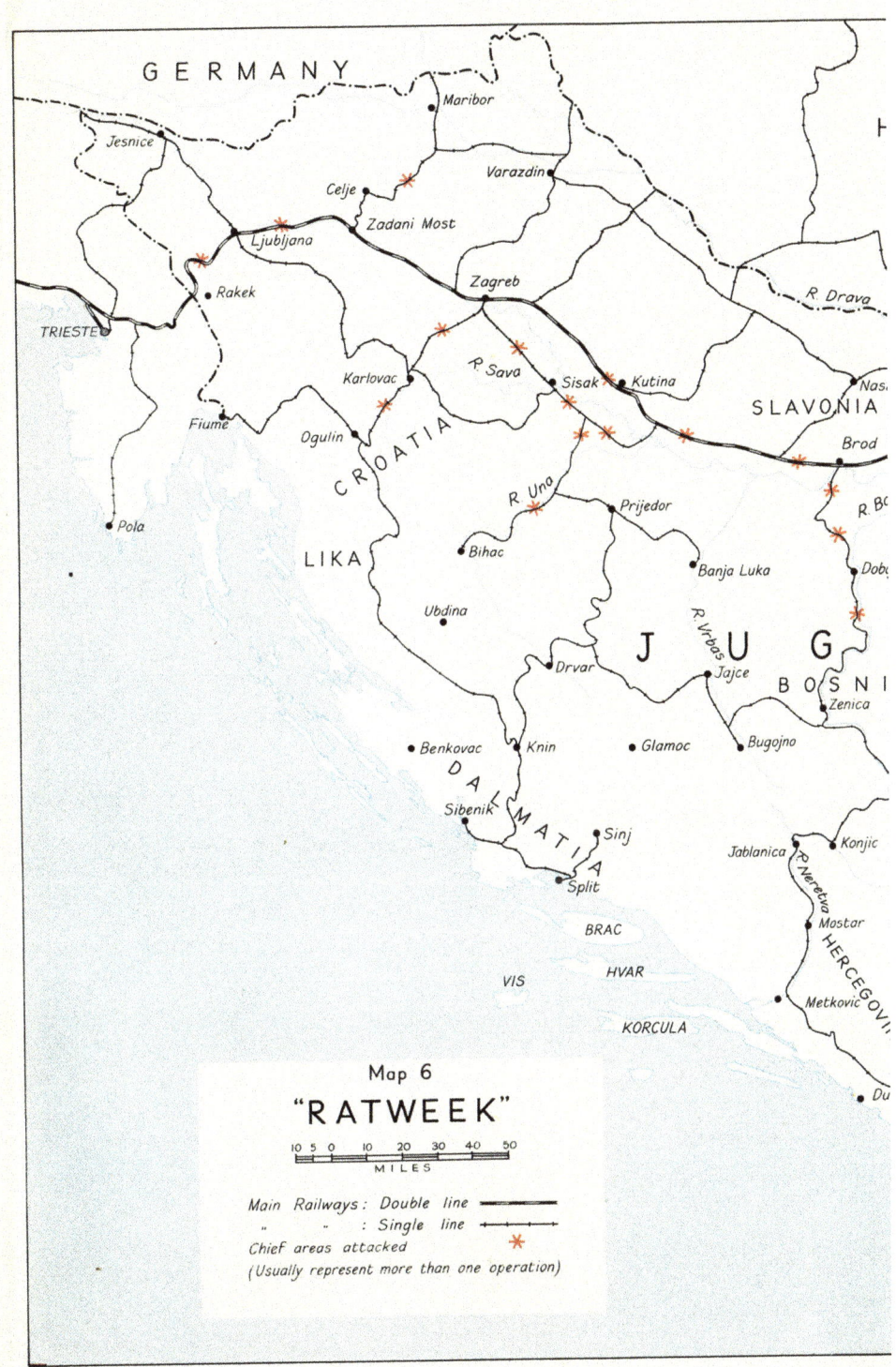

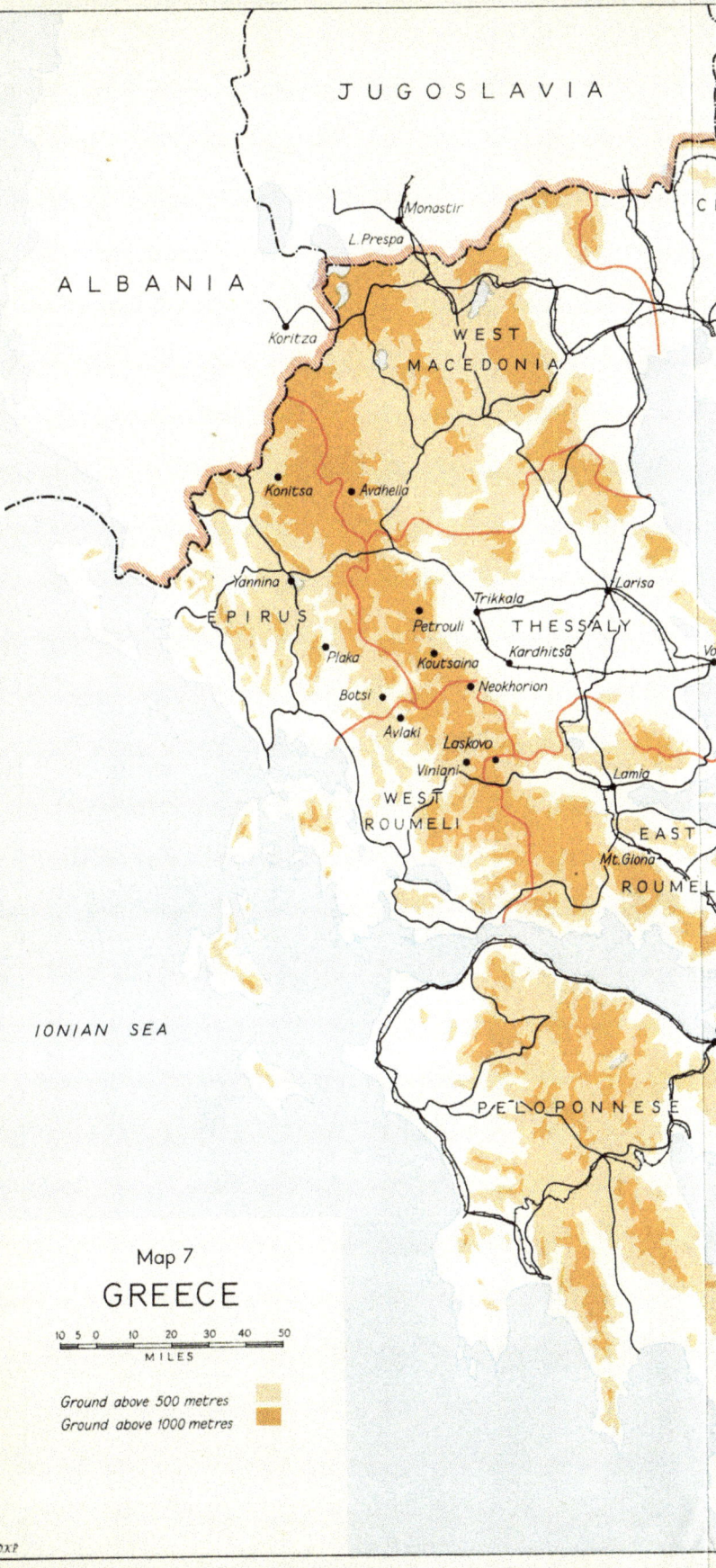

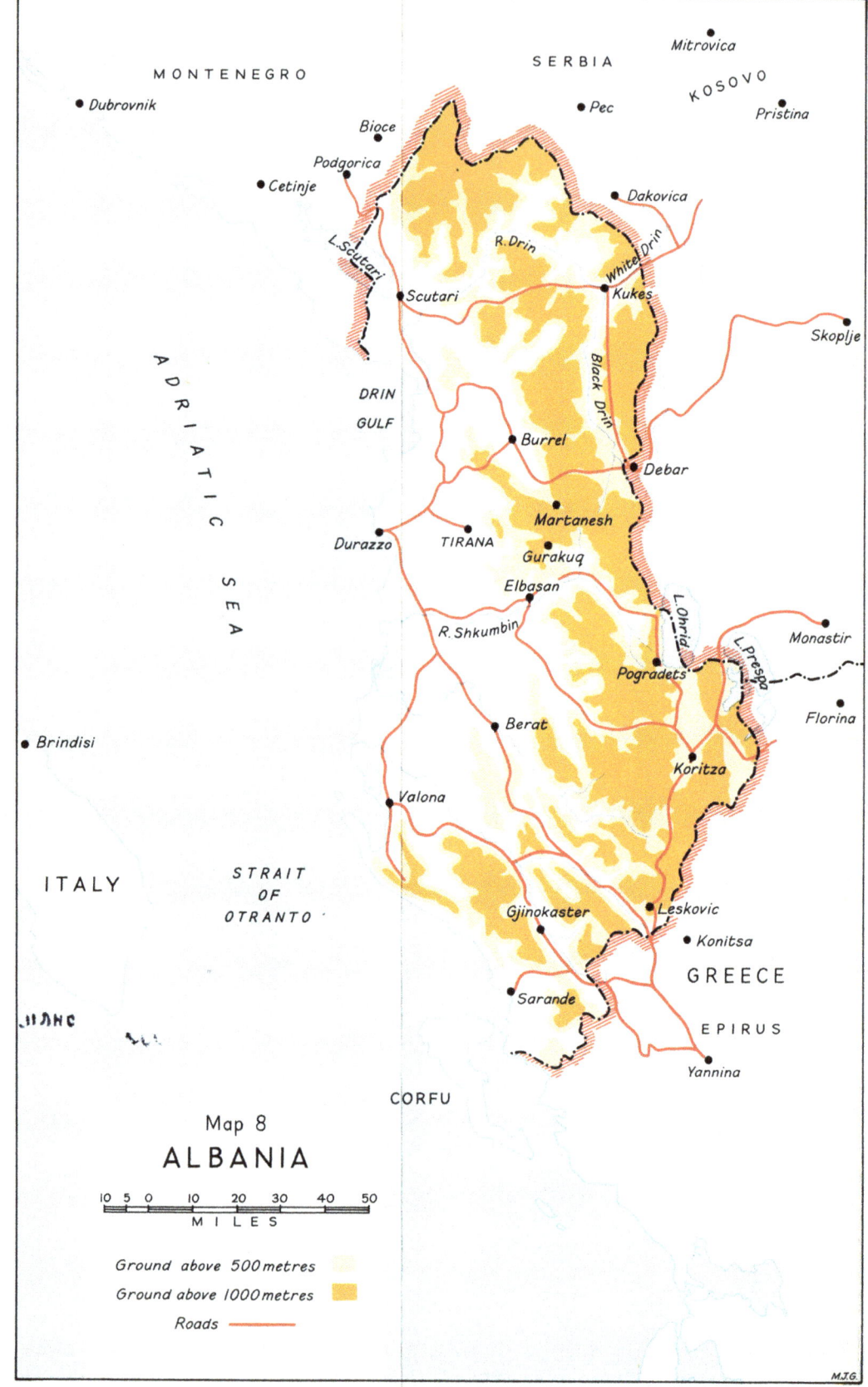

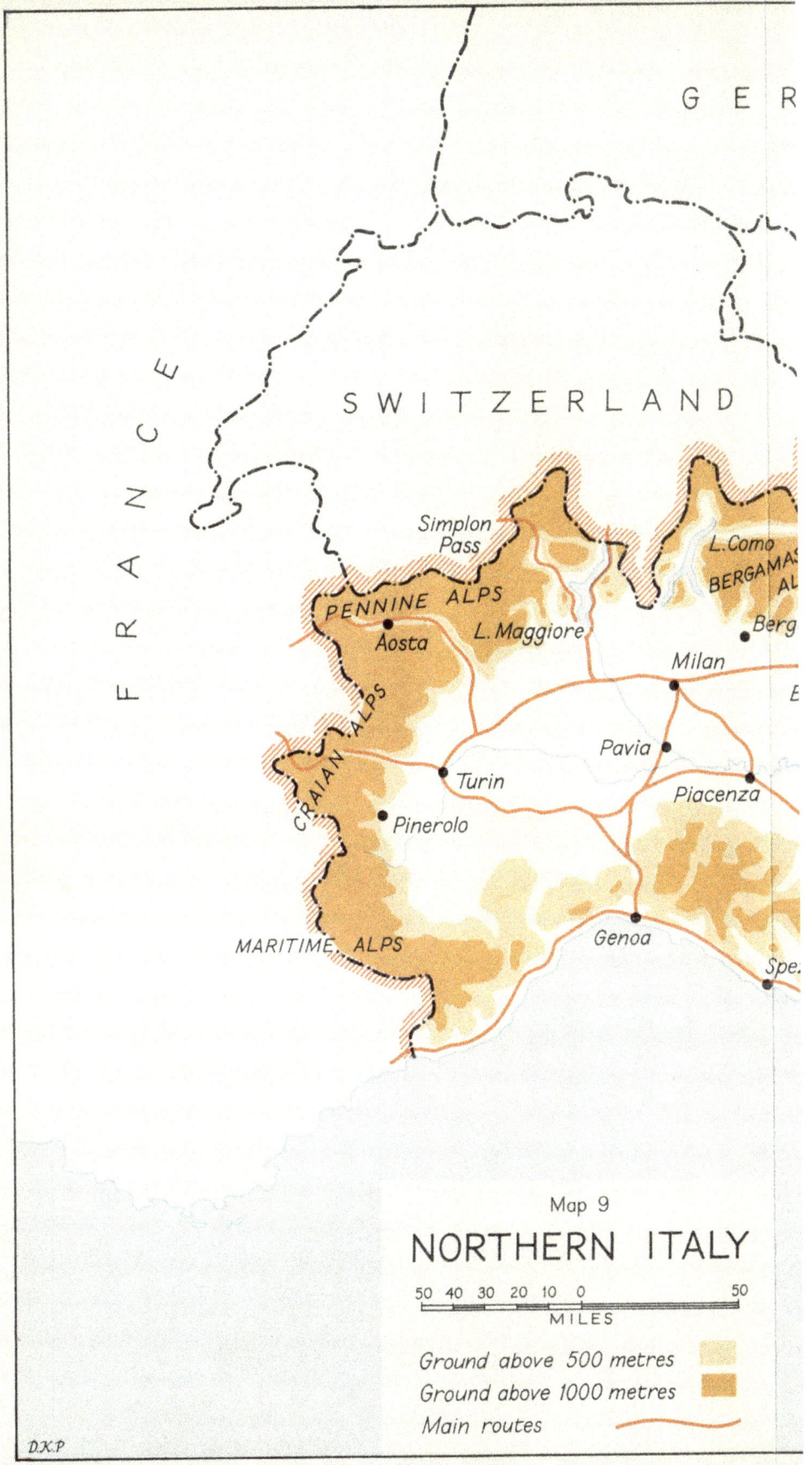

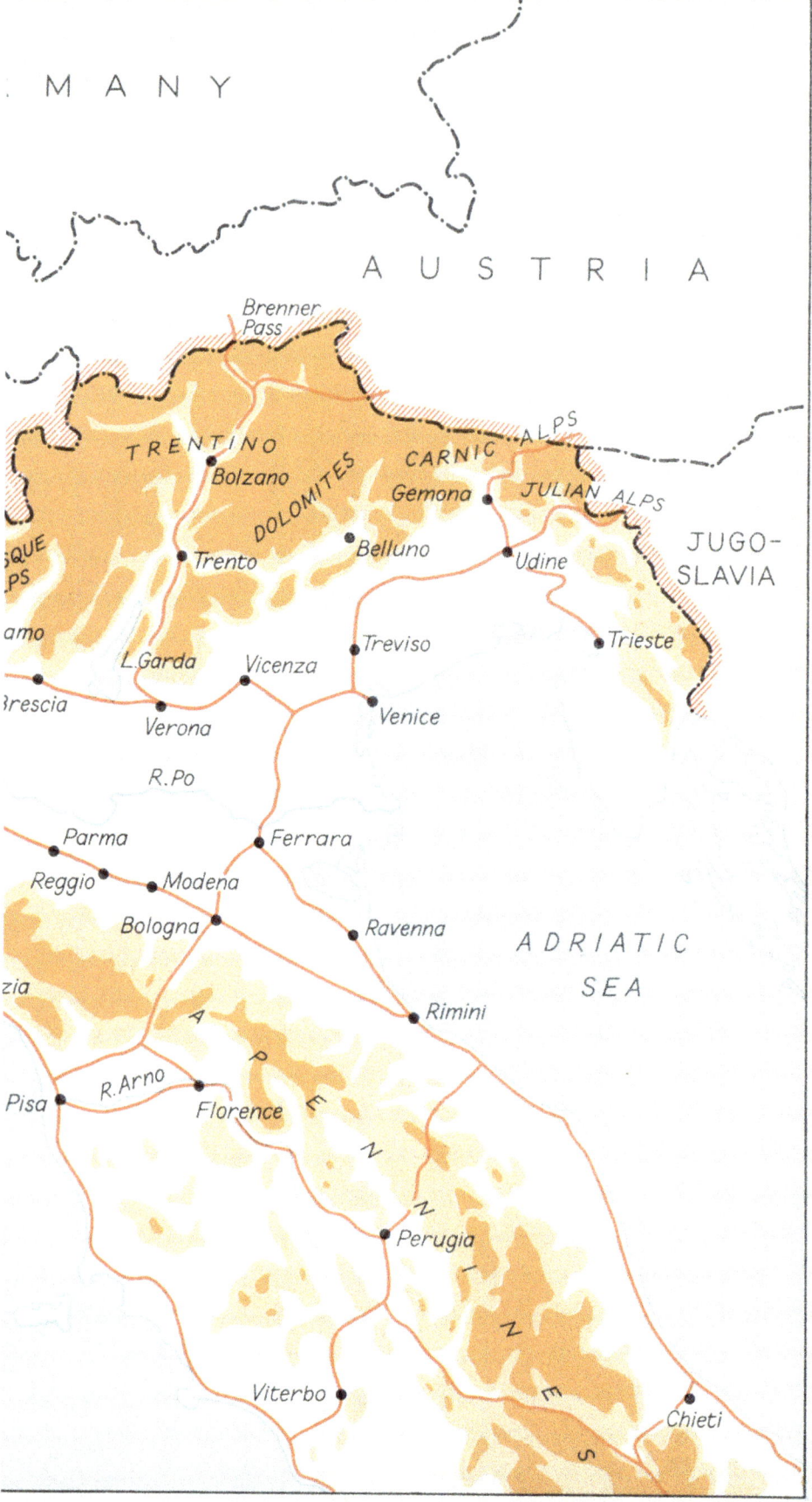

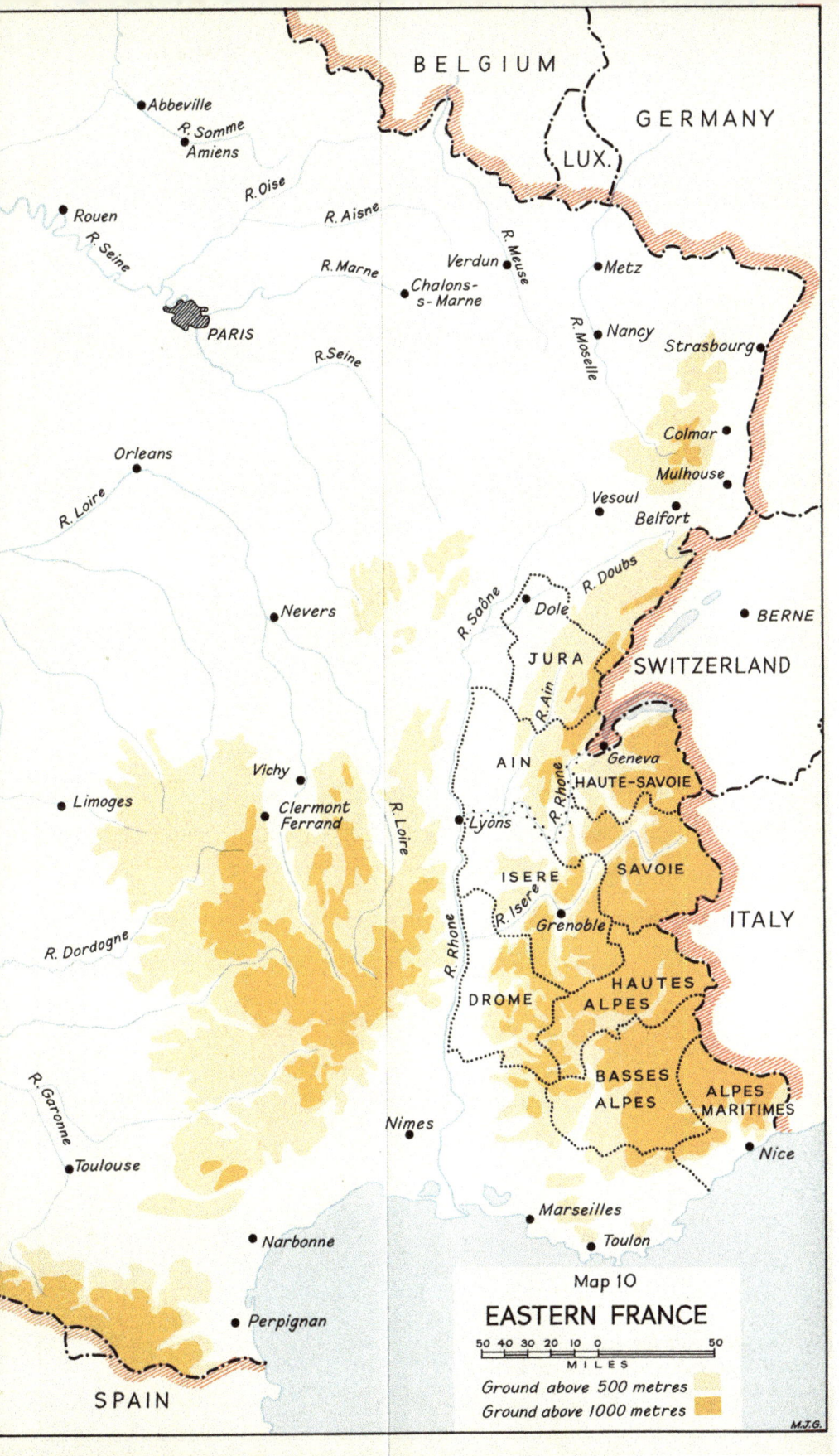

Map 10
EASTERN FRANCE

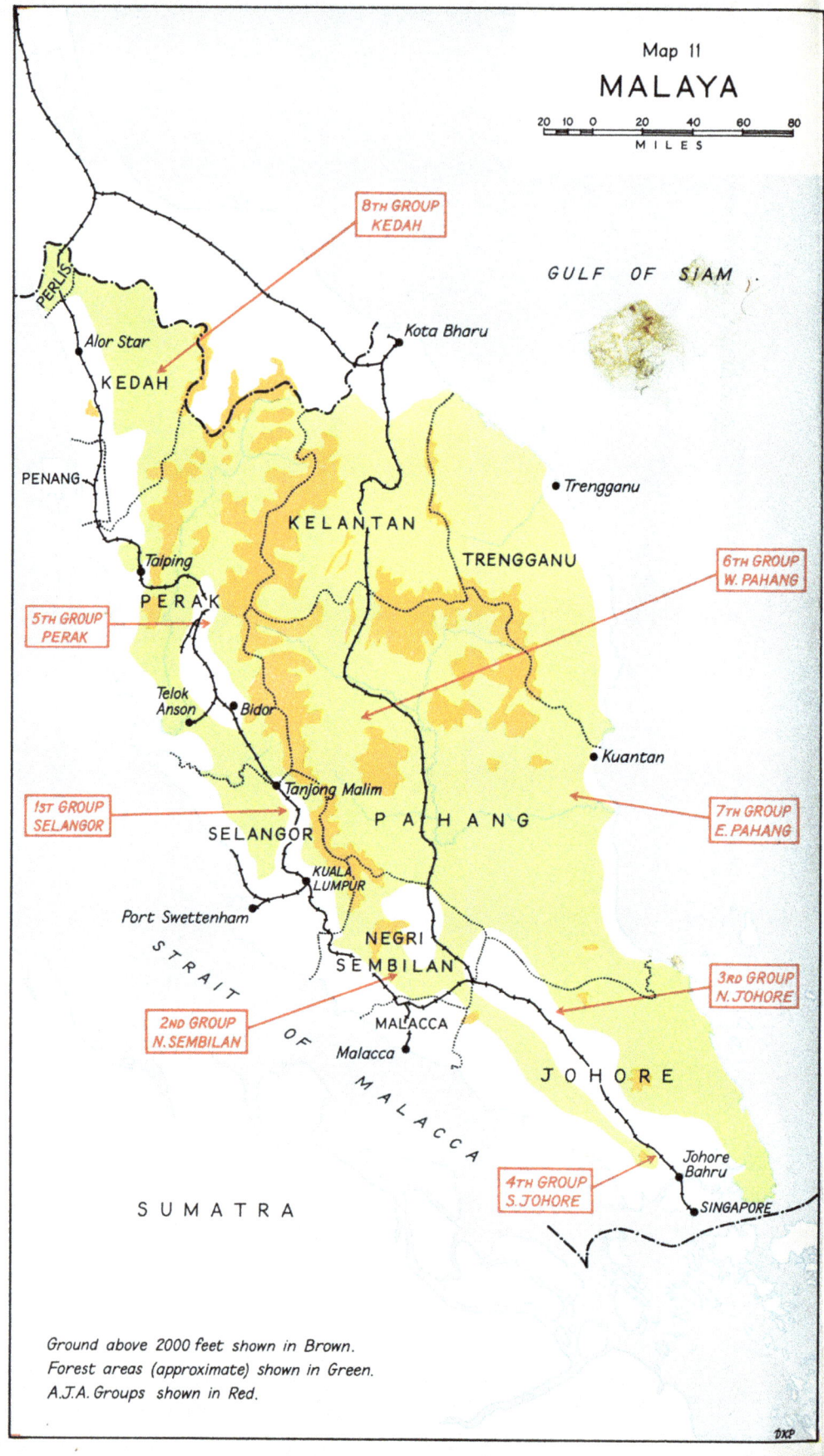

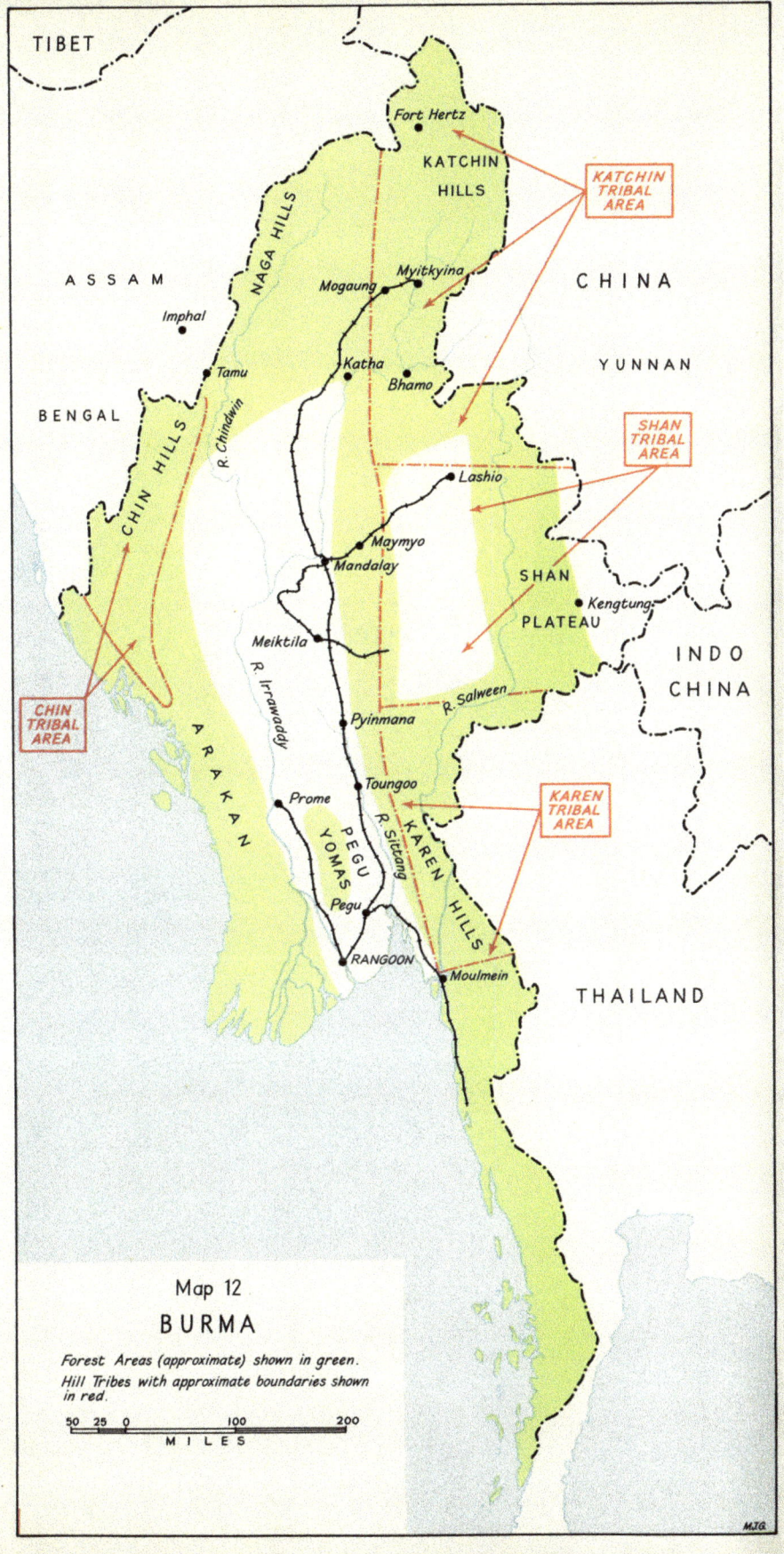

# FOREWORD

## by Lieut.-Gen. Sir James Cassels, K.B.E., C.B., D.S.O.
*Director General of Military Training*

WE as a nation have had much to do with guerilla warfare both in co-operation with guerilla forces as our allies, and in operations to suppress guerilla enemies. While we have made some study in our army training manuals and elsewhere of how to put down guerilla resistance, there is little or no informed guidance on the other side of the matter—the creation, support and strategic employment of guerilla forces fighting on our own side. As explained by the author in his Preface, this book has been produced to satisfy this want, and it should prove a useful stimulant to further study and thought by those of us who may have to deal with such problems in the future. It is, moreover, a very readable and interesting study of one particular aspect of warfare, and as such I commend it to the attention of all officers.

In order that the book should be as informed and authoritative as possible, the author has been given access to official documents and records. It must, however, be understood that the views expressed in this book are the author's own, and do not necessarily represent those of the War Office or other Service Ministries.

# PREFACE

For the reasons given in the body of this Book, guerilla forces may well play a significant part in any future war, provided that they are employed correctly. This requires that those responsible for future strategy, leadership and the maintenance of guerilla resistance should know what such forces can and cannot accomplish. They should also appreciate the many problems that inevitably follow in the wake of guerilla warfare. That those in responsible places in World War II seldom had this requisite knowledge is clearly shown in the various theatre histories included in this volume.

At the moment, there is little documentary information available from which the required knowledge can be obtained, as those Service pamphlets that are in existence deal only with particular aspects of guerilla resistance, and even then at a comparatively low level. It is with the object of filling this gap that this Book has been produced. It firstly emphasises by historical examples the scope and limitations of guerilla forces, the main principles involved and the political factors with which this type of warfare is inevitably bedevilled. It then goes on to consider the lessons learnt and how these can be applied to the future, particularly in so far as the United Kingdom is concerned, if and when we attempt to develop, support or control a foreign guerilla movement in territory occupied by an enemy.

From this study, it is hoped that any commander or Senior Government official who has to plan, operate or support a guerilla movement will gain sufficient background to appreciate the shape and capabilities of the weapon with which he is about to deal. Furthermore, the information contained in the succeeding chapters should, it is hoped, provide an adequate basis for a more detailed and lower level study of guerilla operations should this be required.

C. N. M. BLAIR

*January 1957*

# Chapter 1

# INTRODUCTION TO GUERILLA WARFARE

## (a) Its meaning and scope

*Background*

Although guerilla warfare can be traced back to biblical times and beyond, it was not until the Second World War that it achieved its greatest effect. Technical developments such as aircraft and wireless communications were largely responsible for this; they enabled far-flung and isolated guerilla forces to be supplied for protracted periods and, to a certain extent, controlled from distant bases such as India and the Middle East. Furthermore, the Axis war effort depended on the industrial output not only of its own rear areas, but also on that of the occupied countries. Both the industrial areas and the long lines of communication along which supplies and material had to travel provided the resistance movements with important and suitable targets.

It would seem that in the event of another world conflict, conditions of war, certainly in so far as Europe is concerned, will have changed both in kind and in degree. The advent of the nuclear weapon, with its terrifying power and scale of destruction, imposes a new concept of world war, the full ramifications of which are difficult, if not impossible, to predict. One factor emerges clearly however; nuclear warfare necessitates dispersal, and dispersal in its turn requires communications in all forms. It follows, therefore, that a defender, with his industries, ports, civil population and armed services widely dispersed to withstand nuclear bombardment, is in the most vulnerable position possible for attack by subversive forces. On the other hand, the advantages gained by the dispersal of the enemy are offset by other factors. For example, the widespread devastation and suffering likely to be caused by the initial 'nuclear exchange' will undoubtedly have great and far-reaching effects upon the morale of those remaining alive, and in the general struggle for survival it is likely to be a long time before a spirit of resistance to the occupying power begins to show itself. This means that guerilla warfare, as indeed all other forms of indigenous resistance to an occupying enemy, must be regarded essentially as a long-term weapon. In areas which have avoided nuclear bombardment, this period of inertia will be less, and it is possible that in the Far East, for example, guerilla warfare could be developed at a relatively early stage in the war.

Guerilla forces, therefore, may well play a significant part in future war, provided that they are employed to their best advantage. This requires that those responsible for future strategy, leadership and the maintenance of guerilla resistance should know what such forces can and cannot accomplish, and should appreciate the many problems that inevitably follow in the wake of guerilla warfare. That those in responsible places in the last war did not always have this requisite knowledge may be seen by a study of the various histories included in later chapters of this book.

*Aim of this Manual*

For those wishing to obtain knowledge and understanding of guerilla warfare there is little documentary information readily available. Such Service pamphlets as have been issued deal only with particular aspects and these at a comparatively low level. It is to provide the necessary background and guidance, which up to now has been lacking, that this book has been written.

A glance at the contents will show how the subject has been approached. Briefly, the aim is to provide, on the basis of lessons drawn from recent guerilla campaigns, sufficient information to enable a reader to form a balanced understanding of the scope and limitations of guerillas, the main principles involved and the political factors with which this type of warfare is inevitably complicated.

Before passing on to study certain historical examples of guerilla warfare we must, however, first consider what is meant by this term, and how guerilla operations fit into the overall national resistance movement.

*The meaning of Guerilla Warfare*

There is some ambiguity in the use of the word 'guerilla'. In this country it has even been used in the daily press to describe sudden stoppages of work which have been described as 'guerilla strikes', while in their military manuals on the subject the Americans tend to include under guerilla warfare all forms of active resistance against an occupying power. The official British definition is more limited in its application, for the word 'guerilla' is defined as 'a full-time member of an organised irregular band engaged in open warfare in his own country for a cause other than personal gain.'

Therefore, the first essential of true guerilla operations is that they are undertaken by nationals fighting in their own country. The second is that these operations are carried out openly, and the third is that the guerillas themselves operate in organised units, in other words, on a para-military basis.

This interpretation limits guerilla warfare to one particular phase of resistance, as will be seen from the following short consideration of the various forms which resistance to an occupying power may take.

*Various types of resistance*

In the initial stages resistance to the invader may well be limited to a passive form. That is to say, the population will by all means short of actual violence attempt to hinder and dislocate the enemy's war effort. They may attempt to affect the industrial output of the country by working to rule and other go-slow methods. Machinery may be damaged by lack of lubrication or by pouring sand into bearings, while the transport services may be adversely affected by intentionally inefficient operation and the incorrect routing of rolling stock. These are a few of the many forms which passive resistance may take. Carried out to a co-ordinated plan and by the mass of the population it can be a very potent weapon, even though it may not directly cause damage to enemy personnel and equipment.

As morale improves, controls slacken or hatred of the enemy increases, resistance tends to take a more offensive form, including the destruction of machinery, equipment, and even of enemy personnel, by the use of explosives and other special equipment. This type of active sabotage is carried out clandestinely by individuals or small parties who normally work at their usual profession under the occupying authorities and collect for the specific act of sabotage. Having completed this they return to the cover of their everyday lives.

The next form that resistance may take is when instead of temporary bands operating clandestinely, the resisters form into organised units which do not disperse on the completion of a task. Instead they range the country, openly attacking the enemy and other worthwhile targets whenever a favourable opportunity occurs, then moving rapidly elsewhere before the occupying forces can come to grips with them. This is guerilla warfare, as understood by the definition just described.

*Various degrees of Guerilla Warfare*

As a general guide guerilla movements can be said to fall between the following two extremes. At the top of the scale are those of a country-wide nature of the type that came into being in Spain during the Peninsular War in the early 1800's and in Jugoslavia during the Second World War. In these two countries large para-military forces operated against the occupying power, and even developed their own political and administrative machine in the areas that they controlled. Their success was due largely to the rugged and very difficult country in which they operated.

At the other end of the scale are those small guerilla actions that took place in more developed countries where there existed no safe areas of such extent as the Sierras of Spain and the mountain masses of Macedonia and south-west Jugoslavia. Of this smaller type the 'francs-tireurs' of the Franco-Prussian war of 1870 are a good example. After the Germans had swept westwards to Paris and beyond, these small bands of Frenchmen came into being and operated against the enemy's lines of communication with some success, though their actions were circumscribed by the few areas to which they could retreat. At the same time the web of roads, railways and telegraph systems allowed the Germans to co-ordinate counter-action and move troops to wherever they were required. History repeated itself when in the last war the Maquis operated in much the same way and, until near the end, under the same adverse conditions. The story of the so-called Irish Republican Army in the Irish rebellion of the 1920s is similar, and their activities were confined to minor acts of sabotage and small ambushes.

*Secret armies*

Under certain circumstances even the Maquis form of resistance may not be possible, probably on account of a combination of unsuitable terrain and tight, powerful control by the occupying forces. Although unable to operate in any active way during the enemy's occupation it may be possible to build up an organisation and prepare it to assist the Allies on the latter's reoccupation of the country. At the crucial moment this organisation, or Secret Army, comes into the open and by various means attempts to aid the Allied offensive.

The success or annihilation of these Secret Armies depends on the timing of their uprising. If this is too early they will almost certainly be overwhelmed before the Allied forces can come to their assistance. If zero hour is too late their efforts will be of little use to the Allied cause, for the enemy will have destroyed what he wishes and retreated unhindered. A tragic example of premature timing is Warsaw's Secret Army in the Second World War, which came into the open, fought and was obliterated before the Russian Armies came to its succour. A more successful operation was that of the Resistance forces in Antwerp. These were able to capture the dock installations before they could be destroyed by the retreating Germans, and owing to the rapid advance of the Allies were able to protect them until the latters' arrival. As a result the port of Antwerp was in use within a short while of its reoccupation.

*Contents of this Manual*

From the above analysis it will be seen that broadly speaking there are four types of Resistance—Passive Resistance, Sabotage, Guerilla Warfare and Secret Armies. Two or more of these may well be in being in a country at the same time, while there can be no clear-cut dividing line between the various types. So although this book seeks to deal exclusively with guerilla warfare, reference must sometimes be made to other forms of resistance.

No attempt has been made to produce a complete history of guerilla warfare, and no reference has been made to campaigns that took place earlier than the Peninsular War of 1808. Between that date and 1939 a few widely dispersed examples have been included with the object of showing the development of guerilla techniques and the fact that the basic principles of waging this type of warfare have remained unchanged. The greater proportion of this work, however, deals with the guerilla campaigns of the Second World War and the post-war resistance of the Malayan Communists.

From the examples that have been included it is hoped that the reader will obtain a sufficiently detailed appreciation of the characteristics, employment and limitations of guerilla resistance under varying conditions throughout the world to be able to apply this knowledge correctly in the event of any future conflict.

## (b) Examples, 1800–1939

*The Peninsular War, 1808–13*

The word 'guerilla' originates from the Spanish 'guerra' (war) and means literally 'little war'. It came into general use in the sense of irregular warfare during the Peninsular campaign when many Spaniards, refusing to submit to French rule, took to the mountains and continued to fight from there. These 'guerrilleros', working as semi-independent bands, relied on mobility for their survival. This they achieved by being tied to no specific localities, having no fixed lines of communication, and by being prepared and organised to cover long distances and endure great hardships. Using these methods they were able to strike at suitable targets and, equally important, to avoid battle except under the most favourable circumstances. At the first sign of any serious enemy attack being launched upon them, they were able, by relying upon early information gained from the local population and by their knowledge of the ground, to disappear into the hinterland before they could be surrounded.

The country was well suited for such tactics. It was described by the French geographer, Lavallee, as: 'A chaos of mountains and deep defiles, where 300 men might stop an army; of bare plains; of ravines, impenetrable in winter on account of their waters and in summer on account of their steepness; of rivers, having dangerous fords and not many bridges; of isolated towns, surrounded by walls; and of few roads'. His vehemence is understandable when one remembers that thousands of his countrymen were kept on the move, winter and summer, over these very mountains, rivers and ravines, vainly attempting to come to grips with the guerilla bands which operated from all the main mountain masses of Spain. Continually hunted, these bands nevertheless continued to attack where they chose, quickly withdrawing before the labouring relief forces could gain contact. Because of this, large French garrisons had to be maintained in towns and along the main lines of communication, foraging parties and convoys had to be escorted, and messengers failed to arrive unless accompanied by strong bodies of troops. The size of these commitments can be gauged by the fact that these messenger escorts had to be raised to units 300 strong.

The guerillas for their part had many of the weaknesses inherent in irregular forces, even in modern times. The most serious of these was their inability, in most cases, to co-operate with each other. This was partly due to the difficulties of inter-communication and the lack of any one overall strategic plan, but the main causes were the guerillas' unwillingness to leave their own districts, their constant internal quarrels and the jealousies of the various commanders. Another failing in the early period of the war was their determination to fight it out with the better equipped and disciplined French troops. Bitter experience, however, forced them in time to avoid such actions and to adopt evasive tactics instead. Reprisals by both sides tended to increase as the campaign progressed, until they reached such extremes that both the French and guerilleros appear by mutual agreement to have reverted to more civilised methods. As usual it was the local population that suffered most. Supplies were the guerillas' greatest problem. They lived off the country, but so did the French, with the result that many districts were stripped bare long before the war ended. Acts of oppression, often for personal gain, by a number of guerila leaders further tended to alienate local opinion. Great Britain did her best to help the national resistance by the supply of arms, equipment and money; but owing to the difficulty of transport across country held by the enemy these supplies seldom penetrated further inland than those guerila areas that had an outlet to the sea. The insurgents were therefore mainly dependent for arms and equipment on what they could capture from the enemy. Nevertheless, there is no doubt that the operations of the Spanish guerila forces contributed very largely to the defeat of the French by tying down large numbers of French troops which would otherwise have been available for operations against the British Army. At no time, in fact, were the French able to concentrate more than a fraction of their overwhelming strength against Wellington, and for this we have largely to thank the Spanish guerillas.

*The Tyrol, 1809*

While his generals were vainly trying to subdue the Spanish guerillas, Napoleon found himself confronted with risings in other parts of Europe. Amongst these was the Tyrol, which in 1806 he had ceded to the Bavarians. This the Tyrolese bitterly resented after years of benevolent rule by Austria. It was not, however, until three years later, when Austria declared war on France and invaded Bavaria, that the Tyrolese openly revolted against their new rulers. In their struggle they had four great assets. First, the rugged country was well suited to guerila operations and the few roads along which any large military force could move led through a number of major passes. Secondly, they had an accredited leader in Andreas Hofer, who had already made a name for himself by his outspoken attacks on the Bavarians; thirdly, the Tyrolese themselves were mountaineers accustomed to a rifle and to rapid movement across the Alps and lastly, the Bavarians and later the French played into their hands by an inability to adapt themselves to the irregular methods of the Tyrolese guerillas.

For the first few months the Tyrolese carried everything before them. By a series of surprise attacks culminating in the routing of a strong Bavarian force in the pass of Brixen, not far from the Brenner, they caused the Bavarians very heavy casualties and finally drove them out of the country.

With the arrival of fresh French forces they again withdrew into the mountains and repeated their previous successes; amongst other actions they destroyed a French column of all arms advancing from the south through the self-same Brixen pass. Furthermore, they used identical methods. Trees were cut down and avalanches prepared high up in the mountains, and these at a given signal were precipitated on to the road below. It is said that out of a total of 2,000 men some 1,300 were destroyed; the remainder surrendered. Marshal Lefebvre, who had been sent by Napoleon to retrieve the situation, is reported at this period to have worn a private soldier's uniform for fear of being shot by Tyrolese snipers.

The Tyrolese, however, could never hope to continue the struggle indefinitely without assistance, and when, in July 1809, Lefebvre defeated the Austrians at Worgle all chance of obtaining such aid seemed to have evaporated. The last blow to their waning morale was delivered, when at the Treaty of Schönbrunn the Tyrol reverted again to Bavaria, and Austria ordered Hofer to cease fighting and to send the partisans quietly to their homes. By December 1809 Hofer was a fugitive and the cause finally died with his death at the hands of a firing squad in February 1810, less than a year after the start of the Revolt.

*North Africa, 1830–44*

France was destined yet again to suffer at the hands of guerillas, for we next find her attempting to quell them in North Africa after the French capture of Algiers in 1830. Here the Emir of Oman, Abd el Kader, successfully fought the French occupation forces for fourteen years. Two French marshals failed to check him and his defeat was only at last achieved by the third French commander, Bugeaud, who set about fighting the Emir and his bands with their own weapons—'the ruse, the raid and the ambush'. Bugeaud's methods are of interest, as he in fact adopted guerilla tactics and methods for his own troops. He reorganised his striking force into small, self-contained mobile columns, each consisting of infantry, cavalry and a small proportion of mountain artillery. As speed and endurance were the first essentials the troops were picked men, trained to withstand the climate and conditions of extreme fatigue. They carried the minimum of equipment. He also organised an intelligence system, the importance of which none of his predecessors appear to have fully appreciated. With these mobile forces and more accurate information as to the whereabouts of the enemy he was able to strike at them far inside their own territory.

Nevertheless, for some eleven years Abd el Kader had kept the French on the defensive, attacking them whenever he got the opportunity and withdrawing long before the deliberate French moves to encircle him could possibly succeed. It was, in fact, a repetition of Spanish guerila tactics; but whereas in Spain the campaign had consisted of a series of independent operations under a number of different leaders, here Abd el Kader was the supreme commander, on whom all depended. He was, in addition to being

Emir of Oman, a Mohammedan priest and was therefore capable of preaching a 'Jehad' or holy war, which he did to great effect. By this and by his personality he held the wild tribes together and controlled not only those round Oman but also the nomads to the south. It was by this control over a vast area that he was able to switch his attacks rapidly from region to region, and so keep the large French forces, by 1837 some 40,000 strong, dispersed and on the defensive. But for all his brilliance as a guerilla leader the overwhelming resources of France were bound to tell against him in the end, and the arrival of Bugeaud merely hastened this. By the middle of 1844, three years after Bugeaud's arrival, Abd el Kader was a fugitive and the war was at an end.

*The Caucasus, 1830–59*

While France was failing to establish a Protectorate in North Africa owing to Abd el Kader, the Russians were being equally unsuccessful in Caucasia owing to the resistance of another mullah, by name Schamyl. He, like Abd el Kader, preached a successful holy war. For guerillas Schamyl could not have had better material than the local tribesmen, accustomed as they were to the extremes of climate, hardship and fatigue, and to living on the most meagre rations and in great discomfort. Their main shortcomings were the diversity of types, religions and even languages. It says much for Schamyl's leadership that he was able to retain their loyalty and their will to fight the common enemy.

The country was ideal for guerilla operations, for it must be among the most difficult in the world in which to carry out punitive action; one province is aptly named Dagh-estan, the land of the mountains. Here Schamyl and his followers fought for some thirty years, defeating in succession every Russian commander sent against them.

The peak of his power came during the time of the Russian War against Britain and France in the Crimea, when Russian units were withdrawn from the Caucasus and Schamyl received money and equipment from the Allies. After these successes Schamyl appears to have been tempted into open warfare, and on more than one occasion his forces were badly mauled by being encumbered with artillery and by his determination to save the guns from capture.

The end of the Crimean War, which enabled the Tsar to pour troops into the Caucasus, brought an end to Allied supplies for the guerillas, and Schamyl was left to his fate. He and his dwindling forces were slowly worn down; strongholds, which it appears he held to the last instead of evacuating, were systematically captured, and he was finally surrounded and forced to surrender in the summer of 1859.

*The South African War, 1899–1902 (see Map 1 opposite page 7)*

The next major example of guerilla operations is to be found in the South African War of 1899 to 1902, when the Boers, having failed to stem the advance of the British forces by regular military means, resorted to guerilla methods. Before this stage was reached, however, they obtained a series of initial successes against the widely dispersed British troops then in South Africa. These gains were largely due to the Boers' superior mobility, skilful use of ground and good individual marksmanship: all qualities which were to stand them in good stead during the period of guerilla operations that was to follow. Had they exploited their gains the results might have been decisive, but there was a lack of cohesion between the various commandos and an unwillingness to submit to discipline or obey orders.

When the greatly reinforced British Armies in Cape Colony and Natal went over to the offensive these Boer shortcomings were aggravated by the strain of constant withdrawals and the subsequent disheartenment. Nevertheless the Boers, as individuals and in independent and comparatively small units, fought skilfully. Even when driven back by superior numbers and weight of artillery they contrived to carry out well-timed withdrawals, inflicting heavy casualties with only small loss to themselves. There was, however, an increasing tendency to avoid fighting in mass and to operate instead as independent commandos against the British flanks and isolated columns, when these could be surprised and ambushed.

By the end of February 1900 the Boer situation was grave. Some half of the Orange Free State had been overrun; the capital, Bloemfontein, was in British hands, and the President, Steyne, and his Government were fugitives. The Boers had been driven from Natal, which they had previously invaded, and the second Boer Republic, the Transvaal, was threatened. Furthermore, British strength in South Africa was still steadily mounting, while Boer reserves were dwindling, and all hope of outside aid had vanished. It therefore showed considerable courage and belief in their cause when the leaders decided to continue the fight, not however by regular methods but by guerilla operations against the British lines of communication.

After a halt at Bloemfontein to rest and reorganise, the main British forces under Lord Roberts pressed steadily northwards, with the commandos making pin-prick attacks from time to time on units that became isolated. Scant attention seems to have been paid to the agreed strategic policy of concentrating against the British lines of communication, and there appears to have been only one occasion on which the railway south of Bloemfontein was cut, and then only for a few hours. By June Pretoria, the capital of the Transvaal, had been captured. Lord Roberts' supply line, dependent on the one railway from the Cape Colony northwards now stretched across some 350 miles of unfriendly country. Still the Boer commandos continued on their independent way, and instead of attacking this vital and vulnerable target they encumbered themselves with equipment and prisoners. These not only became a brake on their mobility but also a drain on their food stocks. Their operations did, however, keep large British forces constantly on the move attempting, in most cases vainly, to capture them.

July saw a junction between Lord Roberts' forces and those of General Buller which had been pushing forward from Natal. British units were now deployed as far North as the Delagoa Bay Railway, which runs from Pretoria to Lourenco Marques. Flying columns were operating even farther north.

Even so, both in the Transvaal and Orange Free State commandos continued to ambush and raid small British detachments. A contemporary writer likens the position to 'an archipelago in a stormy sea infested by pirates, who though powerless to take possession of any of the islands made communication between them always dangerous and sometimes impossible'. One of these 'pirates' was de Wet. Ranging from the Transvaal to the borders of Cape Colony he kept a number of British columns constantly employed in attempts to capture him. It was estimated that in one month some 30,000 troops scoured over 7,000 square miles in an effort to come to grips, while de Wet himself trekked over 700 miles and at the end was still untouched but for his transport, which he had to abandon at one of the critical periods.

While de Wet and the British columns were playing hide and seek in the south, the combined forces of Lord Roberts and General Buller were sweeping the Transvaal. Its President, Kruger, and his followers, now almost immobilised by a mass of equipment and prisoners, were pushed eastwards against the frontier with Portuguese East Africa. Kruger fled into exile, but most of the other Boers slipped through the net, destroying what equipment they could and leaving the prisoners to their fate. This was no isolated instance of the Boers' sacrifice of mobility. Nearly every commando operated with a long administrative tail.

By the beginning of 1901 the British forces totalled some 230,000. Of these about one-third were mounted and formed into flying columns to operate against the Boer commandos. The remainder were strung out guarding the depots and lines of communication. On the Boer side it was estimated that 30,000 could take up arms, but owing to their independence and lack of discipline the actual numbers in the field were constantly changing, and at any one time were considerably less than this total. They had now been fighting with their backs to the wall for over a year. Nevertheless, independent guerilla activity continued in a number of areas, possibly the most successful actions being those of Delaney and Beyers in Western Transvaal. Although chased by a mobile force of 6,000 men and 40 guns Delaney found the opportunity on three occasions to ambush units and take some 1,000 more British prisoners. Beyers on being too hard-pressed in the west slipped between Pretoria and Johannesburg and melted into the Eastern Transvaal. That he could cross the vital railway link between the two main towns of the Transvaal with 1,200 men and a long column of transport shows how fluid the situation still was.

These operations were far from achieving anything decisive but they did adversely affect the morale of the British troops. Furthermore, working in a hostile country British intelligence on the Boer movements was always scanty and often inaccurate. The result was a great deal of time and effort spent by units in forced moves through the country after some Boer commando that was never even seen, far less brought to grips. But the difficulties and hardships of the Boers were incomparably greater. Constantly harassed, very often from more than one direction; always on the move and suffering from a series of hair-breadth escapes, they were now steadily losing their transport and artillery, while the methodical widening of British control, and the commandeering by the latter of all supplies and material that might be of use to the Boers was making the existence of the guerillas progressively more difficult. By the end of 1901 those commandos still in the field were operating in ever-diminishing areas. The end was clearly in sight, but it was not until May 1902 that hostilities finally ceased with the Treaty of Vereeniging.

To conclude this brief description it is worth considering in more detail the effect of the country and of the Boers' mentality on the guerilla campaign. A large proportion of the Transvaal and Orange Free State is open and comparatively flat, while those regions that are mountainous or even broken are limited in area and are surrounded by plains or veldt. Over all the country regular forces can operate. Thus from the guerilla angle, though there were many suitable places for ambushes, there was nowhere comparable to the mountain ranges of the Caucasus and Spain, in which guerilla forces could rest and reorganise with a measure of security. Instead they had to depend on constant movement over long distances, together with rapid evasive actions. These were made more difficult than in previous guerilla campaigns by the development of communications, which allowed better control and co-ordination of the regular columns operating against the guerillas. On the other hand, it was owing to this very openness of the country that the Boers employed field artillery without seriously affecting their mobility and were still able to manoeuvre, even with the large transport columns to which they were wedded.

The country may also have accounted to a certain extent for their failure to operate successfully against their most promising target, the railway from the Transvaal to Cape Colony; along its length there were few places where it ran through sufficiently broken country to provide good demolition targets. The major reason for this failure, however, would certainly appear to have been the mentality of the Boers themselves which, as already explained, made them incapable of working to any co-ordinated long-term plan. Conversely it was these same characteristics of independence, stubbornness and a devout belief in their cause that made them continue to fight long after that cause was lost, and thus forced the British to expend a vast material effort and employ a force some eight times as great as that of the Boers.

*The Far East*

As yet, no mention has been made of the Far East where in its broadest sense there can be said to be three main types of area suitable for guerilla warfare—the vast mountain masses, the open spaces, and the jungles.

Of the first the North-West Frontier of India probably provides the best example. Here the warlike mountain tribesman for many years waged a guerilla battle against the British forces sent to tame them. Their story is, however, little different from that of other guerilla campaigns. The country is somewhat similar to the Caucasus of Schamyl's exploits; the tribesmen had similar characteristics of mobility, toughness and endurance, as well as the jealousies and feuds of other guerilla forces; they combined the good marksmanship and eye for country of the Boers. One important advantage that they enjoyed and which was unknown in the other campaigns mentioned in this Chapter was that they could, if too hard pressed, retire to the safety of adjoining countries, where for obvious reasons the British troops could not follow.

China provides an example of the second type, for here space rather than rugged impenetrable country was the ally of the guerillas. Here from 1937 onwards guerillas played an important part in the Chinese resistance to the Japanese invaders. Here again history repeated itself, for with the Japanese advance into the North China plain and the Yangtse Valley, Chinese guerillas constantly cut the ever-lengthening enemy communications. Never able to cut these for any length of time, they did slow down the movements of the Japanese armies and forced strong columns to be deployed in clearing up areas which had only a short time before been swept of guerilla bands.

Before the Second World War no guerilla operations in the jungle were of sufficient importance to warrant mention in this short survey; what resistance there was in this type of country was carried out by people ignorant of modern methods and armed only with elementary weapons.

## (c) Arab Operations, 1916–18

(*See Map 2 opposite page 13*)

*Summary of Campaign*

The last history to be included in this short selection of pre-1939 guerilla operations is that of the Arabs in Arabia and Syria during the Palestine Campaigns of the First World War.

These Arab operations fall into three main phases, although between each of these there is no clear-cut division. The first phase covered the Arabs' attempt to operate as a field force, the second when guerilla operations predominated, and the third when the guerillas and regular Arab forces were joined by a Secret Army that came into the open as the British drove northwards through Syria. The purely guerilla phase, although limited, is considered in some detail as it is the only comparatively modern example of irregular operations of this type being carried out under desert conditions.

For the same reasons Col. Lawrence's background, methods and achievements form a large part of this narrative in order to provide a picture of the problems and responsibilities which are likely to face those who in the future may become Liaison Officers with Arab irregular forces.

*Initial Revolt, Summer 1916*

To appreciate the cause of the final rising of the Arabs in support of the Allies it is necessary to start this study at the period when it became obvious that Turkey would enter the war on the side of Germany. From then onwards Britain pursued a policy of fomenting unrest in all the Arab lands of the Ottoman Empire. The most promising of these was the Hejaz, where the tribes had been on the verge of revolt against their Turkish masters for years, and the Sherif Hussein, Emir of Mecca, had already made overtures to the British for the furtherance of an ambitious plan to form a confederacy of independent Arab States under the sovereignty of himself and his sons.

Matters were brought to a head by ruthless Turkish attempts to eliminate the Arab movement in Syria, and by the news that a strong Turkish column was moving south with the object of replacing Hussein in Mecca by a Turkish nominee. The revolt started in June 1916. The small and isolated Turkish detachments were soon overwhelmed and only Wejh, in the North and Medina, the railhead of the Hejaz railway, remained in enemy hands. The Medina garrison had little difficulty in holding out, and the ill-organised and poorly-armed Arab hordes soon began to lose interest and to disperse. Only the efforts and leadership of Feizal, Hussein's second son, backed by British material aid, kept any Arab forces in the field. It seemed to many that Arab resistance would soon end unless British troops intervened.

*British strategy*

Now followed a period of intensive debate on the merits and demerits of sending a British force to counter the Turkish threat. There were three schools of thought. The Foreign Office considered troops should be sent, on the grounds that otherwise the Hejaz revolt would be snuffed out and our prestige throughout the Arab world would be irreparably damaged. On the other hand the military view was that it was not only unsound to dissipate even a brigade on what was in effect a side-show, but even if a brigade were to be deployed in the Hejaz it was too small a force to have any material effect on the course of events. The third view was championed by the Arab Bureau, the intelligence organisation dealing with Arab affairs. It reported that the arrival of Allied troops would cause such suspicion and hostility amongst the Arabs as to destroy the little unity at present existing. The issue was further complicated by Hussein himself. Although generally averse to receiving British troops for the same reasons as those of the Arab Bureau he pressed for their despatch whenever a Turkish advance on Mecca appeared imminent. T. E. Lawrence was at this time on the staff of the Arab Bureau. After a visit to the Hejaz he reported against the use of a

British force not only on account of the effect its arrival would have on the Arabs and its unsuitability for operating under the conditions prevailing but also because, in his view, the Arabs were capable of continued action themselves, provided they employed guerilla tactics and were aided by British arms, money and specialist personnel. It was eventually decided not to send troops but to build up, as rapidly as possible, an Arab force with British assistance, including officers for technical advice. Amongst the latter was Lawrence. He was appointed British Liaison Officer to Feizal.

## T. E. Lawrence

Lawrence, then 28 years old, had many qualifications to suit him for such a rôle. While at Oxford he developed an interest for both military strategy and Middle East matters and during his last 'long vacation' he trekked alone through Palestine, Transjordan and Syria. On leaving Oxford he returned to the Middle East as a member of a British Museum Expedition to the Upper Euphrates. Here he worked with short breaks for the next four years, spending his spare time in travelling the country in Arab dress, accompanied by one or more of the Arabs from the Expedition's diggings. He thus gained an understanding of Arab ways, customs and thought, and was so far received into Arab life that he came into contact with certain of the resistance movements which were working for Arab independence. There are many references during this period to his influence over the Arabs. In 1913 he was sent to the Sinai Peninsula to provide the cover for a military team which was reconnoitering the country around Beersheba and Aqaba, under the guise of an archaeological expedition. Shortly after war broke out he was posted to GHQ Cairo as an intelligence officer and joined the staff of the Arab Bureau, as already mentioned. Lawrence thus went to his new appointment with an excellent knowledge of the country over which he was about to operate, an understanding of and sympathy for the people with whom he was to deal, and a temperament and physique well suited to the task in front of him. He also spoke the language.

Lawrence joined Feizal in December 1916 only to find that the Arabs had been driven from a strong defensive position by a comparatively small Turkish fighting patrol from Medina and were in hasty retreat to their base at Yenbo. Here they remained unmolested until early in the new year when Feizal's unwieldy force moved northwards to Wejh. The original intention was to seize Wejh by means of a combined sea and land attack, but in the event, owing to the late arrival of the Arabs, the landing party under the control of the Navy captured the town unaided.

The occupation of Wejh had immediate and far-reaching results. Many miles of the railway were now within range of Arab raiding parties. These, led by British officers, carried out increasingly successful demolitions, and the Turks were not only forced to abandon their advance into the Hejaz but also to send down further reinforcements from the North. On the political side the results were equally satisfactory. Sheiks and envoys streamed into Wejh to offer their allegiance to Feizal, and the spread of the revolt into Syria now became a practical proposition.

*Plan for Guerilla operations*

GHQ Cairo were now, however, pressing for an immediate intensification of operations in the Medina area in order to draw off Turkish forces from the Palestine front, where the first Battle of Gaza was about to open. With this in view it was intended that the Arabs should assault Medina and at the same time block the railway to the north, thus forcing the Turks to send down further troops to clear the railway if Medina was to be relieved. Knowing from experience how unsuited the Arabs were to such operations, Lawrence put forward an alternative plan which was to cause a continuous drain on Turkish resources by constant raids on their long lines of communication. To enlarge the areas of these raids it would be necessary to extend the revolt northwards to Damascus and beyond. As a first step he proposed to capture Aqaba, at the head of the Red Sea, by a surprise attack not from seaward but from the north. Lawrence's proposals were accepted and it is from this agreement that the second or guerilla phase of the Arab campaign stems.

As guerillas, two of the main Arab limitations were their unwillingness to operate far from their tribal areas and their inability, due to inter-tribal jealousies and feuds, to work as an integrated force. To overcome these difficulties Lawrence's plan for the extension of his activity against the Turkish lines of communication was to move through the country with a small picked cadre of leaders who would employ the local tribes to carry out specific operations in their own districts.

*Operations, summer 1917*

It was by this method that he intended to carry out the attack on Aqaba. Starting from Wejh his first objective was the Huweitat tribe, who lived some 250 miles to the North, in the Wadi Sirhan. His party consisted of an escort of thirty-five picked camel men, four Arabs of high standing, £20,000 in gold and six camel loads of demolition stores. All the Arabs had specific tasks. One was Feizal's representative to the tribes in the North, another was the Sherif of the Huweitat, a third was a Syrian for liaison with the tribes in that country and the fourth was the leader of the operation. Lawrence remained, nominally, the adviser. As on all his operations Lawrence travelled light. Each man carried six weeks' rations (45 lb. of flour) on his camel, while for water they were dependent on the string of wells along their route. They eventually joined the Huweitat at Nebk after a difficult and, at times, hazardous journey of nineteen days.

Lawrence was now able to make his preparations for the capture of Aqaba. A force of Huweitat were recruited for the attack; the goodwill of the local Emir was secured by means of £6,000 in gold; the wells on which the force would have to depend were reconnoitred; while Feizal's representative was despatched to sow the seeds of revolt further north. All seemed to be going well when a number of the party determined that the next objective should be Damascus and not Aqaba.

Disagreements of this kind were constantly occurring, and one of Lawrence's greatest assets was his ability not only to iron out differences between the Arabs themselves but also to get agreement to his own plans, even though these ran counter to those put forward by the Arabs. A combination of guile, auto-suggestion, tact and patience is said to have been his recipe, but the fact was that Lawrence could live and think as an Arab. This, combined with his wider knowledge and greater intellect, enabled him always to keep ahead of his companions both in thought and in subterfuge.

Once Lawrence had succeeded in uniting the aims of the Arabs, the force, now 500 strong, set off from Wadi Sirhan on the approach march to Aqaba. At Bair they halted for a week, to collect supplies and to stage a deception operation by making a raid on the railway north of Amman. On their next bound, the oasis of Abu el Lissal, Lawrence's force attacked and practically annihilated a Turkish battalion which had, by coincidence, only just arrived there. News of this enemy unit had been received from the local tribesmen and enabled the Arabs to mount a surprise attack before dawn. From prisoners taken it was discovered that the garrison at Maan—already bypassed by Lawrence's force—only consisted of two weak companies. Upon hearing this, the Huweitat, now forming the bulk of his force, clamoured to turn back and attack Maan, and it was only with great difficulty that Lawrence persuaded them to continue the advance on Aqaba. The action at the oasis and this contretemps had not only tired and disorganised his followers, but the delay had caused food supplies to run low. The Aqaba garrison was, however, quite unprepared for an attack from the land side and surrendered after a half-hearted resistance. They little knew that the Arab force had eaten nothing for nearly two days and had little prospect of finding food had the garrison held out.

Soon after the capture of Aqaba, trouble began. The Huweitat, dissatisfied by the continued shortage of food and lack of any reward for their part in the operations, started to negotiate with the enemy. The situation was saved by a substantial interim payment to their Sherif and by Lawrence's diplomacy.

With the arrival of Feizal and the main Arab forces from Wejh, Aqaba became more secure and raids against the Hejaz railway steadily increased. These, and particularly the destruction of rolling stock, had an effect not only on Medina but also on the main Turkish front, for both areas were provided with locomotives and wagons from one limited pool. This could not be replenished from the north owing to a change of gauge near Beirut. The most successful of these raids were carried out under British guidance, but in the process the liaison officers concerned had to deal with the constant wranglings and lack of co-operation between the various tribes; any successful action seems always to have been followed by the complete disorganisation of the raiding party owing to their lust for loot.

*Spread of resistance*

Throughout 1917, Feizal's influence spread steadily northwards. One factor was the successful campaign against enemy communications. Uncertainty as to where the Arabs would next strike was being stimulated by propaganda and by the clandestine issue of handbills warning the inhabitants not to travel by rail since attacks were imminent. But an even greater factor in Feizal's increasing success was his own personality and powers of leadership. Not only did the Emirs of Northern Arabia and Syria acknowledge him as their leader, but by his diplomacy, patience and obvious sincerity he induced them to bury their personal vendettas. Thus when in the autumn he was asked by General Allenby to co-operate in the British offensive about to be launched against the Gaza–Beersheba positions it would have been possible to start a general revolt in the Turkish rear. The 12,000 armed Arabs this would have brought into the open should have been able not only to cut the Turkish communications but also temporarily occupy Damascus. The risks, however, were very great, for unless the British advance was deep and rapid the Arab insurgents would be overwhelmed and in the ensuing reprisals hundreds would be massacred. There would then be no chance of any second rising. So, in view of the limited gains of previous British offensives, Feizal and Lawrence decided that the time was not yet ripe for calling out the Arabs in a general revolt. Events proved them to be right.

However, in order to dislocate communications in the Turkish rear and at the same time prove to General Allenby the value of the Arab irregular force, Lawrence proposed to make a hazardous attack on the railway north of the vital Deraa Junction, 240 miles from Aqaba. Here the track crossed the Yarmuk gorge by two bridges; it was estimated that the cutting of either would stop traffic for a fortnight.

Lawrence's methods were to be the same as for the Aqaba affair. A small cadre would move North to the area of Azraq and from there the remainder of the party would be recruited from local tribesmen. The assault was a failure, chiefly because one of the Arab leaders deserted to the Turks at the last moment. On the return journey, inspired by the insistence of the tribesmen to have something tangible to their credit, a train was successfully derailed. It was full of troops and the Arabs only escaped with difficulty and considerable casualties. An interesting insight is given in Lawrence's closing paragraph on this action: 'I . . . paid rewards, compensated the relatives of the killed and gave prize money for the sixty or seventy rifles we had taken. It was small booty, but not to be despised. Some Serahin, who had gone into action without rifles, able only to throw unavailing stones, had now two guns apiece. Next day we moved into Azraq having a great welcome, and boasting—God forgive us—that we were victors.'

## Events, winter 1917–18

With the capture of Jerusalem in December 1917, Allenby gave Feizal the tasks of protecting his right flank and at the same time of interfering with the Turkish grain traffic from the East. To carry out these commitments Feizal moved parts of his so-called regular force from Aqaba northwards. With their arrival, the campaign entered into a phase of more regular operations, although the policy continued to be that of pin-prick attacks and avoidance of direct opposition to regular Turkish forces. A number of successful actions followed, including the destruction of the grain fleet on the southern shores of the Dead Sea, and the near-annihilation of a Turkish column. The latter was the result of Lawrence's handling of a mixed force of Arab regulars and local tribesmen.

There now followed a lull, for the winter is severe in the uplands around Maan and to the north, but by March conditions had improved and the Turks started counter-operations. The Arabs could do little to oppose these, and to relieve the pressure on Feizal's forces General Allenby attempted a raid in strength on Amman. Its failure, due mainly to the weather, and the subsequent British retreat to Jerusalem, had a serious effect on the Arabs, who believed it a major defeat. Turkish reprisals and rumours that a British withdrawal from Jerusalem was imminent gave a further downward impetus to Arab morale. Even so the British threat to Amman had achieved its aim, for troops were hastily moved back from Maan and the pressure on Feizal's hard-pressed forces lessened.

By now Lawrence's responsibilities and power far exceeded those of a normal liaison officer and he is often found controlling operations in addition to his many liaison duties and constant work of dealing with Arab internal troubles. The strain was beginning to tell. In the spring of 1918 he went to Cairo with the idea of throwing in his hand, only to find himself embroiled in planning for the autumn offensive which aimed at the capture of Damascus. To provide full support for this it was decided that Feizal's Arab Army must be moved further north, and that to accomplish this with security Maan must be captured and Medina at least isolated.

## The Final Phase

The remainder of the Arab campaign is of diminishing interest from the guerilla warfare angle as the lion's share was now taken from the local tribesmen by Feizal's so-called regular Northern Arab Army. Lawrence, however, continued to dominate the scene, and take a leading political and military part in events. The preliminary operations against Maan and the destruction of a long stretch of railway north of Medina are of interest, as they showed the difficulty of co-operation between regulars and guerillas. The carefully planned and timed attacks of the regular force were constantly frustrated by the inability of the tribesmen to keep to any such programme. For the latter only the most flexible plan was suitable. Furthermore, they had to be guided rather than ordered. It is therefore not surprising that there was friction between the two, while loot, or rather a surfeit of it, again caused the disintegration of the irregular part of the forces before the task of isolating Medina had been completed.

For the success of General Allenby's new offensive it was essential that the Turkish High Command should have no inkling of the great preliminary concentration of British troops in the coastal strip. A very comprehensive deception scheme was therefore evolved. In it the Arabs were to play an important rôle, not only by clandestine propaganda and spreading of rumours of intended British movements eastwards, but by themselves threatening the left flank of the Turkish rear areas. Just before the main attack was launched they were also to attack Turkish communications north of Amman with the two-fold object of blocking supplies to the forward Turkish troops and of drawing reserves eastwards and so away from the path of the cavalry's break-through.

The move of the main Arab force to its northern base at Azraq was completed in time, while diversionary attacks were made on the Hejaz line south of Amman. At the agreed time the Arabs carried out major demolitions to the railway north, south and west of Deraa Junction, though not before an Arab regular force had been driven from its objective and Lawrence had had to destroy a bridge (his 78th successful effort) with a small British raiding party in armoured cars. As the Turkish defences crumbled and the British cavalry drove northwards up the coast Feizal called out the population in open rebellion. These, together with the regular and irregular Arab units, played an important part in the subsequent rout and destruction of the Turkish armies.

*Value of Arab guerillas*

It is difficult to say how much the Turkish defeat was due to Arab guerilla operations, but the fact remains that not only was a Turkish Corps swallowed up in Medina, Maan and the many detachments along the Hejaz railway, but further troops were drawn from the main front to protect the Jordan flank and to guard against a possible Arab rising in the Turkish rear areas. Furthermore, the destruction of irreplaceable rolling stock which had to serve all three Turkish armies must have had an adverse effect on their administrative machine. General Allenby, however, thought little of the Arabs as a fighting force. In explaining the rôle allotted to the Arabs by the British commander for the Final Offensive Lawrence writes: 'he did not reckon us as part of his tactical strength. Our purpose, to him, was morale, to keep the enemy command intent upon the Transjordan front.' This was in fact achieved, mainly by propaganda, by spreading of false rumours (not a difficult task where gossip is the spice of life, and with an enemy as gullible as the Turk) and by raids on the Turkish lines of communication: all tasks well within the scope of the Arab irregulars.

*Main Arab characteristics*

General Allenby's poor opinion of the Arabs' fighting potential was well founded, for they showed themselves unsuited to long and deliberate operations and were volatile and uncertain even in minor actions, when all did not go well. Although capable of enduring hardships and at times extremely brave, few were patriots in the British sense. It was the chance of reward, either in the form of loot or British gold, that was their chief incentive. Feizal's influence brought inter-tribal strife to a halt, but jealousy and animosity persisted, with the result that the Arabs remained a mass of independent groups unwilling to co-operate with each other and controllable only by their local sheikhs. Nevertheless, because of their mobility, endurance and knowledge of the country, these tribesmen were well suited to carry out raids against the long Turkish lines of communication, provided they were well led. The majority of successful raids were, in fact, carried out by parties accompanied by BLOs who though nominally only advisers were in reality the controlling influence.

*Reasons for Lawrence's success*

Lawrence's own outstanding success seems to have been due to five main causes: his grasp of tactics and strategy; his capacity to live and think as an Arab; the fact that he was the 'goose that laid the golden sovereigns'; his legendary endurance and bravery; and last, but not least, the support he received from Feizal. Even though Lawrence may have been the power and brain behind the Arab operations, Feizal was the leader of the Arab Movement, a position Lawrence as a Westerner and Christian could never have held. Lawrence fully appreciated the importance of never seeming to presume to this leadership and throughout the war scrupulously kept the relationship between himself and Feizal to that of Adviser and Commander.

This alliance stood the strain of many stresses and was a very important factor in the success of the Arab revolt. But Feizal's leadership, Lawrence's efforts and Turkish misrule would have failed to produce the results achieved had it not been for British aid in supplies, weapons and gold. It is of interest to note that for his negotiations and operations in support of General Allenby's final offensive Lawrence was provided with a credit of £300,000 in gold: not an unreasonable price to pay for the results achieved.

# Chapter 2

# JUGOSLAVIA: SECOND WORLD WAR

## (a) The Guerilla Campaign

*Introduction*

A glance at Map 3 opposite will show that Jugoslavia is divided into two main areas, the lowlands of the north-east and the uplands and mountains to the north, west and south. The lowland area lies astride the River Danube and its tributaries the Drava and Sava. It includes those regions known in 1939 as Southern Slovenia, Central and Eastern Croatia, Slovenia, the Voyvodina and northern regions of Serbia. The second area, that of the mountains and uplands, extends from the borders of Italy and Austria in the north-west to the frontiers of Albania, Greece and Bulgaria in the south and south-east. This mountainous area covers some three-quarters of all Jugoslavia and it was here that the Jugoslavs fought their guerilla campaign during the years of Axis occupation.

Apart from the barren belt of mountains and plateaux, known as the Karstland, that stretches for some 450 miles along the Adriatic Coast the mountains are well forested. Hot summers, followed by cold winters with the temperature well below freezing-point, are the general rule, with rain the whole year round. The heaviest falls of rain and snow occur in the Karstland above which there are thick cloud belts most of the year, and this factor had a serious limiting effect on the scale of air supply flown into the Jugoslav guerillas during this campaign.

Across the mountains movement is generally difficult and restricted, this being particularly so between the Adriatic coast and the hinterland. Few lines of communication exist and these must, of necessity, follow the deep river valleys. The most important route is that which runs up the Morava valley from Belgrade and down the valley of the River Vardar into Greece. The main railway line following this route has a branch at Nis, from which a line cuts through the mountains of Eastern Serbia into Bulgaria. Elsewhere in the mountainous regions of the south, railways are scarce and then mainly narrow gauge. In the plains and through the mountains of Slovenia in the north there is, by Balkan standards, a fairly dense railway system. Roads in Jugoslavia are inadequate and some two-thirds of those existing in 1939 were only fit for animal transport. For this reason waterways played an important part in the country's communication system, the Sava being navigable for over 300 miles of its course while the Danube is navigable throughout its length in Jugoslavia.

Jugoslavia was of importance to the Axis not only because she lay astride the great Danube highway between east and west and the Morava route to the Aegean, but also on account of her minerals. The latter were of great importance to the German war economy, the chief being the chrome industries of the Skoplje area and the copper mines of Bor in Eastern Serbia, which were reputed to be the largest in Europe.

So much for Jugoslavia's geographical background. The historical and political factors which had a bearing on the Guerilla campaign are described, briefly, in the following paragraphs.

At the end of the First World War the new Jugoslavia, the 'Kingdom of the Serbs, Croats and Slovenes' was proclaimed. The event represented an attempt by the statesmen of 1919 to unite the turbulent peoples in that part of the Balkans so frequently called 'the cockpit of Europe'. The new kingdom, however, born in the shadow of world war, and beset from its inception with a series of frontier disputes and internal administrative problems, was too weak and inexperienced to be able to reconcile the age-long political, religious and ethnic differences between its members, especially those which existed between the Serbs and the Croats. The history of Jugoslavia between the two world wars is thus a story of uninterrupted political strife carried out to the traditional Balkan accompaniment of assassinations, rioting and revolution.

By March 1941, one month before Germany invaded Jugoslavia, the position was acute. Serbian nationalists, infuriated by the government's policy of appeasement to Hitler's continued demands upon Jugoslavia, and strongly supported by the younger men of the officer corps, had just staged a successful coup d'etat by which the young King Peter was placed on the throne. A new government was formed under General Simovic, and the recently-signed pact with Germany, which had temporarily satisfied Hitler's demands, was publicly denounced. From the military aspect there was little to back up this show of resistance. The Army and the Air Force were equipped with obsolescent weapons, had little mobility, and were totally inadequate to defend the 1,600 miles of land frontier along which Jugoslavia faced six hostile countries. The German invasion of Czechoslovakia had sealed off Jugoslavia's main source of weapons, the Skoda works, while by this time her allies were either overrun by the Axis or were fighting with their backs to the wall and in no position to help with the supply of arms.

Early on the 6th April, 1941, Germany invaded Jugoslavia. The inadequacy of the Jugoslav Armed Forces, coupled with the fact that mobilisation had been delayed to the last minute on account of the hesitation and timidity of the new government, made the situation a hopeless one from the start. Almost at once, the Jugoslav High Command lost touch with the forces in the field. By the 17th of April, little more than two weeks after the enemy had crossed her frontiers, Jugoslavia was in Axis hands; the King, Simovic and the Government were in exile, and the Jugoslav High Command had capitulated.

The break-up of Jugoslavia was soon completed. Large portions of her frontier areas were annexed and parcelled out among the Axis partners: Germany, Italy, Hungary, Albania and Bulgaria each taking their share. Croatia—now including Bosnia and parts of Serbia—although in theory made into an independent state under Pavelic and the extremist Croat party known as the Ustasi, in fact came under firm German control. Finally, Serbia, now denuded of Macedonia and those areas included in the new Croatia, found herself under the rigid rule of a German 'Economic Dictator' and a 'Quisling' government headed by a former Jugoslav Minister of War, General Nedic.

Almost at once the country was subjected to the usual systematic exploitation of resources and manpower. Political and religious persecution developed rapidly, and the standard of living, never very high, deteriorated severely. Thus as living conditions in Jugoslavia became more and more intolerable, so the 'flame of resistance' began to burn steadily brighter.

*The Resistance Organisations, 1941*

The failure of the Government to mobilise the armed forces until too late was an indirect blessing, as many never reached the army before it capitulated. Many more were able to fade away from their units after the surrender, but before the Germans had time to take control. Some of these men returned to their villages, but others took to the mountains with their arms and equipment. Here they were joined by an increasing flow from occupied parts of the country, as Axis demands for labour and conscription in the Quisling organisations mounted. The growth of this embryonic guerilla movement was the result of spontaneous action by a brave and traditionally independent people. As was to be expected under these circumstances, there was no co-ordination and little connection between the scattered bands that came into being. Neither was there any leader, such as the late King Alexander had been in the 1914–18 war, to serve as a national rallying point for these elements of resistance, while only two organisations within the country had the necessary resources to co-ordinate guerilla activities to any degree. These were the Communists and the Cetniks.

*The Communists*

Although the Jugoslav Communist Party had been declared illegal as far back as 1921, it had continued to work underground with some success. The discontent and low standards of living had been fruitful ground on which to work, and by 1941 its ranks included a number of young, energetic and frustrated individuals. Sympathy with the Movement had also been strengthened in the country by the fact that the Communists had been in no way responsible for the mis-government and evils of the police state which had existed between the wars. They were virile, experienced in clandestine methods, and had an organisation spread throughout the country. Furthermore, a number of their leaders had taken part in the Spanish Civil War and thus had a practical knowledge of guerilla resistance.

The events of 1941 found the Jugoslav Communist Party unprepared, but Tito, the Party leader, immediately set about preparing the organisation for an eventual rising. The situation was made ambiguous by the fact that Russia and Germany were still in alliance. This obstacle was removed in June by the German attack on Russia, and from then onwards the Communist policy, under Tito's direction, remained constant: resistance to the occupying forces and their satellites regardless of the consequences.

## The Cetniks

The other potential resistance organisation, the Cetniks, differed profoundly from the Communists. Their creed was militant Serbian nationalism, and their history dated back to the 1914–18 war when they had distinguished themselves in keeping resistance alive in Serbia after the retreat of the Serbian Army to Corfu. Being essentially a Serb organisation, they were distrusted by the non-Serb elements in the country. Nevertheless, this was the official organisation charged with the task of preparing for guerilla action in the event of the country being overrun. To this end the Cetniks had been organised on a country-wide basis with a central Headquarters and administrative centres throughout Jugoslavia. The more responsible posts were held by serving regular army officers with reservists in subordinate appointments. The rank and file consisted of civilians and ex-soldiers who carried out peacetime training and could be called up in much the same way as the Home Guard in the United Kingdom. Owing, however, to the laxity of peacetime preparations, the efficiency of the Cetniks for war was questionable and their resources in arms and equipment very limited. The Commander in 1941 was Kosta Pecanac, a hero of the 1914–18 resistance in Serbia.

Another whose name came to the fore at this time was Colonel Draza Mihailovic. This officer avoided capture, and with a group of other army officers and gendarmes moved into Western Serbia and set up a Headquarters in the mountains near Valjevo. Mihailovic was a Serbian regular army officer with a good fighting record but little experience outside his limited military education. He was more of a staff officer than a commander. Extremely hardworking and liable to worry over detail, his promotion in the army seems to have been even slower than was normal. He had, however, sufficient acumen to see that the accepted Jugoslav High Command policy of perimeter defence along the frontiers was a suicidal one. He had therefore constantly stressed the need for mobility and guerilla tactics as the country's only hope in any future war. As a result he had obtained some distinction as an expert on guerilla warfare amongst the less conservative army officers.

One of Mihailovic's first actions was to try to appoint the Cetnik leader Pecanac as commander in South Serbia. Pecanac, however, possibly influenced by the memory of the massacre that followed his abortive rising against the Germans in 1916, went over to General Nedic's 'Quisling'

Government, and a number of other Cetniks followed his example. Thus from the first the Cetniks were split into two factions, although the differences between them lessened as time passed. Mihailovic himself opposed action against the Axis on the grounds that, with his own weakness and the overwhelming strength of the enemy, any acts of defiance would be worthless and would merely result in reprisals and loss of life. The Serbian aim, he considered, should be to build up a Resistance organisation which, in the first place, could help the Allies when they eventually began to liberate the Balkans and which, secondly, would form the nucleus of a post-war organisation for the control of Jugoslavia.

*Growth of resistance, 1941*

By the summer of 1941 guerilla bands were forming in most parts of the country where suitable areas lay. Their ranks were steadily increasing, particularly in Western Croatia and Bosnia, as the result of an outburst of terrorism against the Serbian minorities. This was led with great ruthlessness by the extremist Croat faction, the Ustasi. The strongest guerilla forces were in the hills and mountains of Serbia where the greater proportion of ex-army men were concentrated. Here Tito had set up his Headquarters near Uzice, some thirty-five miles south of Mihailovic. Resistance had also started in the hills of Italian-held Slovenia, while a spontaneous but somewhat premature revolt by the Montenegrin people in July caused the Italians considerable uneasiness and a number of casualties.

The occupying forces were as yet thin on the ground and fully occupied consolidating their hold on those communications and centres within Jugoslavia which were vital to their war effort.

By August the Communists in Western Serbia had started offensive action in the area of the upper valleys of the Western Morava and Drina. In collaboration with the Cetniks they cleared this area of the comparatively weak enemy garrisons, capturing a number of towns including Uzice which was of great importance to them since it contained an armaments factory. They also held the stretch of the Belgrade–Sarajevo railway in this district. There was an uneasy alliance during this period between the Cetniks and Communists. Tito appears to have been willing to compromise in an attempt to ensure unified effort, but the great obstacle was Mihailovic's determination to avoid any action which might bring reprisals. At the second of two meetings between the two it was, nevertheless, agreed that, in return for a share of the ammunition produced in Uzice, Mihailovic's forces would take common action with the Communists against the enemy. Even so there were clashes between units of the two movements, each side accusing the other of being the instigator, and the Communists on a number of occasions blamed the Cetniks for not pressing home their attacks.

*The First Offensive, winter 1941*

By now German forces in the district had been strengthened and in the middle of November they launched an attack, later known as the 'First

Offensive'. Its aim was to clear the Sarajevo railway. It was preceded by a large scale massacre in Kragujevac. This may well have influenced Mihailovic and his followers in the subsequent fighting, for they made little attempt to assist the Communists and instead dispersed into the mountains. Some even came to *ad hoc* agreements with Nedic's 'Quisling' forces who had been operating with the Germans.

By the end of November the Communists had been driven out of the Western Morava valley and back into the mountains of Southern Bosnia, the Sandzak, Herzegovina and Montenegro. With them went some of Mihailovic's men who were determined to fight the enemy. The loss of the Uzice armament factory was a serious blow and the Communists were now entirely dependent for arms and ammunition on what they could capture. In fact they relied on enemy sources for everything except food, which they obtained from the countryside. In their moves over the sparsely cultivated and often barren regions through which they now passed food also became extremely difficult to obtain. Even so their losses were replaced and their strength continued to increase.

The Communist appeal was two-fold. First, it offered the hope, when the war was ended, of a change from the corruption and lack of liberty which had been suffered under the old regime, with its vested interests and narrow nationalism. Secondly, it gave the more immediate guarantee of retaliation against the invaders and those who sided with them. Thus every village that was sacked and every hostage shot swelled the numbers of embittered men that joined. The Partisan units soon consisted of men of every class, type and political belief. With this broadening of its character the Communist strain became less conspicuous. For this reason, the more general term 'Partisans' will henceforth be used when referring to Tito's Communist guerillas.

The main strength of the Partisans now shifted to Bosnia. Here the original resistance differed from that in Serbia. Instead of a preponderance of ex-army men from the liquidated Jugoslav Army, the bands consisted of local villagers who had risen to defend their lives and property against the Ustasi. Here, Cetnik and Communist combined in resisting the plundering by the forces of the new Croat State. With the arrival of the Partisan forces driven out of Serbia by the 'First Offensive' operations began in Bosnia, and the civil Communist administration that controlled all Partisan-occupied areas came into being.

The local Cetnik leaders—the village merchant, the policeman, and similar individuals—saw themselves drawn into a movement which aimed at social change. Their only reason for taking up arms had been to preserve their former position and way of life, and these, as they saw it, would be imperilled by a Partisan victory. Furthermore, the Partisans' determination to fight the invaders regardless of the consequences would, they felt, further jeopardise their precarious position as a minority in Bosnia. Therefore when punitive measures became imminent certain of the Cetnik leaders came to agreements with the occupying powers, with the object of avoiding extinction and husbanding their resources on the lines followed by Mihailovic in Serbia and broadcast at this period by the BBC.

## *The Second Offensive, early 1942*

Tito's headquarters, and the main Partisan concentration in Bosnia were now in the area Northeast of Sarajevo. In January 1942 a 'Second Offensive' was launched against them by a combined German and Ustasi force from three directions. Cetnik units were operating with the Partisans but appear to have been divided in their intentions. Some Cetniks, apparently forewarned, withdrew into the woods before the encircling movement started. The remainder were scattered during the operation but a number of the leaders are said to have escaped into Serbia with the help of Nedic's men. The Partisans by rapid marches across difficult country broke through the cordon, crossed the snow-covered Romanija Mountains, and climbed into the high and rugged regions at the headwaters of the Drina (after demolishing lengths of the Sarajevo railway). The less mobile German units did not follow them up and the 'Second Offensive' ended without the Germans having attained their object of destroying the main core of Partisan resistance.

## *Communists versus Cetniks in Montenegro*

Leaving Tito's Partisans to lick their wounds in the mountains of Sarajevo, let us return to events in Montenegro where, as already mentioned, the local inhabitants had risen in the summer of 1941 against the Italian occupation forces. Considerable quantities of arms and equipment had been captured by the Revolutionaries. It was not long before these were being used in internecine strife, for the extremist elements of the Communist Party attempted to gain control by force. Their excesses alienated the rest of the country and in the counter-measures that followed the Cetniks, with the support of the majority of the people, drove the Communists into the mountains, inflicting reprisals on them no less brutal than the previous outrages of the Communists. By the winter of 1941 the pendulum had begun to swing back. The Communists, reinforced by a proportion of those driven out of Serbia by the First Offensive, started to re-infiltrate into Montenegro. By the spring they had regained control of a large part of the country. The now customary reprisals followed. Somewhat prematurely they proclaimed Montenegro an 'integral part of the USSR', for the Italians were strongly reinforcing their Montenegri garrisons and a large part of the population was now hostile to the Communists on account of their brutal reprisals.

## *The Third Offensive, Spring 1942*

It was partly due to these excesses that the 'Third Offensive', which the Italians now opened against the Montenegri Communists, saw the Cetniks fighting openly alongside the two Alpini divisions specially allotted for the operation. The end of May saw the Communists for the most part driven into Herzegovina and Bosnia, and the Cetniks assisting the Italians in the control of the country. For this the Cetniks were provided with arms, equipment, food and, in a number of instances, pay by the Italians.

*Cetnik Policy*

Mihailovic had by now moved his headquarters from Western Serbia to near Mount Durmitor on the northern borders of Montenegro. He appears to have had little control over the initial actions of the Montenegri Cetniks, but his policy concerning their relations with the Italians is given in a report from the British Liaison Officer (BLO) who was with him at the time. It reads: 'Mihailovic is against fighting the Italians until the last moment. He insists that the Italians will shortly collapse and he will get arms and equipment to defend Montenegro against the Germans. He says that if he starts action now the Germans will come in and he will lose for ever the chance of getting Italian arms, and will lose the people as well. If he sabotages the Italians they will no longer feed the Cetniks. He gives no propaganda or hot news against the Italians or their friends here'.

Thus Mihailovic continued on his policy of non-agression to the Axis, and most of his commanders followed suit. Some had already gone even further and were working within the Axis framework as in Montenegro, where the Cetniks were now formally established under Italian auspices.

From now onwards, with some minor exceptions, Mihailovic and his Nationalist Cetniks ceased to be a guerilla movement in the sense of a force opposing the invader and instead turned upon the Communist Partisans whose suppression they considered of even greater urgency to the future of Serbia than the expulsion of the Axis. By efficient propaganda the Germans did much to increase the hatred between the Partisans and Cetniks in the months and years that followed.

*Cetnik Organisation*

By the summer of 1942 Mihailovic's Cetniks were mainly concentrated in Serbia, Montenegro, Herzegovina and Dalmatia. In the last two regions their relationship to the occupying forces were the same as in Montenegro: Cetniks controlled certain areas with the consent of the Italians, while in Dalmatia the Cetnik commander had, with the aid of the Italians, gone so far as to create a force known as the 'Volunteer Anti-Communist Militia'. Mihailovic's main strength lay in Serbia, however, where his forces held numerous areas in the mountainous regions to the west, south and southeast. At this time it was estimated that in Central and South-East Serbia there were about 10,000 Cetniks, of whom 6,000 were—according to Mihailovic's commander in this region—without weapons.

Communications between Mihailovic and his Cetnik forces were poor since, except for couriers, they had to rely on an odd assortment of wireless sets, including Jugoslav army models, civilian sets and many home-made efforts. It was one such home-made set that gained contact with London in August 1941 and started the train of events by which Mihailovic became Minister of War in the exiled Royal Jugoslav Government and the accredited leader of all Jugoslav resistance.

With such inadequate communications it must have been difficult for Mihailovic to control his outlying commanders. Nevertheless, when in subsequent months a number of these failed to carry out his directions, it was not through lack of communications but owing to their own shortcomings.

Cetnik units were also affected by the lack of efficient junior commanders. Many of the regular army officers were prisoners-of-war, and others, determined to fight the invaders, had joined the Partisans. Thus a large proportion of the Cetnik junior commanders on the Company level were promoted Jugoslav Army non-commissioned officers who had little aptitude for leadership and little knowledge of man management or training. Petty jealousies within units grew up, training was poor and discipline lax. This was further aggravated, as time went on, by the lowering of the morale of the rank and file by discomfort and by long periods of inactivity. Nevertheless there appears to have been a strong sense of discipline and loyalty amongst many of the Serbian regular officers, and some of these, while disagreeing fundamentally with the policy of inaction, implicitly obeyed Mihailovic as the King's representative.

*Serbia, 1942*

In general it can be said that within Serbia most of the broken country away from the towns and main industries was under the influence of local Mihailovic commanders, whilst control of most of the rest remained in the hands of the Nedic ('Quisling') authorities. In the countryside not occupied by the Nedic forces there were numerous tracts inhabited by non-Serb minorities which were in no way controlled by the Cetniks. Even in Cetnik-controlled localities no attempt was made to set up new administrative machinery, nor were they in any way liberated areas as in Partisan-held territory. They were rather spheres of influence allowed the Cetniks by the Nedic authorities with whom local agreements were made by the Cetnik commanders. This understanding was initially on the basis of 'live and let live', but as the Partisans gained strength and thrust into Serbia it developed into combined action by the Nedic forces and the Cetniks against the Partisans.

The Germans at first distrusted Mihailovic's Cetniks and could not decide whether to treat them as friends or foes. This German uncertainty can be appreciated when one considers that Mihailovic's forces were ideally placed either to attack a large number of areas of great strategic importance to the Axis war effort, or to hold these against the Partisans. The Cetniks dominated the vital route through the Morava and Vardar valleys into Greece and the subsidiary one from Nis into Bulgaria: they overlooked the dangerous Danube narrows in the Iron Gates sector, while units lay in areas surrounding many of the places whence the Axis were obtaining their badly needed minerals, particularly the chrome of Skoplje and the Bor copper mines. None of these vital targets were ever attacked in any force by the Cetniks, although some raids were carried out on communications, generally as the result of strong and persistent pressure from the Allies.

*Partisan Development, 1942*

We left the Partisans in the mountains south of Sarajevo, having successfully avoided the German attempts to surround them in January 1942. As soon as the German offensive had spent itself Tito returned to the attack and by the summer of 1942 he had regained the regions lost earlier in the year. Reinforced by the Partisans who had been driven out of Montenegro during the Italian 'Third Offensive' he continued operations in the new Croat independent state and by that autumn was in occupation of various areas in Western, Central and Northern Bosnia, as far north as Slunj. Amongst other towns occupied by the Partisans was Bihac. Here on 26th November 1942 the first National Civil Authority was set up, when representatives from many different parts and sections of the country formed the Anti-Fascist Council of National Liberation (AVNOJ). The aims of AVNOJ were: first, to act as the central organ of the Government; secondly, to provide the machinery for producing authoritative statements on policy; and thirdly, to co-ordinate the work of the ODBORS (the local civil administrative authorities set up in areas under Partisan control). The first act of AVNOJ was to draw up a six-point programme which was given the widest possible publicity both inside and outside the country. This programme stressed the fact that the aims of the Partisan Movement were to liberate Jugoslavia and then form a new Jugoslav State on democratic and federal lines. Its liberal outlook had the effect of broadening the support of Tito not only within the country but also abroad.

In the meantime, organisation within the Partisan Forces had been progressing. A start had been made after the 'First Offensive' in Serbia to form military units from the many bands then in being and the 'First Proletarian Brigade' had been created soon after. There were now two so-called Divisions and the end of 1942 saw seven divisions in being. The Partisan forces were now officially designated the People's Army of Liberation (JANL), the High Command of which was responsible to AVNOJ.

*The Fourth Offensive, early 1943 (see Map 4)*

The Germans could not let this development continue, for not only were the vital rail communications between Zagreb and Fiume threatened, but the existence of the National Organisation, with its rapidly growing strength, was a challenge to the Axis New Order itself. They, therefore, launched a campaign in January 1943 with the object of annihilating the main Partisan force and its government. The Map opposite shows in outline the disposition of the various formations and their subsequent moves. The German plan was a two-pronged thrust from the north and north-west which was to drive the Partisans southward, where the circle round them would be closed by other forces holding strong defensive positions on the line of the River Neretva. German and Ustasi forces were to carry out the drive from the north, moving into the mountains from the Sava Valley, and the German Prince Eugen Division would thrust down from the north-west through Slunj and Bihac. Italians and Cetniks were to hold the Neretva line.

At the beginning of the campaign JANL formations within this circle were scattered over a wide area. The First and Third Divisions were spread over Central Bosnia. The Second Division was in the mountains north of Split in Dalmatia, and the Seventh Division was north of Bihac. JANL Headquarters received news of the German plan and concentration before they had been completed, and it was decided to attempt to break across the Neretva before the Italians and Cetniks could strengthen this position.

Accordingly, the First and Third Divisions were sent by forced marches to attack in the area of Jablanica, while the Second Division pushed on to the Neretva, near Mostar. By this move it cut off and destroyed the Italian Murge Division, capturing its equipment and weapons. While the Seventh Division bore the brunt of the German attacks from the north-east the main body, slowed down by large numbers of wounded and thousands of refugees fleeing from enemy reprisals, trekked southwards across very difficult country. For food and transport they had to rely on the countryside through which they passed. Their privations were increased by air and ground attacks. Towards the end typhus broke out.

The Neretva positions withheld the initial Partisan attacks, thus allowing the Germans time to move further divisions against the Partisans' left flank. Heavy fighting continued for weeks but finally the Neretva defences were pierced, and the German attacks held off until the Partisan main body had crossed the river. In the Neretva battle the Cetnik forces, estimated at some 12,000, disintegrated. The majority fled into Montenegro, pursued by the Partisans. Mihailovic and his BLO escaped to Serbia. Thus once again the main Partisan forces escaped encirclement, but at the cost of heavy casualties. It was not, however, until March, some two months after its start, that the campaign finally ended with the JANL safely south of the Neretva.

*Reasons for Partisans' strength*

From the aspect of guerilla warfare there would seem to be three main features of the 'Fourth Offensive' which are worth studying in rather more detail. These are: first, the fact that the Partisan High Command obtained news of the German plan and impending movements in time to act before the enemy's forces had deployed; secondly, the methods of withdrawal of the large Partisan forces over very difficult country and for such long distances; and thirdly, their capacity to maintain their morale and offensive spirit throughout some two months of constant withdrawal and fighting under appalling conditions. These features are considered in the following paragraphs, although the data available is unfortunately limited.

The Partisans seem to have been fully alive to the fact that their very existence depended on good intelligence. Tactical intelligence was obtained through the covering troops that always protected all approaches to Partisan units and formations. In addition, they relied on the inhabitants of the country for news of enemy concentrations in their immediate areas, and owing to the German habit of keeping to the roads whenever possible the Partisans generally had time to withdraw from any threatened area before the cumbrous enemy forces could encircle them. For the 'Fourth Offensive', however, news of the enemy's main intention and movements cannot have been obtained through the channels mentioned above. Someone appears to have had access at a comparatively high level to German military information. It is said that in this instance this was procured by a certain official of the illegal German Communist Party, who had earlier been captured by the Partisans but had been sent back to the Germans as an exchange prisoner-of-war. On his return he had been made Political Adviser on Partisan problems at German High Command Headquarters and from this vantage point had passed high grade intelligence to his Jugoslav 'comrades' in the JANL.

The success of the JANL's long withdrawal was largely due to the fact that although now organised on the lines of a regular field army, with corps, divisions and brigades, the JANL still operated as a guerilla force. The new organisation was a framework for more efficient command and control, but the units themselves acted independently, continued to keep their mobility by remaining lightly armed and equipped; and, except on rare occasions when required to concentrate for a specific attack, they aimed at remaining deployed in small units. Control of these units was a fundamental problem, particularly as Tito's wireless communications were hardly less tenuous than those of Mihailovic. Not only was equipment scarce but sets, batteries and charging equipment were difficult to carry under guerilla conditions. Operators were few and, although training of others was constantly being carried out, it was not possible to maintain a high standard of efficiency. Thus the wireless network could only carry a very limited amount of the JANL'S signal traffic.

They were therefore forced to rely to a great extent on couriers. An extensive organisation of these had been set up, closely linked to the underground movement and using the local inhabitants to a considerable extent. Official couriers had priority rights on transport, food and all facilities necessary for their work. Nevertheless this was at best a slow and cumbersome method, and it would seem that the main factor whereby comparatively efficient co-ordination was maintained within the JANL during this difficult fighting retreat was that most of the commanders knew the aim of their C-in-C, were experienced from past campaigns and had been chosen individually by Tito himself. Thus at any given crisis they knew automatically what their next action should be.

The Partisan evasions were also helped by the fact that, normally, enemy troops laagered during the hours of darkness, only operating by day over the difficult country through which the Partisans moved. The latter therefore concentrated on night marches. On the occasions when the enemy did operate by night as well as by day the results seem to have been serious so far as the Partisans were concerned.

It is difficult to appreciate the conditions prevailing throughout the Partisan retreats without taking into account the large numbers of wounded that had to be moved. The latter had none of the amenities expected by regular forces. Doctors were few and medical equipment was at this time almost non-existent. Even the worst cases, many of whom had suffered amputations under terribly primitive conditions, were looked after by untrained peasant girls. If these were not available this task fell to the less seriously wounded. Ambulances consisted of rough unsprung farm carts which had to be pushed, pulled and sometimes half carried over the broken ground and through the dense forest. The wounded were in constant danger of further attacks and were continually on the move. At all times food was short. The conditions for the fighting troops were little better. Short of food, clothing and boots, they retreated, fighting at frequent intervals, over distances up to some hundred and eighty miles over the mountains of Central Jugoslavia, often in bitter cold and rain.

That they were finally able to drive through the Neretva defences and continue fighting into Montenegro would seem to be due to two main factors—their toughness and their morale. Their morale was bound up with discipline, good leadership and a belief in their cause. Discipline was severe. Looting and violence, for example, were severely punished, even in minor cases often with death. It would seem that this rigid discipline was not so much imposed from above but was the outcome of the passionate conviction of many of the Partisans. Observers have frequently commented upon the almost puritanical spirit of the Partisan Army which, amongst other things, enabled men and women to serve together in the same ranks.

It was the custom for detailed post-mortems to be held after each action. Everyone in the units engaged took part, and each soldier had the chance to criticise publicly any aspect of the operation. This method appears to have had good results both from the point of view of morale and also in keeping up a high standard of efficiency and courage among the officers and NCOs. By the same means, the men gained confidence in their leaders. There was also the bitter enmity of the majority of Partisans towards not only the Germans, but also the Ustasi and Cetniks, and their belief, rightly or wrongly, that capture meant a lingering death. Very few prisoners were in fact taken by either side.

It was for these reasons that, having broken through the encircling forces, the JANL's withdrawal changed into pursuit of the routed Cetniks into Montenegro and the mountains of Western Serbia.

## The Fifth Offensive, Spring 1943

Tito's aim now seems to have been to rest and re-organise his forces and at the same time consolidate his hold on Montenegro as a base for future operations. But the Axis were determined to allow no such respite, for they almost at once started to concentrate a mixed force of German, Ustasi, Bulgar and Italian divisions, supported by tanks, artillery and aircraft.

The Partisans appear to have broken one of the fundamental rules of guerilla warfare for they concentrated their formations, possibly to ease the problem of re-organisation which was so urgently needed at the end of the 'Fourth Offensive'. Partisan H.Q. was now in the area of Mount Durmitor, with a force of some 20,000 lightly armed, poorly equipped and weary men. By the end of May, the Axis forces numbered some 120,000 men and a series of powerful thrusts were now launched against the Partisans whom they surrounded.

The initial attempt of the Partisans to break out eastwards failed; then, appreciating that the enemy was weakest in the north-western sector, they thrust in this direction using three divisions with a fourth remaining as rearguard. The enemy hurried reinforcements to this area, and some of the bitterest fighting in Partisan history occurred. Attacked from the air with no chance of retaliation, and opposed by a much stronger and better-equipped enemy, the Partisans suffered very heavy casualties. In addition, there were many who died of starvation and the rigours of living in and moving over some of the most difficult country in Jugoslavia. Although the first BLO was dropped into them at the height of the fighting, the Partisans were still without any material support from the Allies and this fact, coupled with their exhaustion and lack of all essentials, might well have caused them to look on the position as hopeless. But there was no idea of surrender or even disintegration, and after weeks of fighting and movement over the mountains they broke through to the north, and those who remained alive dragged themselves and their wounded into the Romanija Mountains in North-East Bosnia. So ended the Fifth Offensive.

It was typical of their spirit at the time that the Partisans damaged the Sarajevo–Visegrad railway as they crossed it, and that less than a month after their break-out they raided the airport of Sarajevo, destroying a number of German and Ustasi aircraft found there. By the end of August 1943 Jajce and Bugojno had been captured and the Partisans claimed to be in control of an area larger than Switzerland.

## Collapse of Italy

In the following month Italy collapsed, and there followed a rush by Partisans, Germans, Ustasi and even Cetniks to seize the large quantities of arms, equipment and stores that the Italians had dumped on the Adriatic coast. Wide gaps now existed in the Axis dispositions, while the quisling forces in the western areas of Jugoslavia lost their main source of supply for weapons and stores. As a result many of the Cetnik units disintegrated.

The Partisans for their part not only obtained vital supplies of war materials, but were now for the first time able to link up effectively their organisations in Slovenia and the north with their main forces in Bosnia and those further to the south. By their occupation of the Dalmation coast and islands they had also opened up a possible supply channel to the Allies.

German reaction to this threat was rapid. The Partisans had just enough time to remove most of the large Italian dumps of equipment from Split before they were forced out. Their expulsion from the remainder of the towns and ports along the Adriatic followed in quick succession, but the Germans had not sufficient strength left to carry the islands as well.

*The Sixth Offensive, 1943-44*

The Partisans had little time in which to carry out their re-organisation, for by the end of 1943 the occupying forces in Jugoslavia had been increased to fourteen German divisions—with elements of a fifteenth—and five non-German divisions. These formations were now launched against the Partisans in a series of powerful attacks, the general object being to clear the guerillas from the Dalmatian Islands and the mountainous regions of Slovenia, Bosnia and Western Serbia.

In a matter of weeks, the Partisans had been driven from all the Dalmatian Islands except Vis, which was of considerable strategic importance as a base for supplies and for future sea and air operations against the enemy-held mainland. A mixed force of guerillas, Commandos and Special Service troops successfully defended Vis against all German attacks, although they were severely hampered by the enormous number of refugees—some 70,000 —who were concentrated on the island. Later, albeit with considerable difficulty, the Allies were able to evacuate 25,000 to Italy and the Middle East.

After some preliminary successes, the force of the Sixth Offensive on the mainland was soon spent. JANL was now stronger, better-equipped and more co-ordinated than in previous German offensives, and the time had passed when the Partisans could be driven almost at will from region to region. Instead JANL was now able to relieve pressure on any hard-pressed guerilla formations by threatening other enemy-occupied areas. By January 1944, the situation had become stabilised with the Germans holding all the key towns and the more important communication centres, while the Partisans were generally in control of the hinterland. From now on there was never, with one notable exception, any further threat to the Partisan organisation as a whole, although periodic German offensives still caused considerable dislocation and casualties in the Partisan formations engaged.

*Attempt to capture Tito*

The one exception was an extremely well-planned and co-ordinated German attack on Tito's headquarters at Drvar. Partisan intelligence seems this time to have been sadly deficient. German information on the other hand must have been extremely accurate and detailed, for parachute troops were dropped on to the headquarters itself and gliders crash-landed in the same area almost immediately afterwards. The British mission, apparently mistrusting the actions of an aircraft that had been noticed over the area, had moved further into the hills. Tito, however, was at the headquarters at the time of the attack. He only just avoided capture by escaping from the back of a cave while the Partisan guards held off the enemy, but in doing so the guards suffered very heavy casualties.

Escape from this immediate danger found Tito still threatened by three converging enemy columns and, moreover, completely out of touch with the rest of JANL. After an eventful period of near-capture he, his staff and the Allied missions were flown out of the country and a new headquarters was set up on the island of Vis, where by now the position had improved and the enemy threat to the island had receded.

*Partisan Development in Serbia, 1944*

The only region in which the Partisans were not yet organised in any strength was Serbia. Here, Mihailovic and his Cetniks remained quite inactive—a situation which could no longer be tolerated since the area contained installations and communications of vital importance to the Axis. In consequence, the Allies now pressed Tito to develop guerilla operations in Serbia, in particular against the main routes to the Danube and the railways running through Nis into Bulgaria and Greece.

At the time three weak Partisan groups existed in this area, and these were now reinforced by a Partisan Brigade from Macedonia. Attacks against the Bulgar garrisons and raids on the communications down the Morava valley were started, one result of which was the stimulation of recruitment for the Partisan forces. Numbers increased with astonishing rapidity and, by June 1944, it was claimed that five Partisan divisions—each of some 2,500 men—had been formed in the mountains surrounding the Morava valley and to the west. Allied air supply enabled these new divisions to be reasonably well-armed, clothed and equipped.

This rapid expansion heralded a period of increasing Partisan activity throughout Serbia and the first to suffer were the Cetniks in the Leskovic area, who were dispersed without difficulty. Their commander, typical of many who in guerilla warfare reserve their loyalty for the winning team, promptly deserted to the Partisans with numbers of his men. Other Partisan attacks were directed at lines of communication; the railway from Nis to Sofia, for example, was blocked for periods of up to ten days at a time. It was these and other similar Partisan operations which forced the Germans to send reinforcements into southern Serbia, including their 1st Mountain Division.

In July 1944, a greatly strengthened Partisan staff, with a new commander (Lt. Gen. Popovic), was flown in to the Serbian JANL. Their arrival saw a considerable tightening of political control and education, while the opening of training schools, the re-organisation of some formations and stricter discipline improved the fighting efficiency of the Partisans. All this coincided with strong enemy thrusts which seriously threatened the whole Partisan movement in Serbia, but the timely arrival from Montenegro of three more Partisan divisions restored the situation by compelling the enemy to spread his forces and in consequence to reduce his operations against the guerillas. The initiative now passed to the Serbian JANL and they never again lost it.

*Operation 'BEARSKIN', June 1944 (see Map 5 opposite)*

Little mention has yet been made of guerilla activities in Slovenia, in the north-west of Jugoslavia, but here a Partisan organisation had grown up in the mountains and, since the Italian collapse, had developed rapidly.

By the spring of 1944 the Allied efforts to clear the German forces out of Italy were at their height and the opening of the Second Front was imminent. It therefore became important to stop reinforcements from being moved north, out of the Balkans. With this end in view, the Allies proposed that Partisan forces should make a series of simultaneous attacks on the railways running through Slovenia, with the specific object of preventing all movement across the northern and north-western frontiers of Jugoslavia for a period of one week after a given date. This operation, to which Tito agreed, was given the code name 'BEARSKIN'.

To assist the Partisans in organising and carrying out these attacks an experienced sapper BLO was dropped in to Slovenia by parachute. Arrangements were also made to fly in to the various areas 38 tons of explosives which it had been estimated would be required for the whole operation. By the beginning of June, preparations were still far from complete although it was planned that 'BEARSKIN' should begin on the 7th. In the first place, considerable dislocation had been caused by the break-up of Tito's GHQ when the Germans made their airborne attack on Drvar, and this resulted in the Partisan formations not receiving adequate warning for the 'BEARSKIN' operations. It was eventually agreed to undertake the operation on the word of the sapper BLO. Secondly, enemy operations hampered the assembly of the guerilla forces while, finally, bad weather over the Karstland delayed the supply of the necessary explosives by allied aircraft. Operation 'BEARSKIN' consequently got off to a bad start, and it proved impossible to make a simultaneous drive against all the chosen targets. As a result, although traffic was decreased over the intended period, it was not stopped entirely. The main attacks that were carried out are shown on Map 5, but a number of subsidiary targets were also engaged.

*Attacks on the Stampetov Viaduct*

Undoubtedly the most outstanding single operation to take place during 'BEARSKIN' was the attack on the Stampetov viaduct. For this operation it is clear that extremely detailed and accurate intelligence on the disposition of the enemy and on the viaduct itself had been collected beforehand, a fact which contributed materially to the success of the attack and the demolition.

The force allotted for the task consisted of three Partisan brigades supported by four guns whose rôle was the destruction of the enemy pill-boxes at each end of the viaduct. The approach march went well in spite of the fact that a comparatively large Partisan force was taking part and that a ton of explosives had to be carried in carts. The attack itself which was carried out with considerable skill and determination, achieved complete surprise and enabled the demolition party to destroy one pier and two arches of the viaduct. The attack was over and the Partisans had disappeared before the enemy had time to take counter action.

Although operation 'BEARSKIN' as a whole can only be accounted a partial success, there can be no doubt that both the Partisans and the Allied Staffs gained considerable experience in the planning and carrying out of co-ordinated attacks against communications targets; experience which was to prove invaluable in the planning of a second and more ambitious communications offensive later in the campaign. In the first place, the value of co-ordinated operations as opposed to a series of independent and unrelated attacks was proved beyond doubt: before this the Partisans had tended to consider sporadic raids as adequate. Other lessons included the difficulty of concealing large partisan forces near an important target, the effect of an enemy attack during the assembly stages and, lastly, the general inefficiency and insecurity of Partisan cyphers. In addition, valuable data was obtained on the time required for the distribution and preparation of explosives, on the type of weapons and ammunition required against pill-boxes and other defences and on the more technical aspects of railway and bridge demolitions.

*Operation* 'RATWEEK', *September 1944* (*see Map 6 opposite page 46*)

With the exception of operation 'BEARSKIN' in Slovenia the summer of 1944 was for JANL a period of development in Serbia and of consolidation elsewhere. The Germans for their part launched a number of limited offensives against the Partisans in Slovenia, Serbia and Montenegro, but apart from these appeared content to hold the main towns and control the lines of communications through Jugoslavia.

In Italy the Allies were held on the Gothic line and to help them break through into the northern plains it was decided, in August, to synchronise with their coming offensive an attack on communications throughout Jugoslavia. The proposed outline plan for this offensive allotted the lion's share to the JANL. The Allied Balkan Air Force, while supporting JANL's operations, would attack those main communications targets which the latter could not reach. Allied Naval Forces were to concentrate on enemy coastal shipping in the Adriatic, while small raiding parties from the sea were to dislocate roads which were out of range of the JANL along the Adriatic coast. The operation was given the code name 'RATWEEK', and

## THE GUERILLA CAMPAIGN

was timed to begin on the 1st of September, the day after the Italian land offensive was due to open.

By the second week in August planning had reached the stage when it was possible for Allied Forces Headquarters to put forward to GHQ JANL a plan which included a list of the communications it was hoped that they would agree to attack; a description of the Air Forces available and their targets; the phasing of the operation; and the method proposed for communicating Marshal Tito's instructions to his Corps and Zone commanders. This last somewhat surprising detail was included to ensure, as far as possible, that secrecy was maintained. It stressed the need for using high grade cypher or, where this was not possible, the passing of orders by hand of an officer. In addition, a propaganda programme had been designed to give full publicity to JANL successes. It included broadcasts four times daily in Serbo-Croat and once in German, and it involved wide dissemination of leaflets over targets in Jugoslavia, including German troop concentrations. On the 11th August, Marshal Tito's Chief of Staff agreed to the plan for 'RATWEEK' and a few days later Tito's own instructions for the operation were issued.

On August 30th, the main Allied attack against the Gothic line was launched and on the next day, as planned, 'RATWEEK' began. The chief areas in which communications were cut by the Partisan forces are shown on Map 6, but a number of other supporting attacks were made including the sinking or damaging of barges on the Danube. Throughout 'RATWEEK' the Partisans were given the maximum possible air support, not only by means of the vast quantity of supplies dropped to them, but by the number of ground targets attacked by Allied bombers and fighter bombers. The German reaction was unusually slow, but when towards the end of operation 'RATWEEK' they did attempt to regain control of the communications and the areas that had been taken by the Partisans, they only achieved limited results.

As a guerilla operation 'RATWEEK' was an unqualified success: road and rail communications were cut in hundreds of places throughout the country and all enemy movement was greatly restricted at a most critical period. 'RATWEEK' had been carried out primarily to assist Allied operations in Italy, but it also happened to coincide with the collapse of Roumania and the invasion of Bulgaria by the Russian Armies. It thus had a far wider and more significant effect on Allied operations than was originally planned.

*The closing stages*

From the German point of view the situation continued to deteriorate rapidly. On the 8th September Bulgaria capitulated and without more ado turned on her late allies, while the Russians crossed the Danube and pushed on towards Belgrade. Vast territories and an ever-increasing number of towns were falling to the Partisans.

One major problem that arose is worth mentioning. This was the attitude of JANL as a whole when it became obvious that the greater part of Jugoslavia would be in their hands in a matter of weeks, and the effect this attitude had on the wider Allied war strategy. So far as JANL was concerned there had been no difficulty at first in prolonging 'RATWEEK' operations after the 7th September, but with the complete liberation of their country within sight the Partisans understandably became more and more averse to destroying Jugoslav communications. JANL no longer wanted explosives from the Allies but arms and materials to equip the vast numbers of new recruits that were pouring into the Army.

On the other hand it was obvious to the Allied High Command that a withdrawal of all remaining German forces from Jugoslavia and Greece was imminent, and that for this reason continued and concentrated attacks against communications were still essential, as the JANL could not possibly defeat in regular military operations the far more heavily-armed and better-equipped German formations. Thus the Allies continued to fly in explosives as first priority.

From the aspect of guerilla warfare there remains only one more event to record during the Jugoslav campaign and that concerns the withdrawal of the German 21st Mountain Corps from Albania and Montenegro during the winter of 1944. By this time the Russians held the Morava valley, Belgrade had fallen, and to the west the JANL had occupied the coastal areas with the aid of British air and sea support. Thus both the eastern and western routes were blocked and the only way of escape open to the 21st Corps was through the rugged mountain masses of Central Jugoslavia. Preliminary moves of this formation made it clear by the end of November that it intended to withdraw by this route.

British artillery was offered to the Partisans to assist them in their operations against the 21st Mountain Corps but for reasons which it is believed were largely political they refused to accept it. Nevertheless, the guns seem to have been sent to them although their consent was lacking. Whatever the true state of affairs, the artillery was so mishandled by the Partisans that it took no effective part in the subsequent operations. Allied air support was also provided, but apart from this the JANL forces had only the limited equipment of their previous guerilla campaign with which to oppose the German corps.

The 21st Mountain Corps drove forward under appalling conditions and along routes that were little more than cart tracks through country ideal for delaying actions. They lost all their heavy equipment and transport, but by the middle of January 1945 their rearguards were over the Drina. JANL, even with air support, had failed to stop them. It was an object lesson of the limitations of guerilla forces.

*Summary of results*

With the completion of this short record of the Jugoslav guerilla campaign let us consider in outline its contribution to the overall Allied war effort. The summary that follows is based to a large extent on German appreciations and reports.

Probably JANL's greatest contribution was the fact that it forced the Axis to keep in Jugoslavia large forces that were badly needed elsewhere. In the earlier years, before the Italian surrender, on an average some nine German divisions of varying types and ten Italian divisions appear to have been employed on security and garrison duties in Jugoslavia, with various satellite or quisling formations and units in addition. But the occupation troops reached their greatest strength at the end of 1943 when the Germans reinforced their Jugoslav army to make good the Italian collapse. At this time there were fourteen German divisions, with two regiments of another, as well as five satellite divisions and a protective formation, under German command, in Jugoslavia: a total of some 140,000 German and 66,000 satellite troops. These do not include Bulgar formations which were of little value, or Ustasi, Cetnik and other quisling units, all of which were put by the Germans at between 150,000 and 170,000. JANL at this time was estimated to be 220,000 strong. Thus as a very rough estimate of proportionate strengths it seems fair to believe that JANL were tying down an equal number of enemy troops, without taking into account the 150,000 to 170,000 quislings also operating for the enemy.

Judging from available German reports Jugoslav guerilla operations had little or no effect on the country's economic contribution to Germany. As previously mentioned, Jugoslavia's minerals were of vital importance to the Axis, but the Germans asserted that once they had repaired the initial damage done to the mines in 1941, production of these minerals, with the exception of bauxite, continued uninterrupted and in many cases increased under German control. Neither was delivery of these minerals to Germany ever seriously affected.

As regards communications, German statistics show that considerable damage was being done to railways by 1944, although before this guerilla successes appear to have been limited. For a time during 1944 some 30 per cent. of the railways in Croatia were out of action (probably during operation 'BEARSKIN') but although main line communications were frequently interrupted and secondary lines cut daily, the damage was generally soon repaired. Up to the time of 'RATWEEK' it would in fact seem that no significant results were achieved by JANL against communications.

The failure of the Partisans to attack economic and communication targets was due to two main causes, both common to other guerilla campaigns. First, the majority of these targets did not lie in the mountainous areas where JANL could operate in comparative safety, and secondly, for much of the war JANL was in vital need of arms, clothes and equipment, which could only be obtained by operations against German and satellite units and detachments. Hence their preference for these targets as against those of less immediate value to them. Later, when JANL's requirements were being supplied by the Allies, and when the end of Axis occupation was in sight, the Partisans hesitated to attack targets such as industries or bridges, which in the near future they themselves would require for the restoration of their own economy.

There is no doubt, however, as to the importance of the part played by JANL in the German withdrawal from the Balkans, and German reports confirm JANL's success in blocking their lines of retreat. In addition there is German proof that the Red Army's advance from the south-east was considerably quickened by JANL operations against the German lines of communication through Jugoslavia during 'RATWEEK'.

To sum up, JANL's main contributions to the Allied war effort were that they tied Axis formations to Jugoslavia at a time when they were badly needed elsewhere; and that they hastened the withdrawal and dislocation of the German armies in the Balkans, once Allied victory was in sight.

## (b) Politics, Liaison and Support

*Introduction*

With the preceding survey of the guerilla campaign in Jugoslavia as a background, the build-up of Allied liaison and support to the Jugoslav resistance movements will now be considered. In this examination, it will be seen how, at almost every stage in the campaign, unresolved political issues greatly increased the various problems with which BLO's and planning staffs were faced.

*First attempts at liaison*

News from inside Jugoslavia ceased abruptly with the Axis occupation and it was not until some three months later, in July 1941, that reports began to seep through to the outside world. These brought rumours of increasing resistance and by the following month it was clear that some form of guerilla activity had been started in the mountains in Jugoslavia. It was at this time that the Prime Minister asked the British organisation concerned with clandestine activities of this type, The Special Operations Executive (SOE), what contacts they had with these groups and how best they could be helped. There was so little to tell the Prime Minister. Nothing definite was known and so far SOE had failed to infiltrate any agents overland into Jugoslavia. Preparations were, however, at that moment being made in consultation with the Jugoslav Government in exile to send a party in by sea. It was to consist of two Jugoslav officers, nominated by the Jugoslav Government, a Jugoslav wireless operator and an SOE officer—Captain Hudson. The party was in effect a Jugoslav Mission sent in to that country under the auspices of their Government to establish contact with any groups resisting the Axis. The SOE officer was not therefore formally in command.

Hudson himself was a young mining engineer, then aged 30, who had already worked in Jugoslavia for five years. He knew the language and people well but had no political and little military experience. His equipment included a substantial sum of sovereigns, and two wireless sets. One of these, a battery set, was too weak for regular transmissions, while the other, although more efficient and powerful, was dependent on electric mains—a rare item in the wilds of Jugoslavia. So little was known at the time about the situation in Jugoslavia that Hudson's brief could only be in the most general terms: it was to contact, investigate and report on any groups resisting the enemy, regardless of race, creed or political leaning.

On the 16th September 1941 the party was put ashore from a British submarine on the coast of Montenegro. Their first contact was with a group of Communists calling themselves 'The Montenegrin Freedom Forces'. These passed Hudson and one of the Jugoslav officers on to their headquarters in Western Serbia, where he was well received and was favourably impressed with what he saw. Here he met Tito.

In the meantime the situation was developing in London, for soon after the Mission's departure signals were picked up in Malta from a Colonel Draza Mihailovic, who claimed to be in command of the Royal Jugoslav Army in the field. The authenticity of these signals was confirmed a week or so later by the arrival in London of a representative from Mihailovic himself. On the strength of this, Hudson was told to investigate and on the 28th October he made the comparatively short journey to Mihailovic's headquarters in the mountains to the south of Valjevo. He was politely but coolly received. It appears that Mihailovic considered himself the senior representative in Jugoslavia of the Royal Jugoslav Government and therefore the only legal authority with whom Hudson should deal, and Mihailovic made it clear that good relations were dependent on Hudson having no contact with Tito and his movement. Hudson's only channel of communication was through Mihailovic's wireless link. He was thus only able to get through short and fragmentary signals, often garbled in transmission; as a result considerable reliance was placed on Mihailovic's own reports.

*Developments outside Jugoslavia*

While Hudson was groping for the facts in Jugoslavia, matters continued to develop in London. Early in October 1941 the exiled Jugoslav Prime Minister, General Simovic, started to press for military aid to Jugoslavia. King Peter saw the Prime Minister on the same subject a few days later, and in the middle of the month the Chiefs of Staff were asked to consider what could be done.

From the British military point of view the time was most inopportune. Russia, with the Germans at the gates of Leningrad and Moscow, was in a critical condition and the only theatre where any diversion could be made was North Africa. Here an operation for the relief of Tobruk and a subsequent advance were in a late stage of preparation and the necessary forces and equipment were being collected with the greatest difficulty. It is therefore not surprising that the Chiefs-of-Staff were lukewarm and considered the Jugoslav uprising premature. They nevertheless agreed that, as resistance had started, everything possible should be done to help the guerillas—provided that such help did not prejudice current operations. The Commanders in Chief Middle East were therefore asked to give what help they could, bearing in mind this proviso.

At about this time both the Jugoslav Government and SOE appear to have decided that Jugoslav resistance should be hitched to the star of Mihailovic. The decision was taken blind, before any clear picture had been obtained. It is easy to be wise after the event but there were cogent reasons at the time for this step. It was SOE's task to foster resistance wherever it might appear, and here was a definite resistance movement and the only one of any apparent size of which anything was known; in addition it had the support of the exiled Royal Jugoslav Government, now our allies. Furthermore Russia was urging that all possible aid be given to any diversion in Jugoslavia, irrespective of its origin, while further pressure came from Mihailovic himself in an impassioned signal begging for arms, supplies and money with which he claimed he could build up a large and powerful army 'in a few days'.

From the Allied point of view the great difficulty was that short of jeopardising current operations the material to support any such campaign was not available, and the outcome of a meeting presided over by the Prime Minister in November 1941 was a signal to the Chiefs-of-Staff Middle East on the same lines as the previous one, but with the following added: 'At present we are not in a position to give the Jugoslavs substantial military aid.' Assistance was not therefore refused but became second priority. In this period of acute shortages, second priority meant no priority at all, and the files of SOE are filled with disheartened and recriminatory telegrams about requirements and the failure to meet them.

*Attempts to unite resistance*

As November passed the picture obtained in London and Cairo cannot have been promising, for Hudson's signals told of fighting between the Communists and Mihailovic's forces, and of many leading Cetniks openly preferring the quisling Nedic to Tito and the Partisans. Hudson asked that broadcasts be made from London and Moscow in an attempt to stop the internecine strife and suggested that Mihailovic be told that, unless he attempted to co-ordinate Jugoslav resistance under his command, he would receive no British assistance.

Hudson's suggestions were acted on without delay. General Simovic broadcast an appeal for unity, and Russia was asked through both British and Jugoslav channels to take similar action; but the broadcast that followed from Moscow did little to further co-operation between the two rival movements. King Peter made a further appeal to his country on 1st

December, Jugoslavia's National Day, while a signal was sent to Mihailovic informing him of the action being taken and telling him to do everything possible in the field to unite Jugoslav resistance. With the object of raising his status for this task he was promoted to the rank of General in the Jugoslav Army.

The main outcome of these actions was a meeting between Mihailovic and Tito at which Hudson was present. It was inconclusive, neither side giving way; Tito because his forces were now stronger than Mihailovic's, and Mihailovic because he believed that he would have British assistance in establishing himself as unconditional Commander-in-Chief.

In a somewhat vainglorious report Mihailovic sums up the results of the meeting as follows: 'I have done everything and succeeded in breaking off the patricidal strife provoked by the other side. In the fighting up to now I have exhausted almost all my ammunition. I am making the greatest efforts to unite all the nation's forces and to complete reorganisation for decisive struggle against the Germans. It is most urgently necessary to receive arms, munitions, money, clothes, boots and then the rest.' To say that this was an overstatement is to put it mildly, for at this period, just before the German First Offensive broke over Western Serbia, Mihailovic was making no attempt to organise any decisive struggle against the Germans. But both SOE and the Jugoslav Government appear to have taken his report at more than its face value and the seal was set on the policy of backing Mihailovic when he was made Minister of War in the exiled Jugoslav Government.

As these negotiations were being conducted over Mihailovic's tenuous wireless link, the German First Offensive, as described earlier in the chapter, was launched. It drove the Partisans, with some of the more determined Cetniks, into Southern Bosnia, while Mihailovic's forces as a whole disintegrated. In the resulting confusion Hudson was cut off from the Cetniks without any wireless communication of his own, and Mihailovic also went off the air. Thus at this delicate stage in the attempt to build up a unified Jugoslav resistance all touch with the field was lost and some three weeks elapsed before Mihailovic reopened communications, while Hudson was not in contact with his base again until some six months later.

During the next few months all SOE's efforts to reopen communications failed. Attempts to parachute two parties in had to be abandoned, while a further two, after an abortive journey by submarine, were dropped into Jugoslavia without any arrangements being made for their reception on landing and were never heard of again.

*Allied problems*

The abortive submarine attempt mentioned above exemplifies the difficulties of SOE and the acute shortages of the time. This submarine, although already en route for its destination with the SOE party on board, had to be recalled owing to the sudden need to concentrate all available submarines against the enemy supply line to North Africa, where the Libyan campaign had reached a critical stage. There were, in fact, only two submarines in the Mediterranean which were suitable for SOE needs, and for the use of these two SOE had to compete with those demanding transportation of vital equipment and personnel to beleaguered Malta. As an alternative the employment of local craft had been investigated, only to be turned down on account of the distances involved. Thus there only remained aircraft and one can see desperation in the SOE demand for the exclusive use of one squadron of long-range bombers, as it bore no relation to the availability of suitable aircraft. There was only one type, the Liberator, that had the required range, and these were being delivered to Britain very slowly at this period and the few that were available were urgently needed for the Battle of the Atlantic.

Thus it was still a question of priorities, and between December 1941 and the following April conferences at Ministerial level went over the ground on three separate occasions in an attempt to find some solution. The results were always the same: the Jugoslav case was supported by the Foreign Office and less forcibly by the Army (whose order of battle showed 17 Italian, 5 German and 4 Bulgar divisions in Jugoslavia) while the Admiralty and Air Ministry were obdurate that assistance could only be provided at the expense of interests which all agreed were more vital.

Ignorance of affairs within Jugoslavia during this blank period was, understandably, abysmal. In March, when in fact the Third Offensive was at its height in Montenegro, and Cetniks with Italian Alpini were driving the Communists northwards, an enquiry was passed to Moscow through the Soviet Ambassador asking whether the Soviet Government had any means of communicating with Mihailovic, and if so 'would they be prepared to assist His Majesty's Government in making with the General such arrangements as are necessary to enable supplies to reach him from British sources.' Two weeks later Mr. Maisky replied that the Soviet Government had no communication at all with Jugoslavia.

*Allied attempts at co-ordinating resistance*

By this time Mihailovic was back on the air and those concerned were satisfied that his signals were genuine. Apart from tirades as to lack of aid, for which Mihailovic had some justification, his signals were mainly concerned with Communist acts of aggression. Attempts to enlist the help of the Soviet Government in stopping this civil strife were fruitless, and it is at about this time that doubts were beginning to be expressed by the Russians as to Mihailovic's 'bona fides'.

In the early summer of 1942 the Russian-sponsored wireless station 'Free Jugoslavia' started to broadcast, and through this the world heard of Partisan operations. The British and exiled Jugoslav authorities discounted much of what was said in these inspired communiques, but it was at least obvious that the Partisans were operating with some success against the Axis.

Mihailovic for his part continued to bombard London with accusations against the Communists. A second attempt at a combined approach to the Cetniks and Partisans was made, but it became still-born when a Soviet memorandum was delivered to the Jugoslav Ambassador in Moscow, accusing Mihailovic of treason.

In fact any possibility of agreement, even if it had ever existed, had by now vanished, but London and Cairo were not to know this on the scanty information available. Three main facts were, however, clear. There was fighting between the Partisans and the Cetniks; the Partisans were also fighting the Axis, but the Cetniks did not appear to be fighting anyone but the Partisans. Having no contact with the latter and with the Russians refusing to make any attempt to assist in uniting the rival movements, the Foreign Office and SOE were set a problem which was further complicated by a radical change in the Allied military situation. Instead of considering the Jugoslav revolt premature the Chiefs-of-Staff were now pressing for as strong a diversion as possible in Jugoslavia to pin down German forces while the North African operations were taking place.

*Relations with Mihailovic, 1943*

By now, Hudson had his own signal unit and as a result it appears that SOE were obtaining a clearer picture of the situation for they also were expressing doubts about Mihailovic's true intentions.

It was therefore decided to put Mihailovic to the test and accordingly a signal was sent from General Alexander calling for an all-out attack on Axis communications and at the same time hinting at important impending events in North Africa. This was reinforced by a telegram from the Jugoslav Prime Minister in the same vein. Mihailovic's reply was that he had ordered stronger action, that sabotage was in progress and that no more could be done without further supplies of arms and other essentials. There was justification in this last complaint, as British supplies to him were still negligible. The ball was therefore back at the feet of SOE and the Foreign Office without their having obtained any clearer idea of Mihailovic's real policy, although its aggressiveness was now still further doubted. It was therefore decided to attempt to draw him into action by attaching BLOs to his subordinate commanders.

The time had also arrived when Hudson should be relieved, for he had been in the field for a year under trying conditions. His successor was a Colonel Bailey, aged thirty-seven, who had been a member of the Middle East SOE organisation. He, like Hudson, was a mining engineer and had worked in Jugoslavia before the war. It was not until Christmas Day 1942, however, that Bailey finally parachuted into Jugoslavia.

In the meantime the Partisans had claimed that their Anti-Fascist Council of National Liberation (AVNOJ) set up at Bihac in November 1942, was the supreme constitutional authority of the new Jugoslav State, and Russia had finally become committed to supporting Tito.

Reliable intelligence on the Partisan movement was still lacking in London and Cairo, although it was now clear that the Partisans were a thorn in the Axis flesh. Many felt that Mihailovic was not. Nevertheless, at the end of 1942 when Bailey reached Mihailovic, Foreign Office and SOE policy was to create unity behind Mihailovic as the representative of the only legitimate Jugoslav Government. Bailey's first signals confirmed what Hudson had already reported: that Mihailovic was inactive. Both were also in agreement that there was no prospect of reconciliation between Tito and Mihailovic.

In implementing the policy to attach BLOs to the subordinate Cetnik commanders, SOE Middle East had during the preceding months been collecting and training a number of parties, and in February the first of these joined Bailey. Other BLOs continued to arrive, and by May 1943 there were some eight separate parties, each consisting of one or more British officers with wireless operators. Few of these men knew much of the Balkans, but they were desperately anxious for action against the enemy and thus were a good channel through which to gauge the willingness for action of Mihailovic's subordinates. Although formally under Bailey, their wireless link was for security purposes direct with Cairo. They thus provided what were felt to be independent and unbiased sources of information —indeed Bailey complained that his task was made unbearably difficult by his ignorance of where the parties were sent and what they were doing and saying. Without exception they reported unfavourably on the Cetniks.

Unfortunately relations between Bailey and Mihailovic became strained after the former had been with the Cetniks some six weeks. These reached breaking point when Mihailovic chose a public meeting, with Bailey present, to make a violent attack on the Western Allies, accusing them of using the Serbs for their own ends, failing to support him materially and of directing their propaganda against him. He clearly indicated that if the British would not give him arms the Italians would, and that he had found the latter to be the better allies. It may well have been that this outburst was the result of the reverses the Cetniks were sustaining on the River Neretva at the hands of the Partisans during the Fourth Offensive, but there were also grounds for his complaints regarding lack of supplies.

Only two sorties had reached his units during the last five months, and there is no doubt that these supplies could not compare with what could be extracted from the Italians by various means. The BBC had also been following a questionable policy of advertising Partisan operations with the idea apparently of shaming Mihailovic into action. In fact it merely infuriated Mihailovic and made the task of the BLOs still more difficult.

The lack of supplies combined with constant demands from London for action was a source of embarrassment both to Hudson and Bailey throughout their missions. It was also a subject for forthright speaking from SOE Middle East, as can be seen from the following signal, originated by Cairo at the end of 1942: 'It is quite useless, repeat useless, sending any strong or other message from HMG to Mihailovic with a view to spurring him to further activities when we lack almost entirely means of supporting him.'

*Allied Policies and implementation, 1943*

From the arrival of Bailey's first report late in January 1943 there was almost continuous discussion between SOE and the Foreign Office. Broadly speaking, there appear to have been four alternative plans which were considered in London: first, unconditional support of Tito; secondly, unconditional support of Mihailovic; thirdly, equal support of both parties; and finally, a policy of temporary inaction.

Consensus of opinion was now swinging towards equal support for both parties, with the reservation that support should not be given to Tito until after Liaison Officers had been attached to the Partisans and had reported favourably on them.

The first move to set up liaison with Partisan forces was made in the latter part of April when two parties were dropped 'blind' into Partisan territory and reported favourably on what they found. As a result a signal was sent from the Allies saluting the Partisans and offering aid in the form of small highly trained missions. This offer was accepted in principle by Tito.

At the same time as this approach was being made to Tito a directive was sent to Mihailovic from London stating that the British Government hoped shortly to send him considerable assistance, provided he gave satisfactory assurances on certain points, the most important being that he would collaborate closely with the Commander-in-Chief, Middle East; that he would have no further contact with the Italians or the quisling Nedic; and that he would take no aggressive action against the Partisans but would make every effort to reach agreement with them.

Discussions on the contents of this directive had started in London at the beginning of April 1943, but for various reasons Mihailovic did not receive it until 28th May. During the intervening period the Fourth Offensive had developed, the Cetniks on the Neretva had been broken and Mihailovic and Colonel Bailey were withdrawing into Serbia. The flare up in the Partisan–Cetnik strife had shifted the emphasis from making the Cetniks into good guerillas into putting an end to a serious civil war. With this in view GHQ Middle East despatched on their own initiative what was in effect an ultimatum to Mihailovic, requiring him to withdraw east of the River Ibar and to leave the Partisans all territory which was not strictly Serbian. This document, which became known as the 'Ibar telegram', was sent to Bailey and was prefaced by an extremely outspoken appreciation of the resistance potential of the Cetniks and Partisans.

This was delivered to Mihailovic, unbeknown to the Foreign Office and SOE London, on the very day after he received the London directive. Rightly or wrongly Bailey handed him the message verbatim, and Mihailovic was thus confronted with some unvarnished statements on his shortcomings, at a time when he was already smarting from the veiled threats of the London directive. This had unfortunate results, as his reply to London was almost entirely taken up in attacking the Communists and in stating that the demands made of him in the 'Ibar telegram' from Cairo could not be the foundation of any discussions, although he was prepared to discuss the plans set forth in the London directive.

To complicate the issue even further, Cairo now accepted an invitation from Tito to send Liaison officers to his headquarters. Again, it seems that London was not consulted on this point. Colonel Deakin with another officer were accordingly parachuted in to the Partisans in May 1943, just when the German Fifth Offensive was at its height: JANL had in fact to hold the dropping zone against enemy attack for the night of their drop. By these two actions it is fair to say that GHQ Middle East accelerated the British Government's commitment to support Tito, while they indirectly added another large nail to Mihailovic's coffin. It would seem that this was a General Staff and not SOE (Cairo) policy, and was initiated in a desperate attempt to clear up the thoroughly unsatisfactory situation in Jugoslavia and to obtain some tangible action against the Axis.

*Major decisions, summer 1943*

There followed a period of vehement discussions, on the one hand between Cairo and London and on the other between the Foreign Office and SOE (London). From these emerged three main results. First, the ultimatum to Mihailovic contained in the 'Ibar telegram' was cancelled and another attempt was made to pin him down to the terms of the London directive, which it will be remembered aimed at ensuring that his actions were aggressive and only directed against the Axis. Secondly, it was decided to strengthen the mission with Mihailovic, and at the same time to send a powerful mission to the Partisans, with Lt. Colonel Fitzroy MacLean, M.P., at its head, as the Prime Minister's personal representative to Tito. The ultimate object was that these two missions would work for a combined Jugoslav effort under British direction. Thirdly, an instruction was sent to the Air Ministry and SOE to plan 'subject to operational requirements elsewhere' for increased supplies to Jugoslavia and Greece to an ultimate total of 500 tons per month.

The new approach to Mihailovic elicited his fairly explicit acceptance of the clauses of the London directive, and it was on the strength of this favourable reply that the decision was made to expand his mission. In actual fact his acceptance made little difference to his actions, and in exasperation Bailey on his own initiative presented Mihailovic with another ultimatum in the name of GHQ Middle East to the effect that all supplies would cease unless he carried out the terms of the directive. On hearing of this Middle East repudiated Bailey's ultimatum and sorties to Mihailovic's units continued. Tempers were becoming frayed all round. . . .

## Armstrong's Mission, 1943

As the result of the decision to expand the mission to Mihailovic, Colonel Bailey now became political adviser and a regular Army officer, Brigadier Armstrong, was appointed as its Head. Armstrong's directive was sanctioned by the new Special Operations Committee, Middle East, and followed the lines of the London directive. It laid down that Mihailovic was to be supported provided he ceased to collaborate with the Axis, did not fight the Partisans except in self-defence and collaborated with the Commander-in-Chief, Middle East. Enlarging on this policy, it continued that the first aim was to reconcile the two resistance groups with each other. It was hoped, it stated, that King Peter would return to Jugoslavia as constitutional Monarch and it explained how propaganda would be directed towards achieving this object. Arrangements for American representation were also included.

During the latter part of September 1943, Brigadier Armstrong together with his GSO I, GSO II and RE Staff Officer, and with two American officers, reached Mihailovic's headquarters. From the first there seems to have been little chance of success. Armstrong was soon convinced that Mihailovic was dominated by the single thought of how to overcome the Partisans, to whom he was bitterly and irreconcilably hostile. He appeared completely disinterested in attacks on communications, and while not wishing the British missions to be withdrawn he stated that not one was serving any useful purpose. By the end of October Cairo reported to London that Mihailovic appeared obsessed by internal problems to the exclusion of anti-Axis activity, and that until Armstrong was given a status above that of Senior BLO, and until the Foreign Office guaranteed post-war Jugoslav security and frontiers, Mihailovic would continue to devote his whole attention to purely domestic Jugoslav problems.

Matters continued to drift, with Mihailovic doing everything possible to avoid being forced to take aggressive action against the Axis. By November Armstrong resorted to letters to Mihailovic but these were as fruitless as his interviews and on 18th November a joint signal from Armstrong and Bailey stated that further pressure was, in their judgement, hopeless: the alternatives were complete abandonment of Mihailovic territory or an attempt to displace Mihailovic—an act fraught with difficulties and complications. As frustration increased in the field, so a mass of evidence against the Cetnik movement was building up in Cairo. The crisis was reached when in December 1943 Mihailovic made no attempt to carry out the destruction of two bridges requested by G.H.Q. Middle East, although sufficient stores and explosives had already been delivered to him.

## Break with Mihailovic, 1944

In the same month SOE Middle-East submitted an appreciation to the Commander-in-Chief stating that in their opinion further support to Mihailovic was useless and dangerous and that a break was desirable at the earliest possible moment. This went before the Special Operations

Committee, with the support of the Commander-in-Chief. The Ambassador with the Jugoslav Government in Cairo cabled the Foreign Office recommending the same course.

Knowing that a decision to cease sending supplies to Mihailovic was imminent, SOE Middle-East were already preparing for the difficult task of withdrawing the British Missions from Mihailovic's territory. On the 12th December supplies to Mihailovic's forces were stopped, and three days later all BLOs who wished to do so were given permission by SOE to make their own way to the Partisans.

Amongst those who took advantage of this was Hudson who thus left Mihailovic after some two and a half years. It will be remembered that Bailey had originally been sent in to relieve him, and it is not clear why Hudson was not brought out then for consultations, as his first-hand knowledge of the personalities concerned and the conditions in the country would have been of immense value at a critical period. Contrary to expectations the order to stop supplies was not immediately followed by formal permission to evacuate the Mihailovic Missions, and it was not until February 1944 that HMG clearance to do so was obtained.

Bailey then moved out overland, and reached London on 3rd March, as the first individual of any seniority, either British or Jugoslav, to come out with first-hand knowledge of Mihailovic's story. It was decided that the remainder of the missions should first concentrate at Mihailovic's Headquarters, and that from there an attempt would be made to fly them out. The rigours of the winter, the long distances, illness, casualties and enemy activity all made this concentration difficult, and it was not until May that all missions were eventually gathered into the area of Mihailovic's GHQ. Throughout this period Mihailovic avoided all contact with Armstrong and his subordinates remained passively unco-operative, but there was no treachery and no enemy interference throughout the long concentration period and the final evacuation by air.

This was accomplished on the three nights from 28th to 30th May when a total of 110 persons, not all mission personnel, were flown out in Dakotas from an improvised landing strip. Thus ended contact between HMG and Mihailovic.

## *MacLean's Mission, 1943*

Let us now return to the summer of 1943 and follow the implementation of the decision to send a powerful mission to Tito, with MacLean at its head.

MacLean himself had certain outstanding qualifications for the task; he had served eight years in the Diplomatic Service, during which he had undertaken various expeditions to the wilder parts of the Caucasus, and he had also gained some experience in irregular warfare behind the enemy's lines in the Western Desert. He was a Member of Parliament and, in addition to a knowledge of French, German, Italian and Russian, he knew a certain amount of Serbo-Croat. There was, however, some opposition to his appointment on the grounds that he lacked military experience and was not staff trained, both of which it was felt would be serious disadvantages since his appointment involved co-ordinating the activities of an army of some 100,000 men with Allied strategy. In addition, it was argued that it was unsound to have a primarily political personality controlling a mission whose functions were mainly military.

In the light of history it seems questionable whether any of these objections were valid, and they are recorded here to bring out the point that it is the personality and general experience of a man that count in a mission of this kind, rather than any specialised military training. MacLean's directive after stressing that HMG's policy was to support all anti-Axis elements wherever they might be, subject to the availability of the necessary resources, went on to point out the need for detailed information about the Partisan movement both from a military and political aspect, its attitude towards the King, the Jugoslav Government and Moscow, and also the need for intelligence on non-Partisan movements and how best the quisling rank and file could be persuaded to join anti-Axis resistance. It was also stipulated that MacLean, whilst serving as a member of SOE, was to consider himself in political matters a member of the Minister of State's staff in Cairo, or alternatively on the Staff of His Majesty's Ambassador to the Jugoslav Government, in the event of the latter transferring itself to the Middle East. This would in fact seem to have been the main objection to the whole arrangement, for in effect MacLean was serving two masters, neither of whom had full command.

Brigadier MacLean, as he now became, selected a strong and experienced staff, the principal appointments of which were a GSO I, GSO II, CRE, GSO III and GSO III Intelligence. This party, together with a large signal team, dropped into Bosnia on the nights of 17th and 18th September, 1943. The mission was later reinforced by several other officers.

With the great increase in resources over those of Deakin's preliminary party, reports enlarging on the latter's information soon came pouring in and it became increasingly clear to higher authority that they were faced with the supply, not of isolated guerilla bands, who would be thankful for small mercies received, but of a formidable army, centrally controlled by a man of very considerable ability and power, and organised and equipped on regular lines.

In the months that followed GHQ Middle East and the still comparatively small SOE Middle East organisation recoiled under a series of demands, requests and protests from MacLean. These were mainly centred round air support for JANL operations in the field, aid for the vast numbers of Dalmatian refugees resulting from the German Sixth Offensive and later their evacuation from the Adriatic Islands. The BBC, which had already infuriated not only Mihailovic but also the missions attached to him, also came under fire from MacLean on account of its inaccurate reporting.

*Allied propaganda*

So far as Jugoslavia was concerned there can be said to have been two main classes of propaganda. The first was that dealing with affairs outside Jugoslavia, such as the progress of the war in Europe and the casualties to German aircraft in their attacks on the United Kingdom. The second type was that which centred round events within Jugoslavia itself or on affairs directly connected with that country.

In the first category British propaganda was good. Its accuracy, as opposed to Nazi exaggeration, was known and appreciated by most of the more enlightened Jugoslavs. On the other hand, British attempts to put over the second type of propaganda, concerning Jugoslavia, seem not only to have been unsuccessful but to have done considerable harm. This was accentuated by the astute use the Germans made of British inaccuracies, while they themselves used current news from within Jugoslavia to illustrate their own points and ridicule BBC statements. This was comparatively easy for them, as they were in occupation of the country and thus on the spot. For the same reason they were in a far better position to appreciate what was likely to affect the local population at a given moment. They also had excellent propaganda material with which to aggravate disunion in the many opposed nationalities and religions within the country, in addition to their main source of material—the Cetnik-Partisan rift.

Thus the value of the British world news was largely nullified by our failure in the more local sphere for, to the average peasant and guerilla, affairs in his own country were more important than those in the outside world. There are many examples of inaccuracies and ill-chosen BBC statements, which had adverse repercussions on relations between the guerillas and their BLOs. Pictures, rather than broadcast or written news, appears to have been the best method of impressing the Jugoslav guerilla-peasant.

*Doubtful value of Allied BLOs*

While Middle East were being bombarded by the mission at Tito's headquarters the volume of reports and requests was rapidly increasing from other directions, for once the decision was made missions began to pour into subordinate Partisan formations.

The policy was that support should not be given to Tito until after liaison officers had been attached to the Partisans and had reported favourably on them, but it seems doubtful whether these many missions (by December there were eleven in addition to MacLean's) were sound policy at a time when supplies were so restricted that they could not possibly be dropped in any reasonable proportion to the number of missions in the field. Generally speaking the BLOs concerned knew nothing of guerilla warfare and little of the Jugoslav language, history or politics, and their reports were of limited value. Very few actions were ever fought which would not have taken place without the missions, and as one description states 'half a ton of ammunition and explosives would in most areas have been more effective than half a ton of BLOs.' Their presence was also a source of suspicion to the Partisans.

Possibly with this in mind Tito, supported by MacLean, insisted that liaison officers should not be sent to Partisan subordinate formations without his consent—thereby causing considerable confusion in the Cairo administrative machinery.

*Partisan Mission to Middle East, December 1943*

About a month after MacLean's arrival Tito made a formal proposal for a Partisan mission to be sent to GHQ Middle East. Having been told that no further action should be taken until further details about the delegation were available, MacLean came out early in November through the Dalmatian Islands and thence to Cairo. Here, at a meeting with Mr. Eden, the British Foreign Secretary, on the 16th November, it was agreed that the delegation should come to Egypt, provided it was purely military in character and aim: it could meet the Commanders-in-Chief, but not in Cairo. MacLean then returned to Jugoslavia and began preparations for the evacuation of the delegation.

During MacLean's absence an important political step had been taken by the Partisans, when on 26th November 1943, the Anti-Fascist Council of Liberation met at Jajce for the second time. At this meeting the Council assumed supreme power, proclaimed a new federal Jugoslavia, having denounced the exiled King and Government, and promoted Tito to the rank of Marshal. The meeting ended by sending greetings to Mr. Churchill and President Roosevelt. These declarations were well timed, for they coincided with the Teheran Conference, at which it was agreed that 'the Partisans in Jugoslavia should be supported by supplies and equipment to the greatest possible extent, and also by commando operations.' With this guidance and two excellent papers by MacLean and his staff as background, the Allied authorities had a clear picture of the organisation and likely demands of those with whom they were about to do business.

The Jugoslav mission, however, had serious difficulties in reaching Middle East. It was originally intended that it should come out by sea, but by this time the Partisan gains on the Dalmatian coast had been lost in the Sixth Offensive. An attempt to use a captured Dornier met with disaster, as the operation became known to the enemy and the plane was attacked as the mission was embarking, one of the delegates and two British officers being killed. Eventually the mission was flown out by an Allied aircraft from an improvised landing strip, in the first air landing operation to take place in Jugoslavia.

The two delegates, who reached Alexandria on the 4th December 1943, were well chosen: Colonel Velebit, a peacetime Judge and personal friend of Tito, and Colonel Miloeje, an officer with a brilliant fighting record. They were well received and during their stay discussed their problems with the three senior Service officers in the Middle East. Their first conference, with the C-in-C Levant, dealt with naval matters, including the infiltration of supplies by sea and the provision of small craft. At the meeting on 13th December with the C-in-C Middle East, General Sir Henry Wilson, Velebit raised the possibility of establishing a bridgehead on the Dalmatian Coast in order to open up a supply line into Jugoslavia. He also asked about the provision of artillery and tanks for JANL. The last conference, at which AOC-in-C Middle East was present, discussed air support and supplies for JANL and the formation of a Jugoslav Air Force.

Few decisions were reached but these conferences provided the foundation on which support for JANL during 1944 was developed. In addition, owing on the one hand to the excellent reception given to the Jugoslav delegates, and on the other to the latter's punctilious avoidance of all politics, considerable goodwill seems to have accrued on both sides.

Soon after this private recognition of JANL, the Partisans received public recognition as an Allied force in a speech by the British Foreign Secretary. Thus by the end of 1943 the Allies were committed to Tito's Jugoslavia, and to many Partisans 1944 must have opened with the promise of impressive Allied assistance.

*Allied difficulties and shortcomings*

Some time was to elapse, however, before adequate support materialised, and it was unfortunate that the Partisans could not have been made to appreciate more fully the difficulties attendant on a change-over from small-scale specialised operations to the support of an army of some 220,000 men. As it was, they were exceedingly bitter at the Allies' failure to support them during the critical months of the Sixth Offensive, particularly in view of the massive support being given at that time to the Armies in Italy. In a forthright speech on 15th January 1944, Tito openly accused the Allies of having no desire to help JANL. This was followed shortly afterwards by a broadcast over 'Free Jugoslavia' to the same effect.

To appreciate the reasons for this failure on the part of the Allies it is necessary to go back to the summer of 1943 when, as previously explained, the Air Ministry and SOE were directed to plan for an increase in supplies to an ultimate total of 500 tons per month. The magnitude of this task can be appreciated by the fact that the best month until then, May 1943, only showed a total of 25 tons dropped. The implementation of the new policy to increase supplies appears to have got off to a very slow start, for it was not until November 1943 that the first major step seems to have been taken, when an RAF wing was established to control air supply. Even so, the total tonnage dropped to the Partisans during the whole of 1943 only amounted to 230 tons, less than half the total planned for one month.

SOE had in the meantime changed over from their previous '*ad hoc*' methods of supply to the standard army procedure, their plans being based on a requirement for 100,000 men. With the Italian collapse they pushed forward an advanced headquarters to Bari, expecting that with the opening up of the Dalmatian Coast sea supply would develop rapidly. The scope of this headquarters in Italy was, however, limited by the fact that GHQ Middle East still controlled operations into Jugoslavia, thus forcing SOE's main communication network with the field to remain centred on Cairo. The manning of the two headquarters meant a further strain on the limited SOE resources in personnel and equipment. When in January the RAF supply-dropping formations moved from North Africa to Italy, it became necessary to concentrate the SOE Jugoslav organisation there also. It was not until some three months later, however, that control of Jugoslav operations passed to Allied Forces Headquarters in Italy and that SOE Rear Headquarters could close up on Bari. A further three months were to elapse before all signal traffic from the field could be finally routed there. The delay over the signals change was due to the amount of technical work necessary, such as the issue of new signal plans, crystals and cyphers to the field, the shortage of high-power frequencies, and the lack of suitable wireless equipment needed for the shortened range between base and the field.

Another problem at this time was caused by the considerable number of other organisations assisting in the supply, support and training of JANL. These expanded and multiplied without any definite plan as the commitment grew, and thus the problem of co-ordinating the activities of these agencies was added to SOE's domestic troubles. During this period such co-ordination and liaison as did exist appears to have been very much on an improvised and 'old boy' basis. SOE cannot be blamed for all these shortcomings, for with their semi-independent charter, extreme security and specialist staff they were not the proper organisation to handle an affair which had long passed from the realm of 'clandestine operations' into that of a full-blooded military campaign. As early as mid-1943 there were obvious indications that the Jugoslav commitment was about to expand enormously in volume, scope and complexity, and would differ completely from the problems dealt with by SOE in the other Balkan and Central European countries. This would seem to have been the stage at which some military system should have taken over control of the rapidly-expanding regular forces and establishments committed to the support of JANL. But it was not till nearly a year later that this was done.

*Development of Allied support, 1944*

In the meantime, while SOE was trying to grapple with tasks which went far beyond their charter and the capabilities of an essentially clandestine organisation, JANL demands were soaring at an alarming rate and in April 1944, at a conference between Major-General Velebit, as he now was, and the Supreme Allied Commander Mediterranean Theatre, 300,000 was made the limit beyond which the Allies could not go on supplying JANL. It was also made clear that the number of aircraft allotted for air supply to the Jugoslavs could not be increased above the present level. At this time air effort employed for Special Operations in the Mediterranean consisted of some five British squadrons, equipped with Halifaxes and Dakotas, a Polish flight of Halifaxes and Liberators and two Italian squadrons of somewhat doubtful efficiency, and most of these aircraft were already being used over Jugoslavia.

One of the first commitments to confront the Allies after the Alexandria Conference was the evacuation of refugees from the threatened Dalmatian islands. As previously explained, these refugees were seriously prejudicing the defence of Vis, and it was considered essential that as many as possible should be removed, and before the German threat to the islands receded a total of 25,000 had been evacuated by sea to Italy and thence to Egypt.

Whilst the defence of Vis and the evacuation of refugees occupied the forefront of the Dalmatian stage, preparations were being pushed forward for sea supplies. Two methods were planned; clandestine infiltration through the enemy-held coastal strip, and the securing of a bridgehead on the mainland. The arrangements for the first method were that the Allies should ship stores and equipment to Vis and from there they would be taken on by the Partisans. For this second phase there was a shortage of craft and a lack of suitable communications, and the flow of supplies remained disappointingly low, only a few tons per month reaching Jugoslavia. The bridgehead operation, known as 'KNOCKHOLT', was an ambitious scheme whereby JANL was to force its way down to the coast and for a limited period hold an area in which transport and supplies of all types would be landed. Planning and preparation had reached an advanced stage when it was finally decided in April 1944 that the operation was impracticable.

On the air supply side a spell of good weather in January enabled 84 sorties to be flown to Jugoslavia. This compared favourably with the previous best monthly total of 54 sorties and was of some importance as this record was reached at the time of the accusations by Tito and 'Free Jugoslavia' that the Allies were deliberately not supporting JANL. These sorties also allowed the completion of the task of flying 20,000 boots to the poorly-shod Partisans. Thus, despite the difficulties, improvisation and lack of long-term preparation, support to JANL did very materially increase during the first half of 1944. Indeed, apart from a decrease in February to 30 sorties, on account of bad weather, there was a steady increase to a total of 970 sorties in June. In terms of monthly tonnage, this represented an increase from 124 at the beginning of the year to 964 by May, while June provided the highest total for the whole campaign, 1,674 tons with, in the same month, 2,237 personnel evacuated.

Air supply on this scale had two principal effects. It permitted the development of new areas, the most important of which was Serbia, and it gave the Allies the power to influence JANL operations either by helping to save them in desperate circumstances or by giving them the supplies necessary to mount offensives which were co-ordinated with Allied strategical plans, an example of which was the 'BEARSKIN' operation in the mountains of Slovenia.

During this period the arrival of Dakotas made landing operations possible. The first of these, the ferrying out of the Jugoslav mission to Alexandria, has already been mentioned but possibly the most spectacular was the pick-up of GHQ JANL after the German airborne attack at Drvar. In all, eighteen landings on an improvised air strip were accomplished over three successive nights and those evacuated included Tito, his staff, the British and Russian Missions and 118 wounded Partisans. Two of the sorties were flown by Russian-manned Dakotas under British command. In one of these Tito was flown out, an event for which the Russians extracted the maximum possible propaganda value.

A further contribution to the Allied support for JANL was made by the training given to Tito's guerilla forces. This training ranged from instruction for the embryonic Jugoslav Air Force to courses in sabotage, and included tank, armoured car and artillery training in widely-scattered places from Vis to Egypt.

As the volume of Allied support in all forms increased, so Tito's objection to the attachment of BLOs to his formations lessened, and thus during the period between January and June 1944 six new missions were created, reinforcements and replacements (including doctors) were sent to others, and an Air Commodore was sent as Air Adviser to MacLean. At Vis a large mission was formed to handle sea supplies, training and liaison between the Partisans and the British garrison.

*Reorganisation of Command and Control, May 1944*

Although by the middle of 1944 Allied support to the Jugoslav Partisans had reached a very considerable scale, the organisation behind it remained loose, unco-ordinated and extremely complicated. For example, Naval operations came under two separate Naval commands, supply operations were the responsibility of a number of different RAF headquarters, while the methods of obtaining direct tactical air support were primitive and seem to have depended almost entirely on personal influence at the lower staff levels. The situation was made even more complex by the anomalous position of SOE (or Force 266 as they were known at this time) who were theoretically responsible for co-ordination and liaison in Jugoslavia, but had neither the military experience, authority or organisation to control the vast scale of operations which had by now developed. Nevertheless SOE—or Force 266—were responsible for controlling all British forces committed to operations along the Dalmatian coast.

The difficulties inherent in such a chaotic organisational structure were increased by two other features. The first was the fact that MacLean was virtually serving three masters: as senior BLO to JANL he nominally came under SOE or Force 266; he was also the personal representative of the Supreme allied Commander, Middle East; and finally he had access—as a kind of Ambassador Extraordinary—to the Prime Minister and the Foreign Office. The second feature was the shortage of staff to deal with the ever-increasing amount of work and, as a result, little planning, co-ordination or staff work was possible. Thus the administrative side seems to have been in a state of chronic disorganisation, a situation which naturally multiplied the misunderstandings between base and field. It was therefore hardly surprising that, by the end of May 1944, it had become imperative to reorganise the whole structure of command and administration which had been evolved to assist the Jugoslav campaign. In the first place, it was decided to apply to trans-Adriatic operations the principle of three co-equal commanders, each responsible to his own Service C-in-C for day-to-day operations, but with one of them responsible for the planning and co-ordination of future operations. Since it was realised that the Air Forces would necessarily play the predominant part, it was agreed that the co-ordinator should be the Air Force commander. Thus in due course all the various formations and establishments concerned with Jugoslav operations came under their respective Service organisations, the Commander of the Balkan Air Force (BAF) being appointed as the co-ordinator. Responsibility for providing the base supply organisation, including the holding, packing and despatch of both sea and air supplies, remained in the hands of the HQ Special Operations Middle East (SOM).

MacLean, his mission to Tito now renamed 37 Military Mission, severed his connections with SOE and came under operational command of Commander BAF, although he remained the Supreme Allied Commander's representative to JANL. This organisation continued, with only minor changes, until the end of Jugoslavia's guerilla campaign.

*Developments, latter half of 1944*

From the middle of 1944 JANL steadily developed from a guerilla force into a field army. There remain but two main aspects of the subsequent campaign which are relevant to this study. First, the supply problems that arose during the initial phase of the German withdrawal and the Allied supply effort during this period; and secondly, the development of Tito's policy for post-war Jugoslavia and the effect that this had on relations between JANL and the Allied missions in the field.

It will be remembered that a limit of 300,000 men had been given as the planning figure and that the scales of equipment were based on requirements for guerilla operations only. However, with JANL already showing signs of developing into a field force, and the withdrawal of German forces about to take place at any moment, it became evident by the middle of 1944 that requirements in the near future would far exceed the present estimates unless Allied responsibility was to remain restricted to the supplying of Partisans in enemy-occupied territory only. That this was in fact the intention was confirmed by AFHQ in June.

In September the German withdrawal started. As expected JANL demands increased alarmingly both in volume and variety, without distinction between military requirements and civilian needs, requests varying from tanks and industrial plant to incense for the parish priest. SOM was still in principle not responsible for supplying Jugoslavs in unoccupied territory, but no other organisation had taken on this commitment. This was possibly owing to the fact that at the Moscow Conference, which coincided with these developments, Russia had undertaken the task of sending supplies to JANL. In practice, however, this could not be implemented for geographical reasons, and the supplying of Jugoslav needs in occupied territory and in those unoccupied areas not in direct contact with the Russians continued to fall on the Allies.

Particularly urgent was the need of relief supplies for the Dalmatian inhabitants. These were to a certain extent provided from an 8,000 ton dump that had been built up in Italy late in 1943 when it was hoped that a sea supply-route was about to be opened up with JANL across the Adriatic. Other requirements were met in various ways, by occasional allotments from AFHQ surplus stocks and—where 37 Military Mission could make a sufficiently strong case of operational urgency—from AFHQ operational stores originally destined for the Allied armies in the field.

It naturally took some little time to see the improvements resulting from the reorganisations that took place during June, but by September there were definite signs that air supply was being placed on a sound footing. Attempts were made to give the field firmer planning figures, while liaison had improved between the field and the RAF units concerned and MacLean's Rear HQ at Bari. But possibly the most important liaison development was the arrival of Jugoslav officers to assist in the despatch of supplies to JANL from Italy. They were appointed at the request of Tito and proved an invaluable asset, both in advising Q of JANL reqirements from their practical knowledge of Jugoslav conditions, and also in representing the British case to their own headquarters.

We turn now to the Allied supply effort during the second half of 1944. Air supply in August had passed its peak. From a June total of 1,674 tons of supplies flown to Jugoslavia there was a steady decrease in monthly tonnages to October when only 472 tons were sent. This reduction was chiefly owing to the main air supply effort being switched to Greece in support of other Allied land operations taking place in that country.

This reduction in supplies to Jugoslavia caused considerable difficulties for, owing to expenditure during 'RATWEEK' and its follow-up, there was by October a shortage of supplies with JANL for operations against the withdrawing German Army. In addition the Jugoslavs interpreted this cut as a political move. For these reasons mass dropping over Jugoslavia was started at the end of October and as a result 1,324 tons of stores reached JANL during November, although the following month the total dropped again to 609 tons. Similarly during this period the number of personnel evacuated by air steadily decreased from 4,880 in July to some 160 in December. This reduction was accounted for by the JANL decision not to evacuate wounded from areas which were unlikely to remain long in enemy hands.

Thus although during the latter half of 1944 major operations did take place, such as the flying of 'RATWEEK' stores, the evacuation of 500 wounded from Slovenia and the evacuation of almost 1,000 in a mass pick-up from Montenegro, the general tempo was reduced, while control itself was now considerably simplified through greater standardisation and less fluid conditions in the field.

The weather was one of the worst enemies to air support during the winter of 1944, and indeed throughout the Jugoslav campaign. Owing to the configuration of the country the worst weather over the whole area (as already explained in Section A) occurred over the Karstlands of Dalmatia. As a result, on many occasions when the skies were clear inland, sorties failed to get through because of the storms and clouds above the high ground immediately inland from the Adriatic coast. Some indication of the conditions can be appreciated from the results of two attempted mass drops in January 1945, when a total of 113 out of 126 aircraft failed to reach their targets. It was not until late in the campaign that it was possible to set up an efficient meteorological service, and this in the end did help matters considerably.

Sea supply during this period was comparatively simple, as with the German withdrawal from Dalmatia it became a normal sea transportation process which had no peculiarity merely because it was a supply route to guerilla forces. Allied responsibility ended at the port of discharge after which all supplies were handled by JANL. The tonnage carried by sea was about three times the volume of air supply, and from 1,299 tons in August rose to 6,105 in December.

*The Closing Phase: Allied–JANL relations*

The last point of interest from the aspect of guerilla warfare is the turn that relations took during the closing stages of the campaign between JANL and the Allied missions in the field, for it is then that Tito's actions in preparation for the post-war era began to dominate the scene.

The events in Serbia during 1944 epitomise what was taking place throughout Tito's Jugoslavia during this period. To Tito the future attitude of Serbia was of extreme importance on account of its strategical, political and economic position within Jugoslavia; but Serbia had been until recently the stronghold of Mihailovic and the Cetniks. For these reasons Tito started, in mid-1944, to take steps to ensure control of Serbia and if possible to rally the inhabitants to his cause.

Up to July 1944 relations between JANL in Serbia and the Allied missions were excellent. JANL staff provided all possible information and intelligence, and as a result the planning for the delivery of supplies was greatly helped. Allied support had in fact been extensive to the Serbian JANL during the first half of 1944, and it was largely owing to Allied supplies that, by the summer, the Partisans in that area had expanded from three poorly-equipped groups into an efficient guerilla force of some five divisions. By then not only was liaison between missions and JANL commanders and staffs outstandingly good but the Jugoslavs were showing considerable gratitude for the efforts made by the Allies to help them. In July, however, drastic changes in command and staff of the Serbian JANL occurred. As already explained, a new GHQ under Lieutenant General Popovic arrived by air from Italy. It included a number of high-ranking JANL officers, a Russian mission and finally a political commissar. With this new HQ came an efficient signals unit which provided Tito's GHQ with the rigid control over Serbian JANL activities which had up to now been lacking. Four of the five divsional commanders were also replaced.

Relations with the missions changed abruptly. Although still friendly they were placed on a rigidly formal footing and from then onwards only very limited information and intelligence could be obtained from JANL. The resultant lack of knowledge about JANL intentions and impending actions precluded any further possibility of forward planning of supplies and in turn made supply dropping and the delivery of particular equipment more difficult and less effective than with the previous regime. The political change was equally marked. Political education of the troops began; the achievements of the Communist Party in the war were built up, and a policy of belittling Allied assistance was developed with increasing energy. By the end of the year not only was the Allied contribution being entirely ignored but a campaign was in full blast to give the impression to the Jugoslavs that it was Russian and not British and American aid that had helped to change Partisan fortunes.

# Chapter 3

# GREECE: SECOND WORLD WAR

(*See Map 7 opposite*)

*Introduction*

At many points the history of guerilla resistance in Greece during the Second World War resembles that in Jugoslavia over the same period. In both countries the rapid Axis occupation and the subsequent exploitation of the peoples were followed by the successful growth of guerilla resistance in the mountains. In both cases this resistance crystallised into two ideologically opposed factions: Communist and non-Communist. The main difference between the two countries lies in the fact that in Jugoslavia the non-Communist element, as represented by the Cetniks, soon succumbed to the Partisans, whereas in Greece the Communist controlled EAM/ELAS failed to liquidate all its rivals, despite a number of efforts to do so.

In Jugoslavia the Western Allies had thus little choice but to support the Communist Army of National Liberation; in Greece the alternatives were numerous and complicated, for the non-Communist guerillas had strong Republican leanings, while HMG championed the exiled King of the Hellenes and his Government. To confuse the issue further, in the earlier phase of the war responsibility for deciding the policy of support to the Greek guerillas was divided between London and Cairo, with a natural tendency on the part of the authorities in the Middle East to think more of the immediate military dividend than of the post-war effects.

With these opposed and shifting currents constantly influencing Allied support to the Greeks, and the guerillas more embroiled in internecine strife than in fighting the enemy, a large part of the Greek guerilla story consists of politics and their repercussion on all those concerned, both inside and outside Greece. It is therefore appropriate to give a short summary of the political events leading up to the emergence of a resistance movement in Axis-occupied Greece.

*Events prior to Axis occupation*

Greece became a republic in 1924. A period of comparative stability followed, but from 1932 onwards the Republican cause was steadily weakened by a series of ineffectual governments and in 1935 King George II regained his throne. His task, already difficult, was made more so by the result of the first general election in which the two main parties, the Liberals and Populists, were so evenly matched that the Communists despite their minute representation held the balance of power. The Communist policy was consistently destructive. Essential revisions could not be carried out and a rapid deterioration in Greek politics followed.

General Metaxas, who had by this time become Prime Minister, prorogued Parliament in an attempt to stabilise the situation, but disorders and strikes, many of them Communist-inspired, continued to increase. On the fourth of August 1936, the day before the trades unions had ordered a general strike, Metaxas, with the King's consent, proclaimed martial law, suspended certain articles of the Constitution and dissolved Parliament. The only way that these actions could have been made valid was by the holding of fresh elections, but these did not take place and Metaxas became dictator, a position he held until his death at the beginning of 1941. During the years that he was in power his strong and sometimes ruthless methods caused growing antagonism which the Communists, whom he had forced underground, did their best to exploit.

With the death of Metaxas and in the absence of any adequate successor, the King took over control himself. There was, however, no chance to set matters right, for within a month Germany invaded Greece and by June 1941 the whole country was in Axis hands. The King and his Government escaped to the Middle East leaving the Greek constitutional problem unsolved and themselves branded with the failings of the Metaxas dictatorship. They left in Greece a strong Republican movement which was to gain ground steadily under Axis occupation.

*The Axis occupation.*

From the Axis viewpoint Greece was of little value as a source of supply. Her industrial output was limited and her food production had never been sufficient to satisfy her own internal needs. It was, however, as a vital link in the chain of communication with North Africa that Germany needed control of Greece, and so long as she obtained free passage for her troops and material through the country she cared little for the fate of Greece as a whole.

Thus, in the Axis partition of the country, Bulgaria was given Thrace and Macedonia, which she proceeded to Bulgarise with her usual ruthlessness, Italy took over control of the greater part of Central and Western Greece, where she did little more than garrison certain main centres of importance, and the German command limited the areas under their direct control to those which were essential to the maintenance of their lines of communication from Central Europe to the Mediterranean. These routes entered Greece in the North by the Struma and Vardar valleys, ran to Salonika and then southwards to Athens and the port of Piraeus.

In Athens, the usual puppet government was soon established. It failed to enlist any capable Greeks, however, and since the Germans showed little interest in the government of the country this attempt at administration was a dismal failure, even judged by quisling standards. The lot of the Greeks

*Table 1*

## Main Greek Resistance Movements

| COMMUNIST | | REPUBLICAN |
|---|---|---|
| Popular Front (EAM) | National Democratic Greek Union (EDES) | National and Social Liberation (EKKA) |
| \| | \| | \| |
| (ELAS) | (Colonel ZERVAS) | (Colonel PSAROS) |

uring the Second World War

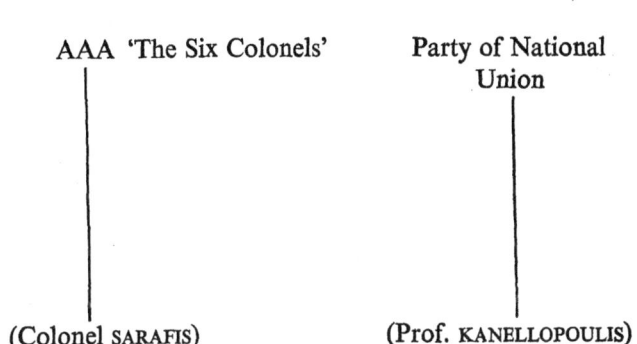

ROYALIST

AAA 'The Six Colonels'   Party of National Union

(Colonel SARAFIS)   (Prof. KANELLOPOULIS)

in Athens and the other more populated areas steadily deteriorated and famine stalked the land. It was owing to this ever-increasing threat of starvation that general resistance to the occupying forces developed during the winter of 1941-42.

*Resistance Movements, 1941-42 (for outline see Table 1 opposite)*

One of the first resistance groups was that of Kanellopoulos, a professor of Political Economy at Athens University. He was the founder and leader of the small 'Party of National Union' which had opposed the Metaxas system of government, but which now stood for national unity behind the King, at any rate until the completion of the war. His followers were mainly drawn from the students of his own university.

A second and strongly anti-Monarchist party began to emerge in the late autumn of 1941. It became known as the Popular Front, or EAM, and was linked to the Greek Communist Party. That winter saw EAM ousting the Kanellopoulos Movement. EAM's rapid growth in power and popularity was due to their more virile organisation of resistance and in particular to their handling of the general strike in Athens, which forced the Germans to improve conditions for the starving Athenians. On account of their efficiency and experience in clandestine work, the Communist element in EAM played an ever-increasing part in its control and actions. The Communists were also amongst the first to spread their authority and doctrines into the mountains, where their slogans and promises were avidly swallowed by the gullible peasants. Here the guerilla organisation that subsequently grew, as part of EAM and under the latter's control, became known as ELAS.

At the same time that ELAS was being born in the mountains, two separate groups of Republican officers in Athens were planning to form guerilla organisations. The first and stronger of these two movements became identified with the name of Colonel Zervas, who at a later date moved into the mountains with the title of deputy leader of EDES, or the National Democratic Greek Union. The second, which came into being some time later, was known as EKKA and during its precarious existence as a guerilla formation its commander was one, Colonel Psaros.

A number of other would-be guerilla leaders, many of whom were Army officers, planned in Athens the build-up of guerilla forces in which they were to hold senior appointments. Among these was a certain Royalist clique to whom at a later date the exiled King and the authorities in Cairo turned in an attempt to form a guerilla movement with Monarchist sympathies. They became known as the 'Six Colonels' and are referred to later. Many of these strategists were entirely unsuited to be guerillas, far less leaders. A number had in fact no intention of moving into the mountains: some did so but made little mark.

So much for the sources from which the Greek guerilla leaders eventually came. Let us now consider the country in which they were to operate.

As will be seen from the map opposite page 65 the greater part of the country is covered by mountains. In these, high crags and rugged valleys mix with pine forests and rolling downs. Roads are poor and few, while much of the country can only be crossed by goat tracks which are often impassable in winter on account of snow.

The people of these mountains matched their surroundings. Indescribably poor, they lived a hard and simple life under conditions of primitiveness reminiscent of the wilds of Scotland in the seventeenth century. Many were illiterate and had little conception of the world outside their mountain valleys. Banditry was endemic and it was consequently only a short step during the Axis occupation for a bandit to become a guerilla. Such material provided excellent guerilla 'rank and file', but could never produce the leaders required to unite the independent bands into a cohesive guerilla force. It was thus of necessity left to the more educated, worldly-wise and politically minded Athenians to initiate, control and co-ordinate the Greek guerilla forces.

Between these leaders from the towns and the rank and file from the mountains there remained throughout the campaign a vast and unbridgeable gap. This cannot be better described than by including part of a report written by Colonel Woodhouse, whose name will often appear later in this Chapter.

It is as follows: 'The distinction between these two components left a permanent mark. Despite all the efforts to bridge the gulf, there remained a more or less clear distinction between those who knew where they were going and those who did not. It was a social and mental gulf far wider than exists between, say, the most experienced general and the most uneducated private in the British Army. It was a difference of degree so vast that it almost amounted to a difference in kind. No British officer could persuade his men to believe the cant and lies which guerilla leaders put into the heads of their followers nor could he hold their devotion, as was so often the case in ELAS, with the mesmeric fixity of sheer terror. The Greek leader was more unscrupulous and crafty: the Greek peasants were more uneducated and superstitious.'

These leaders had by the spring of 1942 already made an impression in the mountains. EAM's representatives were making strides in their recruiting for ELAS, while Zervas was successfully staking a claim for EDES in Western Roumeli and South Epirus; EKKA was still embryonic. All were openly Republican in their sympathies. At this time the guerilla movement was still largely unco-ordinated and spontaneous, and actions against the occupying Italian troops were few and of a minor character.

*Events outside Greece, 1941–42*

Events in occupied Greece were running far ahead of current thought and policy outside that country. This seems to have been due to two main causes, first, the lack of reliable and up-to-date information available to HMG on the situation within Greece, and secondly, the failure of the Greek King and Government to face the fact that Greece was now preponderantly Republican in its sympathies.

Britain had already pledged her support to the Greek King before the German invasion and thus was in duty bound to uphold the King and his Government, quite apart from the long-term advantages of maintaining the monarchy in Greece.

The exiled Greek Government for its part was not representative of the Greek people. At the time of its escape it was predominantly Metaxist and showed its sympathies on arrival in Cairo in no uncertain way by proscribing six prominent republicans, at least one of whom was actively assisting in the organisation of resistance in enemy-occupied territory. Later on, however, the Metaxist influence was removed and attempts made to broaden the exiled Government by the inclusion of more liberal-minded Greeks. But the King and Government still remained strongly opposed to supporting the Republican-dominated guerillas in occupied Greece. HMG at this time appears to have been non-committal, although still sympathetic to the aims of the King and his Ministers, now in London.

In Cairo, however, there were a number of factors which caused those responsible for the prosecution of the war in the Middle East to take a more definite view. Those mainly concerned were GHQ Middle East and SOE. GHQ's chief concern was to hit the enemy as hard as possible wherever he might be found by all available means. In those early days, when all the sinews of war were in short supply, underground resistance in occupied territories seemed to be an excellent and economical method of attaining this aim. SOE Middle East for their part were for all practical purposes at this time under the control of GHQ Middle East, on whom they depended for nearly all their resources except money. Furthermore, they were authorised to undermine the Axis war effort in Greece by stimulating resistance.

Because of these circumstances and the fact that only left-wing organisations were in the Greek resistance field, SOE steadily developed their contacts with the republican resistance movements, supplying them with arms and equipment as these became available. During this period SOE constantly stressed the strength of republicanism in Greece, and even attempted to get the Foreign Office to give the Greek resistance leaders an unofficial assurance that HMG would not impose the Greek King on Greece without some prior expression of popular opinion.

In their attempts to bolster up resistance SOE's insistence was understandable, but so equally was the growing tendency caused by these and other actions to mark SOE as the centre of influence hostile to the Greek King and his regime. This was felt particularly by the Greek King and Government. There was also a feeling in the Foreign Office that SOE were exceeding their charter and were encroaching into the political field.

The arrival of Professor Kanellopoulis from Greece did little to calm the situation, for he confirmed SOE's reports of the conditions in occupied

Greece and proceeded to advocate a policy which was more in accord with republican demands than anything that the King would countenance. It was also unfortunate that, while the King and the Government were in London, Kanellopoulis remained in Cairo as their representative.

The series of Allied reverses suffered in the Middle East, the general strain of war, and the distance between Cairo and London, combined with certain ill-conceived actions and statements by the interested parties all helped to exacerbate the controversy. The main points to note in this unhappy state of affairs would seem to be firstly, the fact that SOE were placed in the thankless position of having two masters (the Foreign Office and GHQ Middle East) whose aims were not identical; and secondly, that the directive given to SOE was too broad to afford them the necessary guidance so essential under such circumstances. These troubles stemmed from the absence of a complete marriage between British foreign policy and British military policy, but it is difficult to see how under the conditions prevailing at the time such a state of affairs could have been achieved.

*GHQ Middle East Plans for Guerilla Action, summer 1942*

It certainly was not achieved in the Middle East where the pressure of military events in the late summer of 1942 called for an all-out effort against Axis communications. The tide by then had started to flow in favour of the Allies, and preparations were in full swing for the counter-offensive against Rommel, who had been halted at El Alamein, while 'TORCH', the Allied invasion of North Africa, was imminent. To support these major operations all the enemy's communications leading to the Middle East, and within reach of Allied forces, were to be attacked. Included in these targets was the main railway route running from Salonika southwards to Athens and the port of Piraeus.

The best targets along this line lay in the mountains, in guerilla territory. As yet SOE had no direct contact with the latter but were in wireless communication with an Athens Resistance organisation, who in turn were in touch with the guerillas, although only by courier. Because of this slow and complicated chain the planning for the attack was in the first instance left to Athens, and they suggested that one of the three steel viaducts in the mountain sector near Lamia, some 100 miles north of Athens, should be demolished. They proposed that a British team with the necessary explosives should carry out the actual demolition, but that the attacking force and covering troops should be found by the guerillas. For various reasons, including the possibility that ELAS might refuse to co-operate, the British team were to be put in touch with two separate guerilla organisations: an ELAS unit in East Roumeli which was best placed for the task, and Zervas in West Roumeli who was the more reliable.

This outline plan was agreed by Cairo who left the final selection of the bridge to be blown to the officer in command of the British team. To be of any use in the overall strategic plan the railway had to be cut by the end of November 1942 at the latest.

The British party selected was twelve strong, including wireless operators. Colonel Myers was in command with Woodhouse as his deputy. Myers was a regular Sapper officer of 36, without knowledge of Greece or of subversive politics, picked at short notice because an engineer was needed. Woodhouse was a young classical scholar of academic distinction aged 25, who had already worked in occupied Crete and had a good knowledge of modern Greece and of the Greek political background. Myers could not speak Greek but Woodhouse could. It was intended that Myers and those who had been included to carry out the actual demolition would be withdrawn by submarine once the bridge had been destroyed, leaving Woodhouse with another officer and wireless operator as a liaison link with Zervas.

*First Allied Contact with Guerillas, autumn 1942*

On the night of the 28th September 1942 Myers and his party set off for Greece in three Liberators but on the following morning all were back at base, having failed to see any signal fires in their dropping areas. In the case of the ELAS group this was due to the Athens agent, who was to arrange the reception party, having been captured by the Italians the day before. There was no sign of Zervas' fires because the area to which the plane went was many miles from where Zervas' reception committee was waiting. The signal giving the location of the DZ had been corrupted in transmission. Cairo, however, had no means of finding this out and a second attempt was made on the night of the 30th. Again no recognition signals were seen in the expected areas, and Myers with his team and stores dropped blind on to the slopes of Mount Giona in East Roumeli, and Woodhouse's party parachuted on to a triangle of fires which proved to be a reception party from a sabotage organisation in Athens, who were expecting a supply of explosives. The third plane again returned to base.

The wireless sets dropped with these parties failed to work and it was a week before Myers and Woodhouse rejoined each other. Having done so, Woodhouse set off across the mountains to establish contact with Zervas, whom he eventually came upon some sixty miles to the north-west. Zervas was at the time engaged in sporadic actions against the Italians but agreed to help in the attack on the bridge. Leaving a proportion of his men to continue harassing the Italians, he and a force some hundred strong set off with Woodhouse to join Myers near Mount Giona.

Meanwhile all Myers' attempts to contact ELAS failed. He reconnoitred three possible bridges, decided that the one spanning the Gorgopotomas was the best to attack, and with his party set about making up the necessary charges. Italian activity, meagre rations and continued bad weather made this period of comparative inactivity an extremely trying one.

The third section of the party eventually parachuted into Greece at the end of October. They lost all their equipment on landing and were themselves very nearly captured, but almost at once fell in with an ELAS guerilla band. Some two weeks later they met Woodhouse who was returning with Zervas's force to Mount Giona, and after some hesitation the ELAS guerillas agreed to take part in the attack.

Thus, three days later, Woodhouse rejoined Myers with a mixed EDES–ELAS force of some 160 men. Of the two, the EDES detachment appears to have been the better led and slightly better equipped, although both groups were armed with a motley collection of small arms; they were ill-fed and poorly-clad, and about a quarter of the ELAS men were without boots.

There were now less than two weeks in which to complete their demolition task, for as will be remembered GHQ Middle East had given the end of November as the latest possible date. Zervas' men, however, needed rest after their long forced march, while the ELAS men were still undecided whether or not to take part. This hesitancy was mainly due to the ELAS system of command, which was organised on the 'Committee of Three' principle, in which the leader of the band had with him a Political and a Military adviser, both of whom had to give their sanction. The Political adviser in this case feared reprisals and casualties and referred the matter back through EAM channels to Higher Command.

*Attack on the Gorgopotamus Bridge, November 1942*

Because of these delays it was not until the 24th November that the final plan was agreed and the force reached an assembly area in the mountains some three hours from the Gorgopotamus bridge. For the actual operation the guerilla force was divided into five parties: the first was to cover the only road down which reinforcements could be sent from Lamia in the north: parties two and three, who were accompanied by officers from the British team, were to cover the railway approaches from north and south and at the same time demolish lengths of track: the remaining two parties were to attack and destroy the Italian garrison at either end of the bridge. When this had been done the demolition team, consisting of British officers and a small Greek covering party, was to move down the ravine and wreck the bridge. The charges for this had been prepared individually and the actions of the demolition team worked out in detail and rehearsed. A headquarters was to be sited some quarter of a mile up the ravine to co-ordinate the operation and signal the withdrawal.

There was snow on the ground, and it was drizzling and bitterly cold when the various parties left the assembly area on the evening of 26th November 1942. All the preliminary moves went according to plan but, although the Italian garrison was taken by surprise, there was still fighting on the bridge at 1 a.m., an hour after the assault had started. It was decided that though the bridge was still not clear the demolition party would have to start work, and they were sent in. But on reaching the main steel pier, which was to be demolished, it was found that its construction was different from what had been imagined and that the carefully prepared charges were useless. These now had to be taken to pieces and remade on the spot. Nevertheless, by shortly after 2 a.m. the demolition was completed, and the pier collapsed, bringing down with it the two 100 ft. girder spans on either side. A second but smaller steel pier was then attacked despite the arrival of enemy reinforcements by rail from the north.

The result of this action was the complete stoppage of rail traffic across the Gorgopotamus for thirty-nine days. Most of the Italian garrison of some 80 men were killed, while there were no British casualties and those of the guerillas were under double figures. During the attack the combined EDES-ELAS force appears to have fought well in the ragged fashion of guerillas, but it was the first and last time that Zervas' forces and ELAS combined in any worthwhile action against the enemy.

There seems no doubt that ELAS's participation in the Gorgopotamus operation was forced upon them by their need for British support and supplies: neither could EAM, at this early stage in their development, afford to let Zervas gain all the credit for an act that was likely to have such far-reaching effects.

With the completion of the operation the ELAS guerillas departed, apparently on good terms with the British mission. The leader was given £250 in gold and a letter to the EAM Central Committee proposing future discussions on the co-ordination of guerila resistance and the question of Allied aid. ELAS asked for a BLO to be attached to them, but this was impossible as Woodhouse had already been earmarked as Zervas' BLO, while Myers and the remainder of his team were due to return to the Middle East, their task completed. Zervas moved back into West Roumeli and, on the 12th December the two British parties separated: Myers' to keep its rendezvous with the submarine on the coast of Epirus, and Woodhouse to take up his appointment with Zervas. Outwardly relations between the guerillas appeared reasonable and, at the time, the British party can hardly have had an inkling of the complexities that lay below the surface.

*Repercussions outside Greece*

The spectacular success of the Gorgopotamus action seems to have dazzled Cairo into concluding that a potent guerilla striking force existed in the Greek mountains. Instead of waiting to get a more comprehensive picture from Myers, which would have seemed the wisest course, SOE decided without further delay to establish BLOs wherever there were indications of guerilla activity.

Myers, with the rank of Brigadier, was to remain in Greece to command this BLO network, while Woodhouse, as a Lieutenant-Colonel, was to move to Athens to become the liaison link with the 'Six Colonels' who both the Greek Government and SOE hoped at this time could co-ordinate the Greek guerillas on a nation-wide basis. Mention of these 'Six Colonels' and their origin was made earlier but as yet their shortcomings were not appreciated in Cairo. Important factors in the decision to use them were that they were all regular army officers who had fought well in Albania under the Metaxas regime, and were monarchists. It shows the great gulf that existed between thought outside Greece and events within since it is difficult to imagine how individuals with such a record would be acceptable to the leaders of the various existing guerilla organisations.

*Events in Greece, winter 1942–43*

The first step in the implementation of this new SOE plan was the dropping of a BLO at Woodhouse's HQ with details of the change in policy. This was on the 17th December, five days after Myers had left for the coast. A runner was sent to recall him but it was weeks before Myers and his party returned. In the meantime the situation developed rapidly. Woodhouse, whose position was complicated by the fact that contact with Cairo was, at the best, intermittent and did not exist with Myers, had a series of visits from different ELAS detachment commanders. These visits were in all cases with the object of obtaining Allied supplies. Under the circumstances it was impossible to satisfy these demands, and unfortunately the only sortie promised failed to materialise owing to bad weather. As a result ELAS were quick to suspect the British intentions.

The climax came at the end of December when a band of several hundred ELAS guerillas appeared. Their leader, who had also led the ELAS force on the Gorgopotamus operation, was under the impression that the whole British party had remained in Greece and was now living at Zervas' HQ, while the latter was being liberally supplied with gold and airborne stores. (In fact the total received by Zervas since the arrival of the British party was a part share of two plane loads.) A conference staged by Woodhouse averted an immediate armed conflict, but failed to produce any agreement between Zervas and ELAS on the co-ordination of their actions against the enemy. On the 1st January the ELAS force left, having been given £250 more in gold: beyond this Woodhouse would not go without authority, which he was unable to obtain.

A week later Myers and his party returned after twenty-seven days of journeying under very difficult conditions and on very meagre rations. With the sudden cancellation of their return to the Middle East—despite the brilliant completion of the sole task for which they had been sent into Greece—it was not surprising that their morale as well as their physical condition was low.

The British party reunited on 8th January and, with Zervas constantly on the move, an independent HQ was established at Botsi, near the borders of Epirus and West Roumeli, and here Myers remained to work out the details of the new plan. Woodhouse went to Athens to carry out his allotted task of getting in touch with the 'Six Colonels'. These showed little enthusiasm for their task and less intention to take to the mountains. Nevertheless good came from his journey, for while in Athens he made contact with leading members of EAM and thus obtained some insight into their intentions. By early February, Woodhouse was back at Botsi, where a somewhat disgruntled mission was chafing in inactivity, an unfortunate state of affairs that continued for most of the mission staff until March 1943.

*Attempts to implement Middle East Plan*

During this period attempts were made to implement the Cairo plan. In effect this visualised something in the nature of a guerilla army on the lines of that developing at this time in Jugoslavia. This was entirely opposed to the conception of Myers and Woodhouse, who considered that the practical answer was to limit the guerilla movement to a few small independent bands who by their very smallness would be able to operate on a hit-and-run basis when and where required in support of Allied strategy. Neither, as a result of Woodhouse's abortive attempt to co-ordinate the activities of Zervas and ELAS, were they optimistic about future attempts to amalgamate these two organisations and far less to place them under the control of immovable Royalist colonels in Athens.

EAM/ELAS were beginning to be seen in their true light by Myers and Woodhouse, and by April 1943 records state that they were convinced EAM was Communist-controlled. A very different picture, however, was reaching Cairo from the BLO who by now was with ELAS HQ. This officer knew little Greek and both his two Greek-speaking officers had been killed in their parachute drop. He was cleverly handled by the local Political Commissar and for some months continued to report on ELAS and EAM as a national uprising which must be given British support so that the democratic parties in the movement might be strengthened, the better to resist the Communist element. With this flow of contradictory statements coming in over the only two wireless links that Cairo had with the guerillas, the need for personal contacts between Cairo and the field would appear to have become greater than ever.

The plan that eventually emerged from these opposed views was a compromise which aimed at the organisation of the Greek guerillas into a limited number of independent areas, each commanded by a senior Greek officer whose previous reputation would give him the necessary standing for the task. These commanders would work directly under GHQ Middle East, and would receive their instructions through BLOs, who would be attached to them and provided with the necessary communications. Myers would be in operational control of these BLOs and their teams. This 'National Bands' ('NATBANDS') project, as it became known, was agreed to by Zervas and also by two other resistance groups which had lately taken to the field: EKKA, under the command of a Colonel Psaros, and a guerilla band led by a Colonel Sarafis. EAM, however, would have none of it. All their interests lay in Cairo's first concept of a guerilla organisation with a centralised control in Greece. If this came to pass they, with their greater strength and more efficient organisation, would obtain a commanding control over their rival organisations.

## Expansion of Greek Guerillas, Spring 1943

By the spring of 1943 EAM were in a strong position *vis-à-vis* their rivals. By efficient organisation they had formed ELAS bands throughout the mountains. They had built up an administrative machine which dealt with such pressing problems as the distribution of food and the maintenance of law and order. Although dictatorial and primitive in its methods it was a form of local government and this was something that had never been seen before in these regions. By such means as this and by various forms of verbal propaganda EAM built themselves up as a national movement, which the simple villagers took at its face value. They flocked into the ranks of ELAS. It was of little interest to the EAM high command that these recruits could not be armed and in many cases were useless as guerillas, for the movement was primarily attempting to construct a state, not a mobile striking force to support the Allies.

Zervas, on the other hand, had neither the capacity, propaganda machine nor recruiting organisation to compete with ELAS expansion. Nor did it suit Allied policy for him to do so, firstly because his area of control included no military targets of importance at this time, and secondly because Allied supplies were limited and it was considered unsound to recruit more than could be armed and equipped. Zervas, having agreed to 'NATBANDS', obeyed the instructions of GHQ Middle East. No such policy governed the other would-be guerila leaders, many of whom had come into the mountains from Athens and elsewhere only when the war had turned in favour of the Allies. A number of new bands were now forming all over Greece.

The Italians, who had been given the unenviable task of controlling the mountain areas, did little to stem the growth of these guerilla bands. They continued to hold the main communication centres only, while occasionally sending punitive columns into the mountains when German pressure or guerilla activities forced them to do so. The guerillas had little difficulty in avoiding capture, but a number of villages were burnt and the inhabitants killed in reprisal or removed as hostages. Away from the main Axis lines of communication and the plains there was, however, almost complete freedom of movement for the guerilla bands.

## The British Military Mission, Spring 1943

By the late spring of 1943 there were ten British Liaison teams distributed in Macedonia, Thessaly, Epirus, Roumeli and the Peloponnese. Three of these were attached to EAM/ELAS. But in the early stages the only two wireless links that were effective were those working to Cairo from Myers' headquarters and from the BLO at ELAS HQ. Within Greece itself contact between the BLOs and mission HQs was extremely difficult, and only possible by personal contact. Myers' own wireless station was static and this meant that he could not go on tour without losing touch with his base. Because of these difficulties of inter-communication between Myers and his BLOs, it was almost impossible for Cairo to obtain a balanced picture of the situation in the mountains. Furthermore, the BLOs and Myers were at a great disadvantage in their dealings with the highly centralised control of EAM/ELAS. During the critical situation that was soon to develop, the latter were able to make full use of the British Mission's inability either to keep its officers posted about the rapidly-changing situation or to coordinate their actions with the agreed British policy.

The situation in the mountains of Greece in the spring of 1943 was therefore briefly as follows: EAM/ELAS had overwhelming strength over rival organisations in some three-quarters of the area; Zervas' followers were mainly concentrated in South Epirus and West Roumeli; of the independent bands that had sprung up two now came into the picture, those of Sarafis and Psaros. There was little Axis interference, there was little the BLOs could do and news of the situation reaching Cairo was most sketchy.

In the world outside, General Paulus and his army surrendered at Stalingrad, the siege of Leningrad had been raised, and the Axis forces in North Africa were being steadily driven back. These defeats and the growth of Allied strength (as indicated to the guerillas by the influx of BLOs and supplies) gave the false impression, particularly to EAM/ELAS, that the end of the war was in sight.

*EAM/ELAS attempts to gain control, Spring 1943*

Mistrusting British intentions and determined to obtain complete control of the Greek resistance movement before the reoccupation of the country by the Allies, EAM decided that the time had come when their rivals must be eliminated. On 3rd March ELAS surprised and captured Sarafis and a number of his officers, accusing them of collaboration with the enemy. They then burst into the southern part of Zervas' territory, effectively loosening his control there and threatening attack on Zervas' main force if he did not hand over the residue of Sarafis' band who had fled to Zervas for protection. Zervas' reply was the liquidation of some ELAS bands that had developed in South Epirus and a deployment of his own forces to meet the threatened attack by ELAS.

It was not until three days after the capture of Sarafis that the news reached Myers at his HQ in West Roumeli. It found the British mission in a poor state to deal with the crisis. Myers himself was still convalescing from pneumonia which had been aggravated by a series of forced moves as the result of Italian attempts to capture his HQ. EAM/ELAS higher command had not yet been identified, much less contacted; while, by ELAS' clever handling of the BLO at their HQ, Cairo was still receiving pro-ELAS reports. They were therefore unwilling to act on Myers' demand for a stoppage of all supplies to ELAS.

The British mission did what it could to deal with the situation. A demand for the release of Sarafis and his followers was sent to the EAM Central Committee in Athens. An attempt was made to re-form the remnants of Sarafis' force, but this proved a failure. Myers himself set off with the object of meeting the leader of the approaching ELAS force and preventing open warfare between ELAS and Zervas. Fortunately, the ELAS force commander, possibly appreciating Zervas' strength and determination to fight, moved off northward. Myers' efforts to save Sarafis and his officers were in the end successful, but Sarafis himself disavowed 'NATBANDS' and went over to EAM, to become the so-called C-in-C of ELAS.

While these events were taking place in Roumeli, ELAS were making successful efforts to absorb their rivals, where necessary by force, throughout the mountain regions from Macedonia to Pelepponese. In these moves to gain control, ELAS acted with great brutality on a number of occasions and, though they strengthened their position militarily, they were now seen in their true colours by many for the first time.

Myers now set out on tour with the twofold object of attempting to reconcile EAM/ELAS to the 'NATBANDS' project and of co-ordinating the efforts of the BLOs. The latter object was achieved to a considerable extent but little good came of his various meetings with ELAS leaders, except for a number of promises which were later broken. He left his HQ on the 14th March and did not return until the first week in June. Thus for the greater part of three months he was out of touch with Cairo and his own HQ during a period of crisis with the Greek exiled Government, and a series of crises with EAM/ELAS.

By June the remainder of Sarafis' forces had been dissolved, Zervas' adherents had been cut down to those in South Epirus and the neighbouring mountains in West Roumeli, and Psaros had been attacked and captured. The latter was released at Woodhouse's instigation and promises made by ELAS to allow him to continue the formation of EKKA undisturbed.

*Attempts to co-ordinate Guerilla Resistance, Summer 1943*

From the point of view of the Allied war effort it had now become quite clear that no plan for the employment of Greek guerillas could succeed unless it took full account of EAM/ELAS: either a bargain must be struck with them in return for their operating against the Axis, or their defeat must be the first British object. The latter course was out on all counts: it remained therefore to make a deal.

Some such arrangement became the more urgent as the next phase in the Allied Mediterranean campaign approached: this was the invasion of Sicily. The Greek guerilla operation in support of this was known as 'ANIMALS'. In this, Middle East planned for a simultaneous attack by the Greek guerillas on a large number of communications, first as part of a deception plan designed to give the impression that the Allied landings were to take place in Greece instead of Sicily, and secondly to prevent the withdrawal of enemy troops from Greece for use elsewhere. It was timed to begin in June 1943.

Improved communications, Myers' tour and another by the head of SOE's Greek Section in Cairo all helped to consolidate the British Military Mission and improve their knowledge of the general situation. The mission had expanded considerably and this resulted in increased supplies by air where most required, and also in detailed reconnaissances being made of the many targets which were to form part of 'ANIMALS'.

EAM/ELAS for their part, having failed to obtain absolute control by force and having alienated large parts of the country by their atrocities, now changed to a more conciliatory policy in an attempt to restore their popularity and following.

In the slightly less tense atmosphere that followed this change in EAM policy, Myers managed to bring together all parties in an attempt to find some compromise 'NATBANDS' agreement. This meeting took place at Laskovo on the borders of East and West Roumeli. In order to strengthen his position in the bargaining that he knew would take place, Myers had asked Cairo to stop supplies to ELAS, but this had been refused on military grounds. At the meeting ELAS, led by their political commissar, held firm to a drastically amended 'NATBANDS' project which had been drawn up by the EAM committee in Athens. This proposed the setting-up of a joint GHQ in occupied Greece to co-ordinate and control guerilla resistance throughout the country, with representation from the various guerilla organisations in such proportion that ELAS would have the controlling influence. After two days of debate the conference broke up on 7th June, having failed to come to any agreement.

With 'ANIMALS' due to start on 21st June ELAS's agreement to cooperate was now a matter of extreme urgency and Cairo instructed Myers to accept their terms as a last resort. Armed with this authority and accompanied by his newly-acquired mobile wireless station Myers set out to secure ELAS co-operation and at the same time to check plans finally with his BLOs. On 14th June agreement with ELAS was eventually reached. It was the EAM version almost in its entirety and, as events proved, the lip-service paid to the Allied High Command by ELAS in agreeing that the joint HQ would be under the direction of C-in-C Middle East, through Myers, meant little or nothing. It was ELAS GHQ who decided whether or not the instructions to GHQ Middle East should be followed.

A week later 'ANIMALS' opened with the destruction of the Asopos viaduct. This was probably the most brilliant action of its kind ever undertaken in the last war, but no Greek guerillas took part . . . ELAS had declared it as beyond their capacity and the feat was accomplished by an all-British party of six. This bridge was out of action for nearly three months. Elsewhere the guerilas, guided by BLOs, were more effective. In the initial plan the responsibility was broadly divided between ELAS in Eastern and Central Greece, and Zervas in the west, for it was considered that none of the other organisations were sufficiently strong or well equipped to be allotted a geographical area. Of the 30,000 Greeks available it was intended to employ only 1,000, together with the 50 British available, against specific targets. Nevertheless, other bands seem to have operated independently and of their own accord.

'ANIMALS' achieved its objects. Within three weeks there were forty-four major cuts in the few existing road and rail communications, as well as many minor actions. Some idea of the success can be obtained from the report of an Italian transport officer. This stated that at the beginning of July it took his division 11 days to travel from Athens to Yannina, a journey which normally could be done by a convoy with ease in three days. In its main object, as a deception operation for the Sicily invasion, 'ANIMALS' was equally successful on German and Greek alike. The conclusion reached by the Greeks themselves, that the reoccupation of the country was imminent, also had its repercussions, as will be shown later in this chapter.

*Events, Autumn 1943*

The completion of 'ANIMALS' was followed by a conference of all available BLOs, with the object of briefing them on the changed circumstances as a result of the modified 'NATBANDS' agreement. At the same time the first meeting of the Joint HQ took place. Both meetings were at Petrouli, in the mountains overlooking the Thessalian plain from the west. EAM were represented by the High Command of ELAS, as usual in its tripartite form, with a military commander, a political commissar, and a military adviser. At this first meeting both Zervas and Psaros attended, although subsequently they were represented by junior officers.

It was a time for optimism, for not only did there seem a good chance that the rival guerilla organisations might at long last co-operate, but the position of the guerilla movement as a whole had markedly changed *vis-à-vis* the occupying forces. Some two-thirds of the country was now controlled by the guerillas, and this included not only the mountains but certain areas in the plains, including the town of Kardhitsa; a wireless training school had been set up; an airfield was under construction and safe areas were being provided for other branches of GHQ Middle East such as ISLD (who collected intelligence) and Force A (who collected escaped prisoners). With the guerilla successes there also came from enemy-held areas a steady flow of refugees and others wishing to join the resistance.

This extension of guerilla territory brought with it many added responsibilities for the Joint GHQ, in the administration both of the local inhabitants and of the thousands of refugees from enemy-occupied Greece. Thus, of necessity, the Joint GHQ became more a government than a military HQ. Because of the resources on which they could call, the Allied missions played an important part, but Zervas and Psaros, or their representatives, had little or no say. It was in fact EAM's government of Greece. Where it was to their advantage EAM's administration was comparatively comprehensive and efficient, for it included communications, law courts, schools, supply organisations, workshops and large numbers of newspapers. In the areas occupied by EAM's rivals, however, much of the administration, including provision for the refugees, fell on the Allied Military Mission, for as Woodhouse very aptly writes, 'the other guerilla groups tried to do the same (as EAM) but suffered the usual disadvantages of the small retailer competing with the chain store.' Nevertheless this was, on the surface anyway, a period of goodwill during which EAM/ELAS recovered much of the popularity that they had lost by their ruthless conduct of some months before. This change in policy seems to have stemmed largely from the final British acceptance of EAM's version of 'NATBANDS', virtually in its entirety. To EAM this implied that they had been accepted as the controlling organisation in Greece, and this impression was strengthened by the arrival late in July of Major Wallace, as the Foreign Office's representative to the Joint GHQ.

A further political development took place the following month when, as the result of an invitation first made during Woodhouse's visit to Athens at the beginning of the year, a guerilla delegation was flown out to GHQ Middle East. Their departure was made possible by the completion of an airstrip in the mountains of West Thessaly. This had taken some 700 men, working in shifts under the guidance of a BLO, a month to clear and level. Not the least of the problems was the payment of these workmen, all of whom had to be enticed away from their own fields at a time when their harvests were ripe. Their 'wages' were dropped to the BLO in the form of golden sovereigns which had then to be changed in the black market in the larger towns, before the peasants could be paid in local paper money. A second major problem was the camouflaging of the airstrip as it was developed. This was done by temporarily planting many hundreds of small trees on the runway and by using large numbers of fir branches to break up the surface of the newly-flattened earth. So successful were these methods that the RAF, having taken an aerial photograph of the strip without warning, reported that the area was quite unsuitable. It was from this landing-strip that the delegation was flown out in a Dakota on the night of the 9th August 1943. It was a party of importance in the guerilla world, consisting of four senior EAM representatives, and the seconds-in-command of Zervas and Psaros: with them went Myers and Wallace.

*Affairs outside Greece, September 1942–September 1943*

To appreciate the situation in Cairo at the time of the delegates' arrival it is necessary to follow briefly the course which events had taken in London and the Middle East since Myers and his party dropped into Greece in September 1942. At that time Professor Kanellopoulos was the Greek Government's representative in Cairo, a post he continued to hold with ever-growing difficulty until March 1943, when he resigned after a serious mutiny had taken place in the Greek fighting forces in the Middle East. The King then moved from London to Cairo, where his Prime Minister formed a new and more republican Government. There followed a period of continued difference of opinion within the Greek Government, and between it and the King as to the conditions under which the monarchy should return to Greece.

One faction considered that the plebiscite on the fate of the monarchy must be held before the King again set foot on Greek soil. The King himself, and others, felt strongly that he should return with the liberating forces and that only when conditions had stabilised should the people be asked to decide for or against the monarchy. In an attempt to find an acceptable solution the King, in a broadcast during July 1943, promised that a plebiscite would be held within six months of his return and that he would abide by its decision as to the future of the monarchy. This met with universal opposition: there was another mutiny in the Greek forces. EAM immediately repudiated the King's offer and a mass of other evidence from occupied Greece showed that opinion there was strongly against the King's return until after a plebiscite had been held.

It was just when discussions over this difficult subject were at their height, that Myers and his party of resistance politicians appeared almost unheralded. GHQ at Cairo found itself faced, therefore, not only with an exiled Greek government already rent in two over the question of the monarchy, but also with a party who regarded themselves as the only people qualified to voice authoritatively the political opinions of the overwhelming majority in occupied Greece.

Matters were made worse from the start by the EAM Communists attempting to gain control of the discussions. The Greek Government, while still divided over the King's return, were united against the Communists, once they had realised their presence. The delegates from the resistance movements, although divided on Communism, were united in their views on the King's return. It was not surprising therefore that from the first hurriedly-called meeting there was deadlock. Eventually, with HMG's agreement, it was decided that the delegates must return forthwith to Greece, if the existing government were to remain in office, but at the last moment their departure was postponed and they remained in Cairo until mid-September. No good came of this respite and they reached Greece disappointed, angry and with the fixed idea that the British Government intended to reimpose the monarchy.

This unfortunate affair had repercussions in other than purely Greek spheres. The King and exiled Greeks tended to blame the Foreign Office and particularly SOE for the fiasco, while so far as these two departments were concerned it came as the culmination of a long and increasingly bitter crossfire of argument and criticism between them over the organisation, support and employment of the Greek guerillas. As mentioned earlier this was largely owing to the opposed policies of backing the King on the one hand and employing Republican guerillas on the other, in turn due to the Allied need for military results. Drastic reorganisation within SOE followed and in the Middle East a Special Operations sub-committee was set up to control and co-ordinate resistance in occupied areas. So far as Greece was concerned the main say was now vested in HM Ambassador to the Greek King, and in the C-in-C Middle East's representative. All matters of policy were removed from SOE's responsibility.

While the delegation was still in Cairo the war was developing rapidly elsewhere. The Italian armistice was signed on 3rd September 1943; on the 9th the Allies landed at Salerno; on the 16th British forces moved into Cos and Leros and seemed likely to clear the Aegean.

## Events in Greece, Winter 1943

In Greece isolated Italian garrisons were in some cases swiftly disarmed by the Germans, in others by EAM; but in Thessaly BLOs were first on the spot and General Infante came over to the British with his Pinerolo Division and its equipment almost intact. The Germans had little difficulty in re-occupying the plains but they met with resistance as soon as they tried to penetrate into the mountains. In these actions the Pinerolo Division operated against their former allies with considerable success: a success resented for their own good reasons by EAM, who took steps to break up the division into small units and so weaken their fighting strength and weight of support for the British Military Mission. Continued attempts by Woodhouse to reverse this policy seemed at first to have borne fruit when by agreement of ELAS, the division was again concentrated on the morning of 14th October, but that same evening they were surrounded and disarmed; many of the officers being arrested on the grounds that they were planning a 'Fascist plot' in concert with Zervas.

The Cairo delegation had returned to Greece on 17th September but without either the Foreign Office representative, Wallace, or Myers. As a result Woodhouse had to face, single-handed and with no adequate brief nor clear idea of the course of the Cairo meetings, the most difficult situation that had yet developed. He now had a junior American officer on his staff: his HQ thus became an Allied, as opposed to a merely British, Mission.

The return of the delegation brought a change in relations. There followed constant argument on minor matters and increasing signs that the days of co-operation which had begun in June with 'ANIMALS' were past. One such proof came when C-in-C Middle East called for guerilla attacks on a number of airfields in Greece, in an attempt to lessen the air bombardment of the now hard-pressed British troops in Cos and Leros. These orders were grudgingly accepted by ELAS at Joint GHQ but were never implemented by them. In only one place, at Larisa, was any attack carried out and that was by a party led by British and consisting mainly of Italians. As events were to show, EAM/ELAS were no longer interested in supporting the Allied war effort. A combination of the results of the Cairo visit, the apparent determination of HMG to impose the monarchy, and probably strongest of all, the course the war was taking, had decided EAM that the time for another bid for complete control in the mountains had come.

## First Civil War, Winter 1943–44

With this in view ELAS opened an offensive in the second week of October 1943 against Zervas and his adherents. Those bands that were outside Zervas' main area in South Epirus were eliminated by ELAS without much difficulty, but in South Epirus Zervas cleared all ELAS units out of existence and continued to hold his own, although his area of control was greatly diminished. By the middle of October it was estimated that ELAS' strength was 25,000 as compared with Zervas' 5,000, but in the actions on the latter's border ELAS' superiority was less than two to one. After the initial impetus of the ELAS assault had spent itself there was a comparative stalemate, as few had any enthusiasm for the civil war. Fighting was desultory and half-hearted.

But before any settlement could be reached the Germans struck. They had already moved formations northwards, thus confirming in EAM's mind that a German evacuation of Greece was imminent. With these troops they now drove into the mountains, burning and massacring as they went. They caught the guerillas completely unprepared, there was little armed resistance, and Joint GHQ at Petrouli disintegrated and its scattered components were driven further into the mountains. In the areas which they occupied the Germans now began to develop Greek quisling organisations on similar lines to those of Nedic and the extremist Cetniks in Jugoslavia. The 'Security Battalions' which they formed were armed and recruited ostensibly to protect the villages against the excesses of EAM. By clever propaganda, including the idea that the British themselves favoured the formation of these battalions as a counter to Communism, the Germans had considerable success with their recruitment.

They were also helped by the fact that EAM in their attempts to alienate opinion against the British (and thence the King and Zervas) also spread rumours that the British were contemplating an alliance with the Germans against EAM and the Russians. Unfortunately, some substance was given to these accusations by the actions of an over-zealous BLO who made contact with the German command in order to discuss what turned out to be a purely imaginary surrender offer. EAM also provided evidence that Zervas was in touch with the Germans through EDES Committees in Athens.

Zervas for his part accused EAM of aiding the enemy not only by playing the German propaganda tune and by their actions forcing many into the Security Battalions, but also because ELAS had attacked Zervas while he was operating against the Germans.

The Germans thus effectively exacerbated the enmity of the Greeks towards each other, and by this means helped to transform the war against themselves into an internal one between Greeks.

Zervas continued to receive arms from the Allies but was none the less getting the worst of the civil war, and was rapidly becoming an unimportant military factor. Arms to ELAS were temporarily stopped and EAM and its known leaders were discredited in the House of Commons and bombarded with stern warnings from Cairo. Even so they continued to gain strength militarily. They appear, in fact, to have looted more arms from the Italians than were ever supplied through British channels.

## AMM and ALO Position, Winter 1943–44

The winter 1943–44 was therefore a testing time for the Allied Military Mission (AMM) and its Liaison Officers. Those with ELAS were almost all on bad terms with their local commands; all were continuously on the run either from the civil war or from German columns, while the complete lack of policy and the absence of any activity against the enemy had bred bitterness and discontent. Where the ALOs functioned at all it was not as a military liaison link but as a relief organisation for the masses of homeless and destitute people now wandering in the mountains. Some 100,000 of these were civilian refugees who were kept from starvation at a cost to the British of £37,000 in gold a month. This was paid to EAM for their food; an unavoidable but far from satisfactory arrangement as a large proportion of this sum was taken by EAM for other than its approved use. Escaped prisoners of war of all allied nationalities and the greater part of the Italian Pinerolo Division also had to be administered by the AMM. It caused a heavy strain on the mission, particularly as EAM/ELAS did nothing to assist and much to obstruct. There was also a steady stream of American airmen who had been shot down. These appear to have received preferential treatment from EAM/ELAS together with a great deal of inaccurate information in an attempt to cause friction between the British and Americans. Very gloomy reports continued to be received by the AMM of Zervas' position and by December 1943 Woodhouse, despairing of him as an ally, recommended that on military grounds he should be abandoned and sole reliance placed on EAM. It was at this time that AMM seemed to have plumbed the lowest depths of disillusionment and despair for the future.

Woodhouse's recommendation was fortunately disregarded, for early in 1944 the situation showed signs of improvement. With the help of Allied supplies and equipment, Zervas held out and even gained some ground. On the other hand, EAM's 'mountain state' was disintegrating as the result of continued and purposeful German operations, and EAM, presumably appreciating for a second time the failure of their attempted coup, resumed the meetings between ELAS HQ and AMM and began negotiations to end the civil war. This also coincided with the lessening of the German offensive, but just as there seemed a chance that ELAS might be prevailed upon to come to an agreement, Zervas launched a vigorous and successful counter-attack and the war flared up again.

As much to provide an object for the guerillas and ALOs to work towards as for any other reason, Cairo now proposed a plan for harassing the German withdrawal, whenever this might take place. To give this scheme some urgency 'NOAH'S ARK', as it was named, was to be ready by April 1944, though it was appreciated by Cairo that the operations were in fact unlikely to be required until considerably later. For 'NOAH'S ARK' Greece was to be divided into areas, Zervas and Psaros each being allotted one: British and American units would be infiltrated later to reinforce the guerillas.

## Preparation for 'NOAH'S ARK', early 1944

With the aim of stopping the civil war 'NOAH'S ARK' was at this early stage intentionally vague, but it implied that the Allies would again be prepared to recognise EAM/ELAS, if they ceased civil strife and set about preparations for 'NOAH'S ARK'. EAM accepted it in this outline form and issued orders to ELAS subordinate commanders for its implementation. At the end of January all available BLOs were assembled in S.W. Thessaly to receive details of 'NOAH'S ARK'. Meanwhile ELAS, on a trumped-up excuse concerning Zervas' boundaries, attacked the latter and drove his forces westwards. Having thus strengthened their bargaining power EAM opened discussions.

EAM's proposals were for the formation of a united guerilla army, for a joint political committee in the mountains and for a public denunciation of all collaborators. This denunciation was framed and intended to embarrass Zervas. After three weeks of debate the so-called 'Plaka Agreement' was signed on 29th February. This put an end to the civil war for the time being and provided a bare basis for mutual toleration and military action. From EAM's point of view the Plaka Agreement was a failure in that it gave them no political status, and in an attempt to gain this they created in March the 'Political Committee of National Liberation' (PEEA). This was ostensibly an administrative organisation but if the opportunity appeared it could well become a government. In order to create the myth that EAM was a national movement PEEA included a number of well-known Republicans and was strongly non-Communist in its composition. Zervas and Psaros, however, remained openly mistrustful.

## Liquidation of EKKA, April 1944

That their distrust was well-founded became clear in April, when an ELAS force made a surprise attack on Psaros. Psaros himself was murdered, his followers killed or forcibly converted, and EKKA as a guerilla organisation vanished. Having swept EKKA from East Roumeli there seemed every possibility of another ELAS offensive against Zervas in South Epirus.

The immediate reaction of Cairo to this was to order the withdrawal of the AMM. The difficulties of doing so, and the disadvantage of not even being able to keep a watch on EAM/ELAS soon became manifest, and with the change in Greek political thought that took place at this time in the Middle East the order was eventually countermanded. Woodhouse and his ALOs thus continued their thankless task of attempting to stop civil strife, prepare for 'NOAH'S ARK' and provide for the destitute and homeless. In an attempt amongst other matters to delineate Zervas' area Woodhouse brought together all those concerned at Koutsaina, south of Petrouli early in May; but apart from an unsuccessful attempt to discredit Woodhouse with the Allied High Command, nothing came of this conference.

## GREECE

*Preparation for German withdrawal, Autumn 1944*

Nevertheless EAM on the whole followed a policy of outward respectability, as the result of which relations between them and the AMM steadily improved, while the responsibility and action of preparing for 'NOAH'S ARK' seems to have had a marked and salutary effect on the morale of AMM and the ALOs. A point of interest was the arrival of a Russian Military Mission to EAM (unknown to the Western Allies until after its arrival) and a number of records mention the fact that the start of EAM's more conciliatory policy coincided with the advent of the Russians.

Preparations for 'NOAH'S ARK' continued, but it was not until August, with the collapse of Roumania, that there were obvious German preparations for withdrawal from Greece. In early September the Allied C-in-C in Italy called a conference to co-ordinate plans for harassing this retreat. Sarafis for ELAS and Zervas for EDES attended. 'NOAH'S ARK' was to be co-ordinated with attacks by the Allied Air Force, and as a second phase a British force would land in Southern Greece to maintain order in the Athens area while the Greek Government was taking over control of the country. The division of responsibilities between ELAS and EDES was agreed, and it was also accepted by both Sarafis and Zervas that no guerillas should move into the Athens area. Here the Greek Military Command was to be in the hands of one of the 'Six Colonels', mentioned earlier in this Chapter.

*'NOAH'S ARK', Autumn 1944*

After some preliminary skirmishes 'NOAH'S ARK' began officially on 10th September 1944, ten days before the British landings in the South. It continued until 1st November, when the last German detachments from the mainland crossed the Greek frontier. It was a series of individual actions which were on the whole a success although the guerillas held back a large proportion of men and arms for their own purposes: ELAS more so than Zervas. The main actions were fought on the only two escape-routes along the eastern and western coastal strips. There were a number of successful attacks on loaded trains, as well as continuous sabotage of the line itself and ambushes of convoys moving through the mountain sectors. Woodhouse estimated German losses by ground action alone as 100 locomotives, 500 motor vehicles and 5,000 killed. To these must be added the damage done by Allied air attack on the traffic jammed on roads by guerilla operations. The guerillas also provided safe areas for the advanced landing grounds used during these air strikes. Finally there was the lost time, weakened morale and equipment destroyed or abandoned because it could not be moved in time.

With the end of 'NOAH'S ARK' comes the end of this narrative of the Greek guerillas, for the fighting that broke out in Athens and the civil war that raged through Greece at a later date lie outside this story.

## Resistance in the Islands

With the possible exception of Crete, there were no islands in the Aegean suitable for guerilla operations, while Crete itself had neither the necessary expanse for providing safe areas in the event of determined counter-action by the Germans, nor important enough targets to warrant the reprisals that would certainly follow guerilla attacks.

Small and scattered guerilla bands did come into being in Crete early in the war, but these were employed, with the help of British officers, in smuggling from the island the large numbers of British still there after the withdrawal of the Allied forces. British policy in Crete, as in the other islands, was to build up the elements of resistance against the time when landings for the reoccupation of Greece took place, meanwhile avoiding any action that might bring heavy reprisals with little or no gain to the Allied cause.

Therefore when General Kreipe, Commander of the German 22nd division, was successfully kidnapped and removed from the island by a British *coup-de-main* party the utmost care was taken not to implicate the Cretans. The uselessness of following any policy of open resistance to the enemy in unsuitable areas was shown in the summer of 1944, when, possibly due to the apparent imminence of Allied landings, the Cretan guerillas began independent actions against the occupying forces. They killed at the most some 150 Germans and destroyed a dozen or so motor vehicles: in reply the Germans burnt 30 villages, and executed 1,000 innocent Cretans.

## Conclusion

In conclusion it is important to mention the close relationship between the overt guerillas in the mountains and the various clandestine organisations of the more populated areas. As already described, many of the guerilla leaders came from these underground groups, while it was through the latter that Middle East established contact and maintained communication with the guerillas during the early part of the campaign. Furthermore, the sabotage operations of the clandestine cells in Athens, the Port of Piraeus and elsewhere played a vital part in the campaign against Axis communications.

Because of this close connection between overt and underground resistance it is extremely difficult to isolate the results achieved by guerilla operations from those obtained by sabotage and other clandestine methods. As a result much of the official statistical data available is of little use in assessing the value to the Allies of Greek guerilla resistance alone. There seems no doubt, however, that the guerillas did contribute to the Allied war effort by their periodic dislocation of communications throughout occupied Greece. They also contained comparatively large enemy forces in the country, at a time when these forces were badly needed elsewhere.

The guerillas' first important contribution was the aid that they gave to Myers and his party in the attack on the Gorgopotamus Bridge—the destruction of which cut enemy rail traffic between Central Europe and Piraeus at a critical period in the North African campaign. Subsequently, while the British offensive was developing in that theatre, it was at least partly the threat of the Greek guerillas that caused six German and twelve Italian divisions to be retained in Greece.

At the time of the Allied invasion of Sicily guerilla operations again played a part, not only in deceiving the Axis as to Allied intentions but also in compelling the enemy to reinforce Greece with two German divisions and extra air support.

During the 'NOAH'S ARK' operation, guerilla activities, coupled with Allied air support, caused the withdrawing German forces heavy casualties and considerable losses of equipment. Thus the Allied object of ensuring that enemy formations would have to be re-organised and re-equipped before being able to fight again on other fronts was fully realised.

Amongst economic targets attacked were the chrome mines, which by the middle of 1944 had almost stopped production, while as a by-product of their other activities the Greek guerillas provided the Allies with considerable intelligence. Lastly they provided safe areas on escape lines, for other organisations operating in the country and as reception organisations for the landing of British regular forces.

Much of this could have been accomplished by comparatively small numbers; 'ANIMALS', the cover operation for the Sicily landing, only required, for example, 1,000 of the 30,000 guerillas available.

Militarily, therefore, there was a strong case for limiting the Greek guerillas to a few mobile, well-equipped and highly-trained units which would operate in support of Allied strategy as required. There are in fact some grounds for arguing that the military results achieved by the Greek guerillas might have been accomplished by the employment of clandestine sabotage organisations and Allied *coup-de-main* parties only.

Initially it might have been possible to impose some brake on Greek guerilla expansion but in those early days the predominant military short-term policy was to arm any resistance group regardless of political creed, provided it was prepared to fight the Axis. Matters were further complicated by lack of accurate and up-to-date intelligence. This might have been remedied had personal contacts between those responsible for policy and those in the field been established, and in this respect the cancellation of Myers' return from Greece in 1942 seems an ideal opportunity missed. By the time the Greek situation became sufficiently clear to those concerned, both militarily and politically, no limitation of guerilla development was possible. For political reasons the EAM leaders had already embarked upon the rapid expansion of ELAS, and SOE could impose little or no control on them. Even had control been possible it is still very doubtful whether the expansion of the guerilla bands in the mountains could have been checked, for conditions under Axis control, the turn of the war and other factors caused many to take to the mountains. It was impossible to turn these people away and, despite their doubtful military value, they had to be supplied with the necessities of life either from guerilla or Allied sources.

Thus with the inevitable expansion of the Greek guerillas it might seem that for post-war political reasons it would have been sound policy to have given all-out support to Zervas and EDES, in order to provide a rival party to Communism. On the other hand it was ELAS that lay astride most of the main military targets of importance and, as the war had to be won before the peace, it is understandable that arms and equipment were supplied and dropped all the time to ELAS. An eventual stoppage of all supplies to the latter might well have caused an increase of internecine strife.

This problem of which movement the U.K. Government should support—the cause of so much wasted effort and expense in Jugoslavia—arose in one form or another in many countries during the Second World War. Consequently it is a theme that frequently recurs throughout the pages of this book.

## Chapter 4

# FURTHER EUROPEAN CAMPAIGNS: SECOND WORLD WAR

## (a) Albania

(*See Map 8 opposite*)

*Comparison with Jugoslav and Greek Resistance*

During the Second World War guerilla resistance in Albania followed much the same pattern as that in Jugoslavia and Greece, albeit on a smaller scale. In all these countries the people and the areas in which operations took place had similar characteristics: in all three the guerilla effort was adversely affected by political and post-war considerations. In Albania, however, national unity was split even deeper than in Jugoslavia and Greece, and in addition to the emergence of a Communist-controlled Popular Front and the antagonism which this bred, there were religious differences, tribal alliances and innumerable family feuds.

*Background*

As can be seen from Map 8, the interior of Albania consists of a tangled mass of mountains which are a prolongation of those of Greece to the south and Montenegro in the north, but unlike Jugoslavia, the Albanian mountains are mainly forested and the many narrow valleys are comparatively fertile. Along the coast is a flat and fertile belt which, on account of its strategic importance at the entrance to the Adriatic, has for centuries been occupied by the various Great Powers which have successively attempted to dominate the Mediterranean. These invasions have left their mark on the peoples of the coast but since there was no incentive for the attackers to penetrate into the almost trackless interior, the Albanian mountaineers have maintained their independence and autonomous way of life including their primitive outlook and customs. Ethnologically and geographically the River Schkumbi, which cuts through the country towards Lakes Ohrid and Prespa, forms a broad division between the two different races of the Ghegs in the north, and the Tosks in the south. Within these two races there are further sub-divisions into innumerable clans which are isolated from each other by the ranges which hem in their valleys. Amongst these mountaineers there are further differences on account of religion, for Catholics predominate in the north, Moslems in the east and centre, and Orthodox Albanians in the south. It is therefore not surprising that clan and family feelings governed their actions, rather than national or even regional considerations.

Most of the very few educated Albanians lived in the coastal belt where, in the south, contact with Greece had its effect on thought and culture. Owing to the lack of schools and universities in the country, however, an increasing number of middle-class Albanians were before the Second World War being educated in Italy, France and other Western countries. From these, a class of more educated and westernised Albanian was developing, a class which was hostile to the existing conditions of feudalism and lack of opportunities for advancement.

*Resistance Movements (for outline see Table 2 opposite)*

From this kaleidoscope of conflicting interests, beliefs and allegiances there eventually emerged three main resistance movements. The first of these, known as the Zogist or Legality Movement, supported the exiled King Zog and his return to the Albanian throne. This Royalist movement was eventually formed round Abas Kupi, an Albanian Army officer who had become something of a hero in Albanian eyes for his spirited attempt to defend Durazzo in the early days of the Italian occupation. He was a Gheg who had gone into exile with King Zog, but had later been infiltrated back into Albania—with British backing—in order to foment unrest against the Italians. Main support for the Legality Movement came from the north, for King Zog himself was a Gheg and during his regime had developed this area at the expense of the south.

A second resistance movement which emerged was known as Bal Kombetar. This right-wing party developed particularly in the coastal belt and foothills, where the larger landowners and others, who had suffered heavy taxation at the hands of King Zog and his Ministers, were opposed to the King's return but at the same time were equally against the spread of communism, as represented by the third movement, the National Liberation Front, or FNC.

FNC grew on similar soil to the Jugoslav partisans and EAM in Greece. Its backbone was the Albanian Communist Party and its junior leaders came from the discontented elements of the country, particularly those of the middle class who were clamouring for a progressive policy. FNC developed initially in the south. Its leader was Enver Hoxha, an Albanian professor who had been educated in France and Belgium.

These divisions only began to become clear in the latter part of 1943 and even then there always lay behind them feudal, tribal and religious rivalries.

Long before this, in the days of so-called peace in Albania, a proportion of the mountaineers had lived by brigandage, and the abortive Italian campaign against Greece had provided them with numerous opportunities for personal gain by the ambushing of small Italian transport columns moving over the difficult mountain roads. With the decline in Italian prestige these actions by independent bands had multiplied, but they remained uncoordinated affairs until the autumn of 1942, when the National Liberation Front proclaimed its programme. This was on exactly similar lines to those

*Table 2*

Main Albanian Resistance Movements during the Second World War

| COMMUNIST | REPUBLICAN | ROYALIST |
|---|---|---|
| National Liberation Front (FNC) | Bal Kombetar | Zogist or Legality Movement |
| (Enver HOXHA) | | (Abas KUPI) |
| *Developed initially in the south* | *Developed particularly in the coastal belt and foothills* | *Developed particularly in the north* |

set out a little earlier in Jugoslavia and Greece, with the promise of an improvement in conditions and all-out resistance to the Axis. FNC's progressive policy and clear-cut opposition to the occupying power won them many adherents and formed a rallying point both for those who were determined to fight the enemy and for those who craved a more advanced and democratic way of life. As in other countries, the Communist aspect of the movement was kept concealed in these early days of expansion and, like EAM, FNC were prepared to use well-known and acknowledged leaders, regardless of their political views. One such individual was Abas Kupi, who, as already mentioned, later became leader of the fundamentally opposed Legality Party. Even at this time he was well known for his pro-Zog leanings.

## British Action, 1941

The first British attempt to foment unrest by infiltration of Abas Kupi and a group of other Albanians was made through Jugoslavia early in 1941. Almost immediately after their arrival in Albania, Germany invaded Jugoslavia and as a result, not only did it become impossible to give Abas Kupi and his followers material support, but all contacts with him were cut. From then on, news from inside Albania was almost non-existent and it was not until some two years later, in April 1943, when a small SOE Mission arrived there, that any idea of the situation in the Albanian mountains reached the Allies. The mission was dropped into northern Greece and, with the help of EAM, eventually made contact with FNC in southern Albania. But the first task, that of finding out the strength and circumstances of Albanian guerilla resistance, was greatly handicapped by the lack of previous information and, initially, by the undisguised suspicion of the Albanians themselves. It was therefore some weeks before the mission was able to obtain a balanced picture of the situation.

## Growth of Guerilla Bands

Meanwhile the guerilla bands steadily increased, recruitment being encouraged by the news of constant Italian reverses in North Africa and, later, in Sicily. As numbers grew, FNC became more and more determined to control all resistance forces before the liberation of Albania by the Allies. Bal Kombetar had by now taken the field and there had already been armed clashes between them and FNC bands when the news of Mussolini's downfall became the signal for a country-wide revolt against the occupying forces. For the time being, this put a stop to internecine strife, and at first a considerable number of casualties were inflicted on the Italians and much of their equipment damaged. There were, however, some five and a half Italian divisions in the country and once they had weathered the first shock they steadily regained control. Very heavy reprisals followed; in one area alone, to the north-east of Valona, 70 villages were burned and some 25,000 people rendered homeless. Just when these operations seemed likely to quash organised resistance, Italy capitulated, and the Italian formations retired to their main garrison areas in the coastal belt.

*The Italian Surrender and German Occupation, 1943*

In the vacuum which followed much of the country was occupied by Resistance forces. In the southern mountains Communist-controlled FNC bands moved into most of the towns and villages. In the north, Abas Kupi —now parted from FNC—held a number of towns with a motley band of Ghegs, while much of the coastal strip declared for the Bal Kombetar. Italian control was reduced to Tirana, Scutari and the ports of Valona and Durazzo.

There were by now four groups of BLOs in Albania, distributed between FNC and Abas Kupi, and the Italian surrender caught them unprepared. Thus there was no transfer of complete Italian units to the guerillas as had occurred in Greece with General Infante's Pinerolo Division. In any case German reactions were swift and efficient, and within a few days their forces had occupied all Italian-held centres of importance and disarmed their late allies without opposition. Within less than three weeks the Albanian guerillas had been driven back into the mountains, although they were able to take with them a certain amount of captured equipment. Some 20,000 Italians also took to the mountains. Most of these were without arms and equipment and escaped in order to avoid internment in Germany. A few, who deserted with their arms and as organised units, operated with the guerillas but the great majority were employed on various menial duties with the guerillas or in the villages. There must have been little to choose between German internment and Albanian slavery.

Having regained control of the coastal belt and opened up their communications with Greece, Jugoslavia and Montenegro, the main task of the German Command was the establishment of an adequate coast defence against the threatened Allied invasion. These defences had been neglected by the Italians and for the first few months of occupation the German forces, which by the winter of 1943 numbered some 40,000, appear to have been too fully employed to undertake punitive expeditions into the mountains.

*German Propaganda, 1943*

German political warfare proved extremely effective from the start. Albania had always aspired to the rich Kosovo Plain which they asserted had a 70 per cent. Albanian population despite Jugoslav attempts to Serbianise it. In the south, the Albanians had for many years claimed parts of Epirus. Both these aspirations had necessarily been passed over by the Allies, and this became, in consequence, fruitful ground for German propaganda in support of Albanian nationalism at the expense of Jugoslavia and Greece. They released the political prisoners whom the Italians had held. They stressed Moscow's control over FNC and the latter's allegiance to

Tito and EAM, whose aim, they averred, was the dismemberment of Albania. They pronounced the inevitability of an Anglo-American war against Russian Communism, and the alliance of Germany with the Western powers in such a conflict. For left wing edification they preached the dangers of British Imperialism, reaching the illiterate masses by such means as leaflets showing Mr. Churchill either carving up Albania or putting Albania's double-headed eagle into a cooking-pot. The strength of this propaganda seems to have been in its clever distortion of facts as opposed to a mass of lies. In this the Germans had the advantage of all occupying powers in being able to keep their propaganda material closely related to current events within the country, while the Allies, with their lack of contacts and the unavoidable slowness of communications, lagged far behind in their counter efforts.

German propaganda was ably abetted when the Communists took as their first target those Albanian resisters who remained outside FNC, and proclaimed their affiliation with movements in Jugoslavia and Greece.

*Threat of Internal Strife*

Fanned by German propaganda, FNC's bid for power caused sporadic civil strife to break out at the end of 1943. The Bal Kombetar movement was too weak to resist FNC unaided; Abas Kupi was too engrossed in holding together his own following to co-operate with Bal Kombetar; with the result that Bal Kombetar and its followers were driven into the arms of the Germans. FNC for their part continued to expand northwards into Gheg country where Abas Kupi was now trying to recruit the local chieftains into his anti-Communist Legality Party.

Despite his prestige his efforts met with only partial success, for the local chiefs, divided by personal ambitions, intrigues and even blood feuds, were unmoved by patriotic and similar appeals. They wanted hard cash and evidence of forthcoming arms and supplies. Abas Kupi had neither the necessary gold nor weapons, for it was British policy to withhold both until he had proved his worth by active operations against the Germans. For his part, he persisted that without money and equipment it was impossible to begin attacks against the occupying forces.

On the other hand, FNC had shown their willingness to fight the Germans, and this was deemed sufficient proof of their good intentions for them to receive Allied arms, equipment and gold. This British preference for the Communists lessened even further the chances of the formation of any co-ordinated right wing guerilla organisation.

In this morass of divided interest, recriminations and animosities, the hapless BLOs floundered, trying in most cases vainly to bring the Albanians to grips with the Germans instead of with each other.

In an attempt to unite guerilla resistance against the enemy and to co-ordinate the efforts of the BLOs, SOE decided to send in a special mission under the command of a senior officer, Brigadier Davies, with a

Headquarters staff. The new mission was parachuted into Albania during the winter of 1943. Davies soon determined that the Allies had little choice but to throw in their lot with FNC, and supplies to the latter therefore continued. During the short time that Davies's mission was in existence, its relations seem to have varied according to the need for Allied arms, supplies and money.

FNC Headquarters was at this time in the village of Martanesh, in Central Albania and Davies set up his HQ some miles to the south. He had with him some ten British officers and men and these were soon augmented by interpreters, Italian cooks, servants, mulemen and others, while probably, owing to the severe winter weather, living accommodation, store huts and stables were built in a clearing in the forest. A steady accumulation of reserve stores appears to have added still further to the unwieldiness of this headquarters.

Inevitably the Germans located the mission, but FNC intelligence gave the British sufficient warning to escape, although a large quantity of stores had to be left. Even so the mission moved out with some sixty mules and horses. Then followed a period when both the mission and FNC HQ were hunted from place to place. The remnants of FNC HQ eventually broke out to the south, but the British mission, depleted and suffering from exposure and lack of food, was finally cornered. In an attempt to shoot their way out Davies and another BLO were wounded and captured. The remainder, under the second-in-command, Colonel Nicholls, escaped. Unfortunately, after enduring further extreme privations under appalling conditions, Nicholls died. (For his outstanding endurance and fortitude he was posthumously awarded the George Cross.) The remainder eventually joined Abas Kupi in the north.

*German Counter Measures, Winter 1943–44*

As a result of these operations, during which German columns had driven into the mountains of central Albania from every quarter, FNC forces in the area were effectively disorganised but, although this meant an end of active operation against the common enemy, it did at least avert the threat of civil war. Abas Kupi's faction still showed little inclination to fight the Germans, and this state of affairs was encouraged not only by the German policy of non-aggression towards the right wing resistance organisations but also by their skilful anti-communist propaganda. In the south, German columns from Pogradets, Berat and Valona succeeded in driving the Partisans deep into the mountains and for a time German communications between Albania and Greece were unhindered, but with the return of the German units to their bases, FNC bands began once more to ambush any MT columns that were not well protected and to harass small detachments along the enemy's line of communications.

The winter of 1943–44 was nevertheless a testing-time for all Albanian resistance. The combination of FNC aggression, German propaganda and lack of Allied support had had its adverse effect on the non-Communist elements, while the small quantity of supplies, arms and equipment which it was possible to drop to FNC during this period of bad weather, combined with the disintegration of the BMM, lessened British prestige and FNC's reliance on the Allies.

In an attempt to augment air supply a small bridgehead had been established in a deserted bay between Valona and Sarande. But only maintenance stores for the British personnel could be brought ashore here as it was in an area controlled by Bal Kombetar who somewhat naturally were unwilling to allow passage for FNC supplies when they themselves were refused such Allied aid. In defence of the British policy to supply FNC only, there seems little doubt that Bal Kombetar units operated against FNC in the Valona area if not in direct support of German formations, then with their tacit consent.

## FNC Expansion, Spring 1944

In January 1944 FNC's total fighting strength was no more than 5,000, but with the arrival of spring their position steadily improved. By April their numbers had increased to some 12,000 and their control had again spread northwards as far as the Elbasan valley. This improvement was due to better weather, to a lessening in German activity in the mountains, and to greater Allied supplies. One of the German divisions had been withdrawn from Albania and its place taken by mercenary troops (Armenians, Kosovo Albanians and Turkestanis commanded by German officers and NCOs). These were poor material and a large number deserted with their arms and equipment to the guerillas.

One consequence of this weakening of the German occupying forces was the opening of a second and larger bridgehead north of Sarande and this time in FNC territory. Here landing craft were used, and the limiting factor proved to be not the capacity of the craft but the ability of FNC to transport the stores inland. On the first two sorties 30 and 36 tons were landed.

With the increase in Allied supplies and the lessening of enemy efficiency, FNC's activity against German communications correspondingly increased in volume and effectiveness. The coast road between Valona and Sarande was held for comparatively long periods by FNC forces. A series of demolitions on the main route from Greece, through Gjinokaster, forced traffic on to the devious and more difficult road to the north-east. German convoys moving through southern Albania now had to be protected by strong escorts of AFVs and supporting troops, and as the weather improved Allied fighter strikes from airfields in Italy were able to add to the dislocation caused by FNC.

In May, FNC's strength was estimated at something over 20,000 under arms and their sphere of control had extended northwards to the mountains east of Tirana, where the so-called FNC Second and Third Brigades, each some 500 strong, were deployed. But FNC's main strength remained in the south where, in addition to ambushing convoys and raiding small detachments, they were now operating against some of the larger garrisons: that of Pogradets, for example, was contained by Partisan forces until the arrival of German reinforcements.

*German Counter Offensive, Summer 1944*

By June 1944 the position was sufficiently serious for the Germans to reinforce the two divisions already in Albania with a first class operational formation, the 1st Mountain Division. With these three divisions they launched a series of attacks against FNC in southern Albania. Operations lasted a month and the Germans succeeded in closing the Allied bridgehead north of Sarande, reopening communications with Greece and scattering the Partisans into the mountains. Here the guerillas re-formed in comparative security and, in August, when the 1st Mountain Division moved to Jugoslavia, and L of C duties were again perforce allotted to second-rate troops, the bridgehead was reopened and communications with Greece were disrupted as before.

Meanwhile Northern Albania had remained comparatively docile under deft German handling, and despite numerous declarations by local leaders of their preparedness to co-operate with BLOs, they gave little practical proof of any determination to operate against the enemy. The few ambushes and demolitions that did take place in the north were almost entirely the work of BLOs.

Abas Kupi and the clans which had declared allegiance to his right wing movement were the best potential guerilla force outside FNC. They were concentrated in the mountains running north from the Debar Burrell road, and so by the summer of 1944 were already on the fringe of FNC's northern expansion. While constantly stressing that, once given material assistance by the Allies, he would operate against the Germans, Abas Kupi refused to do so until this aid materialised. Bargaining on these lines was still in progress when the first clash between FNC and Abas Kupi's 'Legality' forces took place in the Burrell area.

*Full Allied Support for FNC*

In the subsequent fighting, Abas Kupi's forces, Bal Kombetar and occupation troops all fought against the FNC, and in the flood of accusation and counter-accusation that followed Allied policy crystallised on the abandonment of Abas Kupi and Bal Kombetar and the giving of all-out support to FNC.

The fate of those opposed to FNC was thus sealed and by the time the German withdrawal northwards had gathered full momentum FNC had spread its control throughout the length and breadth of the mountains of Albania.

*German Withdrawal, Autumn 1944*

In their actions against the retreating German columns FNC were strongly supported by the Balkan Air Force, while in the south and along the coast British Commando and Special Service troops operated in conjunction with the guerillas. Of these latter operations possibly the most important to FNC was the capture of Sarande in September 1944 by the 2nd Special Service Brigade, for with the opening of this port the flow of Allied supplies greatly increased.

Reports state that during this phase of the campaign FNC fought well in the typically ragged fashion of all guerillas. Attacks were pressed home, particularly where air support was available, and estimates show that, as the result of FNC actions during the enemy's withdrawal from Albania, 6,000 to 7,000 German troops were killed, with considerable damage to stores and equipment. The German 21st Mountain Corps suffered particularly heavily at the hands of the Albanian guerillas and shortly afterwards—as will be recalled from Chapter 2—this formation had to run the gauntlet through Tito's partisans in Jugoslavia.

*The Results*

What of the cost? Records do not show Albanian losses, but there were 20 British casualties among the Mission. 2,334 tons of supplies were infiltrated to Albania by sea and air between May 1943 and December 1944—a total only little more than double the airlift to Jugoslavia for one month during the peak period of the summer of 1944. In terms of money, the Albanian effort cost the Allies some £109,000 in gold over the whole period of the campaign. (Maintenance of the Greek refugees during the winter of 1943 cost the Allies £37,000 each month.) Therefore in striking a balance between cost and result, from the Western Allies' point of view, it would seem fair to say that a comparatively small investment paid a handsome military dividend, while the political consequences, although unsatisfactory, had little effect at the international level.

*Finance*

Before closing this account of Albanian guerilla resistance it is worth while to consider for a moment the question of finance, since Albania affords an excellent example of its application to this type of warfare. As a theatre of operations Albania had a low priority for both supplies and air lift, particularly during the early days of universal shortage. As a result, gold was the only commodity available for the BMM to effect the build-up of Albanian resistance. It was also on gold that they had to rely for the obtaining of their own food stocks, shelter and much of their other requirements during the days when supply sorties were so few and far between.

Every British officer and other rank carried a small sum of gold with which he could purchase food or shelter in an emergency. Larger sums were flown into the mission or to individual BLOs as and when required. In general, authority from base had to be obtained before large sums were expended, and BLOs accounted monthly for their expenditure and acknowledged funds as received. The largest amount infiltrated at any one time was £15,000, which Davies had agreed to pay to FNC for the establishment of food dumps for the winter of 1943. It was dropped to him in two lots of £7,500 each.

It would seem that in the early days officers tended to carry too much gold, owing mainly to the few air sorties available and the need to obtain everything with money. The gold proved heavy, difficult to carry and difficult to conceal, and a considerable amount was lost during the periods when BLOs were on the move avoiding capture.

It soon became known that British personnel invariably carried some gold, and there was thus always the risk of attack and even murder. Altogether some £2,600 in gold are shown in the relevant records as having been 'stolen from liaison officers.' A far greater total was looted on the dropping zones and the formidable sum of over £10,000 is included under the heading 'lost on drops or by enemy action.'

Many unsuccessful attempts to avoid the looting of funds from containers on the dropping zone were made, but it was not until the dropping became more accurate and an increase in sorties made it possible to divide the money into many small sums, that these losses decreased.

This extensive use of money by the mission caused growing inflation in the mountains, while by the spring of 1944 paper money had become so scarce that efforts had to be made outside Albania to procure it. Eventually, sufficient was raised from Italian banks to meet the needs of SOE personnel in their day-to-day purchases from the local population.

Of the total money used in Albania the chief items of expenditure were £56,800 in gold on 'mission maintenance', and £32,900 on FNC. Only £2,800 were paid to other guerilla organisations and of these £2,000 went to Abas Kupi. 'Mission maintenance' included the purchase of supplies locally (a large expenditure in the absence of air sorties), the hire and purchase of mules, pay of guards, guides, mulemen, escorts and agents.

The main lesson learnt in Albania and elsewhere was the fact that material rather than financial aid should be given to guerillas whenever circumstances permit, as the extensive use of gold may have two very serious consequences. First, it may cause inflation owing to shortage of local supplies, and secondly, it may be used for purposes other than those originally intended.

## (b) Italy

(*See Map 9 opposite page 101*)

### Growth of Resistance, 1943–44

Italy surrendered to the Western Allies in September 1943, but the country from Naples to the Alps was still dominated by German forces and thus remained enemy-occupied territory. In the months that followed, Mussolini's authority in this area waned rapidly and more and more Italians in the north came to look on the King and the Allied-sponsored Government of the south as the symbol of patriotism. With this change of allegiance, Resistance in German occupied Italy grew.

It was a movement that grew round the towns and other centres of population, rather than in the mountains. In the mountains themselves the first guerilla bands consisted mainly of fugitives from Fascist conscription, army deserters and others unable for various reasons to remain in the more populated and enemy-controlled areas. These bands formed in the Apennines to the north west of Florence, and in the mountains around Italy's northern frontiers. From the beginning they relied on their compatriots in the valleys and plains for many of the necessities of life, and thus developed as a branch of the resistance organisations in these lowland areas.

Despite twenty years of Fascist dictatorship, politics were not long in reappearing and by the end of 1943 there were six separate political parties in existence, each with its own policy, its own principles and its own clandestine papers. All, however, combined into a National Resistance Movement which until the closing phase of the war continued to work as a comparatively united organisation.

This National Resistance Movement took shape early in 1944. Control and co-ordination of its effort was vested in the 'Committee of National Liberation of Northern Italy' (CLNAI) with its clandestine HQ in Milan. The country was divided into regions and zones, each with its own committee consisting of representatives from all parties. The active elements of Resistance in these regions and zones, such as the sabotage cells and guerilla forces, were combined into a 'Corps of Volunteers of Liberty' (CVL) which, on paper at least, came under control of CLNAI through the local Committees of National Liberation.

Only the Communist Party attempted to build up forces within CVL for its own purposes, but during the war they never attained the military monopoly achieved by the Communists in Jugoslavia, Greece and Albania, although their success was sufficient to alarm the Allies, particularly after the Greek civil war of 1944.

*Support of Allied Offensive, 1944*

The Allied break-through to Rome and the news of the great offensives in north-west France and in Russia gave added impetus to the expansion of CVL. On the other hand the summer of 1944 saw the mounting of operation 'ANVIL', the invasion of Southern France, for which troops were drawn from the Italian theatre. CVL thus now became of paramount importance to the Allies, not only to offset the reduction of the regular Allied forces in Italy but also to give indirect support to Operation 'ANVIL'. Consequently Allied policy was one of maximum support for CLNAI and CVL, without too much thought for the political future.

To this end AFHQ publicly proclaimed the Italian partisans as part of the regular forces of the Italian State, they were allotted a monthly subsidy of 100,000,000 lire, and supplies of arms and equipment were greatly increased. In August General Cadorna (son of a victorious general of 1918) was parachuted into North Italy to act as Military Commander under the direction of AFHQ. His two joint Chiefs of Staff were Longo, a Communist, and Ferrucio Parri of the Action Party, who later was to become Prime Minister. By September there were seventeen British Military Missions in the field to aid in the allotment of Allied supplies and interpret AFHQ requirements.

CVL's rôle in support of 'ANVIL' was to prevent the movement of troops across the French frontier: this the guerillas in the Alps of North-Western Italy were well placed to do. In support of the Italian campaign itself CVL were to cause the maximum possible dislocation to communications through Northern Italy and across the frontiers into Austria and Northern Jugoslavia. The former task mainly fell to the clandestine sabotage organisations in the valley of the River Po and other more densely populated areas through which ran the main routes; but the harassing of enemy movements through the mountain passes of the north and north-east and across the Apennines was made the responsibility of the guerilla forces. Those in the Apennines also provided safe areas for a number of sabotage teams, sent in to carry out specific demolitions, while large numbers of escaped Allied prisoners of war also found protection with the guerillas.

Although it is difficult to assess the part each guerilla force played during the summer of 1944, there is ample evidence to show that CVL as a whole caused Marshal Kesselring's command very considerable trouble in his rear areas, trouble he could do little to counter owing to shortage of troops. The political dividend was also great, for the union of Italy under the Allied-sponsored Italian Government depended on some representation and control in northern occupied Italy, and this CLNAI and CVL supplied.

By the late summer CLNAI was dealing as an equal with the Italian Government in liberated territory, and CVL had reached a considerable size. In the mountains alone it was estimated that their strength was some 85,000. With the guerillas still expanding, the provision of stores, arms and equipment was now a major Allied commitment.

*Difficulties of Winter, 1944–45*

The autumn of 1944 found the Allies held in the area of Florence and it became apparent that the campaign would drag on for a second winter. AFHQ now had to decide upon the tasks of CVL as a whole and of the guerillas in particular, during the months until the offensive could be reopened in the following spring. The main problem during this intervening period would be the continuation of supplies to the guerillas at the summer rate both on account of bad flying weather and of a general reduction of support for the Italian theatre now that the main effort of the Western Allies was in North West Europe. A second factor was a growing nervousness that the Communist Party might gain control of Italian Resistance as had already happened in Jugoslavia, and was at this time taking place in Greece and Albania.

It was therefore decided that the guerillas must reduce their numbers to a minimum, leaving only a strong cadre on which to re-expand when the time came. Operations were meanwhile to be limited to small harassing actions.

To the guerillas, on whom this change of policy appears to have been burst with no warning and little explanation, it had an extremely adverse effect. Neither was it an easy matter to pare down guerilla strength without driving those who became redundant into the arms of the enemy, if only to obtain food through the winter.

The plight of the guerillas was made more difficult with the slackening of Allied pressure on the main Italian front, for this meant that for the first time German troops could be employed against them in some strength. Aided by the severe winter weather, the results were wholesale desertions and the disintegration of several units, even though casualties from enemy action were not heavy.

In December a mission from CLNAI visited Rome. The outcome was an agreement with the Government of Bonomi in which:

(a) The Bonomi Government formally delegated CLNAI to represent them in the struggle in German-occupied Italy.
(b) CLNAI accepted the Bonomi Government as the legitimate authority in such territory as the Allies returned to it and agreed to accept the military directives of Field Marshal Alexander.

The Allies, for their part, undertook to make available 260,000,000 lire a month. This meeting and agreement lessened the fears of AFHQ and the politicians of Communist domination in occupied territory.

During this period more Allied formations were transferred from Italy to the western theatre, and with this reduction in Allied strength it again became important to ensure that full use was made of the guerillas in the coming spring offensive. The chances of their rehabilitation did not at the time seem promising, but a period of abnormally good weather over the first three months of 1945 allowed a marked increase in the air lift above what had been planned, and by the end of March some 770 tons had been flown into Northern Italy. To help in the reorganisation, the existing Military Missions were reinforced by additional liaison officers, and by April there were 59 British officers and 66 other ranks in the field, apart from those sent in by the Americans.

Unlike the Military Missions in some other theatres, such as Greece, those in Italy were not integrated. Instead, SOE became responsible for specific areas and resistance formations: their American counterpart (OSS) dealing with others. This arrangement seems to have worked without friction, although reports show a rather different approach, in that the

Americans tended to concentrate more on quick military results, regardless of possible political repercussions, while British policy paid more attention to political aspects.

In the early months of 1944 a slackening of German activity in the guerilla areas, increased Allied support and better weather all played their part in raising guerilla morale and strength. It was essentially a period of preparation and build-up, and actions were limited: during this time the provision of operational intelligence was the guerillas' most important contribution.

Throughout the winter Allied propaganda appears to have made good use of its many opportunities. In Italy, unlike in other theatres such as Albania, it was possible to obtain comprehensive and up-to-date background information from within occupied territory. With the aid of this, local propaganda programmes were broadcast, in conjunction with the BBC, both to the Italian Resistance and to the enemy. This propaganda was further expanded by the infiltration of newspapers, posters and photographs and by a campaign of rumours.

Not surprisingly, German morale deteriorated steadily throughout the winter and there was a growing tendency for local commanders to come to an agreement on mutual toleration with nearby guerilla forces. Amongst the Italians, Mussolini's adherents were already a spent force.

*Rival Resistance ideologies*

The spring of 1945 was a period of growing confidence for CVL, whose strength at this time was around 89,500. By guerilla standards they were reasonably well-armed and their morale was generally high. Not all were, however, thinking in terms of supporting the Allied offensive as with the approach of 'LIBERATION' the various political factions within CVL were concentrating more and more on the build-up of their organisations for the political struggle that was to come. The Communists in particular had redoubled their efforts to gain more control and to augment their numbers.

At this time the Communist partisan forces were attracting into their ranks much of the Italian youth, not only on account of more efficient organisation but also by their clever propaganda. Their appreciation of the use of propaganda was shown, for example, in their adoption of 'Garibaldi' as their idol. To the Italian people Garibaldi is a colourful romantic whose exploits have been handed down to succeeding generations in song and verse, and the fact that his followers wore red shirts provided a heaven-sent coincidence for the Communists. In point of fact the first Garibaldi unit to be raised by a local Italian patriot had nothing at all to do with Communists, but the possibilities inherent in such a name were such that the Party soon adopted it as their own.

This rapid rise in Communist strength naturally had its repercussions on the opposing Partisan leaders, and at times their fear that Italy might emerge as a Communist dominated state when the war was over, caused them to regard the actual fighting as of secondary importance. There were several instances of Actionist and Socialist formations cacheing the military equipment supplied to them by the Allies, with the intention of using it after the war to fight the Communists once Allied control had been withdrawn. On one occasion in early 1945 a Socialist brigade is reported to have withdrawn from the area in which it had been ordered to engage the enemy in order to preserve ammunition for this purpose. The Communists for their part did no more, and sometimes a good deal less, than their rivals in defeating the common enemy.

As 'LIBERATION' drew near both sides became acutely conscious of the fact that a general election would take place in the not very far distant future, the purpose of which would be to set up a new Italian Government. Consequently all formations strained their logistic resources to the utmost, and welcomed into their ranks anybody whom they could get to join them, with the object not of driving the enemy over the Brenner Pass with one gigantic push but of obtaining the greatest possible number of votes for their respective political parties.

*Spring Offensive, 1945*

Meanwhile, the Allied High Command were planning for the Spring Offensive that was due to open on the 12th April. In this, Italian Resistance was allotted two alternative rôles. Which they were to carry out depended on whether the Germans attempted a fighting withdrawal or whether they surrendered. In the event of a withdrawal, CVL were to prevent destruction of industrial plant and other economic targets ('Scorch') by the enemy and were to harass their columns as they retreated over the Northern passes. Should the Germans surrender, CVL's tasks were to prevent 'Scorch', maintain law and order and mop up enemy units after their capitulation.

The Allied attack opened as planned on 12th April. Within five days the main German defences had been pierced and the Allied forces were sweeping into the valley of the River Po. During this initial phase the Apennine guerillas, some 5,000 strong, successfully operated against the enemy's communications through the mountains and claimed to have prevented a number of enemy demolitions. The Germans for their part were too fully engaged elsewhere to counter these activities in any force. With the break through of the 8th and 5th Armies into the plains to the North the rôle of the Apennine guerillas changed to one of mopping up enemy units left in the wake of the Allied advance, maintaining law and order until the arrival of the Allied Military Governments, and generally opening up communications.

Events now moved rapidly. Allied forces crossed the River Po on the 25th April and drove onwards with main thrusts towards the Brenner, Udine and Trieste. With the crossing of the Po the 'all out' order was given to the guerillas, and in the closing stages of the campaign they joined the regular forces in defeating the German Army in Italy. On the 29th April 1945 the German High Command surrendered.

## Results achieved

In the fluid state of these last few days the contribution of the guerillas in actual offensive actions cannot have been great, although many units did play a part in slowing down German elements in the mountain passes and keeping open the routes for Allied columns in their rush to the frontiers. Furthermore their presence allowed the Allies to leave their flanks and rear unprotected in the knowledge that the CVL would mop up enemy units left in their rear.

It was, however, politically that the Italian Resistance paid its greatest dividend during this final phase. Through its organisation there were in every town and village Committees of National Liberation, and these emerged at once as provisional organs of government. They were, at that time, still representative of all political parties and therefore had the backing of the majority of the population.

Aided by the guerilla and other CVL forces these Committees made easier the eventual assumption of control by Allied Military Governments and the Italian Government in Rome. In the period of vacuum before these took over the Committees did what they could to maintain law and order. But this 'law and order' had a distinct Communist bias and atrocities committed by Communist 'partisans' in the name of 'Liberty' were bad enough to cause many Allied Military Government officials to look upon all Italian partisans as Communists.

There seems little doubt that had the war lasted another three months or so the Communists would have obtained complete military monopoly in the CLNAI. As it was their influence very nearly achieved its object. The Italian Communist Party emerged at the end of the War as one of the largest in Europe, due principally to the effective propaganda campaign representing Communists as those who had done more than anybody else, including the Allies, to liberate Italy from enemy domination.

Thus in Italy, as in the majority of countries where guerilla resistance was encouraged, the effects of guerilla warfare did not end with the war.

## (c) France

(*See Map 10 opposite page 107*)

### Background

There is little good 'guerilla country' in France, for the excellent road and rail systems allow regular forces with their heavy supporting arms to move anywhere comparatively easily, while there are few regions which have sufficiently extensive cover to provide safe areas in which para-military forces can manoeuvre. This is particularly the case in the north and west. In the centre of France there are limited areas of forest in which it is possible to remain hidden, and in the so-called Massif Central the ground is rather more broken. Neither of these areas are suitable for protracted guerilla operations, however, nor are the Ardennes or the Vosges to the east. The only region that is in any way suitable for continuous guerilla activity is the wedge of mountains and plateaux that start in the Jura to the north and extend southwards between the Rhone Valley and the Italian frontier. But even this cannot compare in suitability with the mountainous and almost roadless expanses that exist in Jugoslavia and Greece.

It is therefore not surprising that there is no mention of the formation of guerilla forces in the initial Allied plans for French Resistance. It was generally accepted then, both in France and by the Allied High Command, that the underground movement in France should concentrate on building up a Secret Army which would come into the open only when Allied forces again landed on French soil.

There was one organisation, however, which, from its inception, followed a policy of all-out resistance against the occupying powers and all those that aided them. This was the 'Front National' which included the French Communist Party. By 1943 their growing strength, as a result of this aggressive policy and their mounting successes, made it clear that sabotage could play an important part in the dislocation of the German war potential in France. Thus, while still fashioning a Secret Army for D-day, sabotage now became a second rôle.

With this expansion in sabotage came increased reprisals, and numbers of Frenchmen were forced into hiding. These joined the Maquis (a term derived from a Corsican word meaning a piece of wild bush land).

*Development of the Maquis, 1942*

The story of the Maquis begins in the summer of 1942 with an agreement between the Germans and the Vichy government by which 50,000 French prisoners in Germany were to be exchanged for 150,000 'voluntary' skilled French workers. This bargain, not surprisingly, failed to work and in September 1942 Vichy under German pressure introduced compulsory labour service. By this means the Germans secured their first 150,000 men only one month behind time: by March 1943 they had squeezed out another 250,000 after which 400,000 more were demanded.

Resistance to these conscriptions was spontaneous and universal. Young men liable to compulsory service 'lost' themselves. Many fled to the less populated parts of the country and lived in organised camps and hide-outs. These formed the original Maquis, which grew so rapidly as to cause serious concern for their safety and maintenance. As early as February 1943 General de Gaulle was demanding greatly increased supplies of food, arms and equipment for them. The British Government, on the other hand, were urging him to try to limit the numbers in the Maquis, and to discourage their provocation of the Germans, for fear of unnecessary reprisals with no military gain.

Estimates as to the strength of the Maquis vary widely according to the interpretation of the term 'Maquis' by the group or individual making the report. A memorandum on the subject, prepared for the Chiefs of Staff, put the total strength of the Maquis in France at the beginning of 1944 at about 40,000. Of these some 18,000 were in the south-east in the Departments east of the Rivers Doubs and Rhone.

*Organisation of the Maquis*

In theory at least, control of all the Maquis was centralised in the 'Conseil de la Résistance' in Paris. Each of the twelve Regions of France and each Department had its own Chef du Maquis, while within each Department there were varying numbers of groups, each divided into bands 10 to 50 strong.

In practice, the highest level at which command seems to have been effectively exercised was that of the Department. The departmental chiefs were usually men who had not been appointed by the united Resistance Movements but had emerged as natural leaders from the Maquis itself. They recognised the authority of the Resistance Movement, accepted supplies and financial help from them but enjoyed a large measure of autonomy. Between the Central HQs in Paris, Regions and Departments there was considerable rivalry and clash of personalities: communication between these levels, and the general state of security left a good deal to be desired.

There were therefore many advantages in the Maquis being developed into a number of independent forces, provided there was some body outside occupied France to co-ordinate their activities. A prerequisite was a direct communication system between these independent formations and the controlling organisation.

This the Maquis had not got. They were at this time dependent on the communication set-up of the Resistance organisations, which had by now combined into the 'French Forces of the Interior' (FFI). The existing links between the FFI and the Allied High Command were, to put it mildly, complex. At least three separate organisations in the United Kingdom were concerned with the organisation and supply of the FFI and had their own contacts with the latter.

To decentralise control of the Maquis and at the same time provide them with the necessary direct communications with the outside world, it was decided that in each Department the Maquis should be formed into an independent formation with their own wireless link to base. To co-ordinate their activities and development it was planned to group these formations into districts, each of which would have a co-ordinating HQ, which in turn would be reinforced by an Allied mission. Thus for example the Maquis forces of Jura, Ain and Haute Savoie formed one district and had one mission attached to them.

*Allied Missions*

The Allied missions that were sent to the various districts consisted of a

British, an American and a French officer, together with a W/T operator. They were in no sense in command of the District, but were for liaison between the Maquis and the Allied High Command. In practice their rôle became considerably more than purely liaison, for it was generally they who had to produce some order in the confusion of personalities and politics that prevailed.

The first of these missions, code name 'UNION', dropped into Savoie in January 1944, their district being Savoie, Isère and Drome. Other similar missions followed and, as the Maquis forces developed and activity increased, the original districts were further divided. To cover these new areas more missions, including what became known as 'JEDBURGH' teams were sent in: some came from the United Kingdom, others from North Africa.

Later, after the Allied landings in the South of France, American operational groups were dropped in to strengthen the Maquis. These Operational Groups consisted of four officers and thirty enlisted men. They could be sub-divided into sections of one officer and fifteen men, or squads of six men. Every man was specially trained to a high standard of physical toughness and skill in both demolitions and para-military action, and was equipped to produce a large volume of fire power. Six of these groups which were sent into southern France from North Africa on special tasks remained to assist the local FFI. Similar British units of the Special Air Service operated in France but not in the areas of the guerillas.

*The main task*

The main rôle of the guerillas in the south-east was the support of the Allied landings which were due to take place on the south coast of France in August 1944 (Operation 'ANVIL'). In addition, however, they were whenever possible to contribute to the lowering of German morale and the dispersion of his forces on garrison, convoy and similar duties during the period leading up to the Allies' main landing in Normandy ('OVERLORD') in June 1944.

The generally-agreed concept of how these tasks should be carried out seems to have been the normal hit-and-run guerilla methods until such time as the Allied regular forces were so close that the Maquis and Resistance as a whole could rise safely in open rebellion.

*'Plan Vidal'*

But at some time during this planning stage there appeared another project, sometimes known as the 'Plan Vidal'. This was based on the assumption that certain areas of France could and should be liberated by the French themselves, and that these areas could be held by the FFI against any counter-attacks that the enemy would be able to launch. It envisaged these defended areas serving as 'ports of entry' through which supplies and airborne troops could be received in large quantities, and from which raiding parties could dominate sections of the German lines of communication.

This project was generally damned on the grounds that guerillas could not hold even prepared positions against well-equipped regular forces. In addition it was argued that any such attempt would inevitably lead to a demand for a diversion of Allied resources which would be hard to resist and yet strategically useless. Although apparently turned down by the Allied High Command, the 'Plan Vidal' was not killed and in the end was put into effect with results that fully justified its previous condemnation.

*'Colour Plans'*

A third series of plans which also affected the Maquis guerillas were known as the 'Colour Plans', and were an ambitious and complicated arrangement developed by the French High Command in the UK. The theory was that a comprehensive list of 'D-day targets' should be prepared under different categories: stores for each category were to be sent to the field in containers labelled with the colour of the plan: these stores would then be put aside for 'the day'. Each plan would then be put into effect by special BBC messages. In all there were seven different 'Colour Plans' but in the end only three survived: 'Plan Vert' which was for attacks on the railway system; 'Plan Tortue' for attacks on reinforcements moving by road; and 'Plan Grenouille' for the sabotage of railway turntables. These three plans were put into action in due course with good effect, but as a whole these 'Colour Plans' caused much wasted effort and were too ambitious to be practical for Resistance organisations in the field. It must, however, be remembered that they were drawn up by the French to deal with a number of alternative eventualities, without a full knowledge of Allied intentions. This had been denied them on security grounds, and from reports available this restriction seems to have been more than justified.

*Supply, 1944*

To carry out their allotted tasks the Maquis required arms, and they were woefully short of these, despite urgent and forceful requests from Free French Headquarters in the UK. At the beginning of 1944 it was estimated that, with few exceptions, there were on an average only sufficient weapons to arm one in ten of the Maquis. Most of these arms were of the very short range type, such as sub-machine guns, pistols and shot guns.

This lack of weapons appears to have been at least in part the result of the studied policy, already mentioned, of ensuring that the Maquis did not have the tools with which to provoke the occupying forces into reprisals on themselves and the local population, with no commensurate gain for the Allied war effort. As a result the air lift allotted for the supply of French Resistance as a whole remained comparatively small, while most of that available had to be used to keep the sabotage organisations supplied for their current tasks.

Because of this inability to arm the Maquis adequately, the last three months of 1943 was a period of strained relations between Free French

Headquarters, SOE and the RAF. The Prime Minister was at the time convalescing in North Africa, but on his return in January a meeting was held under his Chairmanship. At this meeting Mr. Churchill left no doubt as to his own views on the subject, and insisted that everything possible should be done to support the Maquis in the fight against the occupying forces. The immediate consequence was a directive to Bomber Command placing the supply of the Maquis second only to the air offensive against Germany. This priority, together with a very substantial acceleration of the aircraft programme, made it possible to plan for sufficient arms for 16,000 men to be dropped to the Maquis in February, over and above SOE's existing programme.

A further allotment of aircraft was made in March, and the total of successful sorties rose by leaps and bounds. From 101 in the last quarter of 1943, it increased to 700 during the first quarter of 1944, 1,665 during the second quarter and 3,573 during the third.

This great effort came at the right time. Made earlier, it might well have inflated Resistance dangerously and prematurely. But as it was, there was a steady crescendo up to D-day and beyond, and the French met the invasion with strong faith in Allied support.

*Mission* 'UNION', *1944*

In January 1944, however, when Mission 'UNION' dropped into Savois, the Maquis of south-eastern France had a long way to go before reaching this comparatively satisfactory state. The officers of 'UNION' found the Maquis morale good, food reasonably plentiful and the peasants fully supporting the local Maquis groups. The groups were in all stages of development from small bands of ragged, unarmed men to comparatively well-organised and equipped units which were already operating.

Little had as yet been done to reorganise on the basis of the French Departments and the top-heavy, centralised channel of control remained. In most cases communications were chaotic. There were instances of a number of different Allied organisations passing instructions to the same group or groups, and in some cases no contact at all existed with the outside world. Thus one small area might be covered by three wireless sets, while a whole Department might have only one. Some were in contact with London, others with Algiers.

Many of the guerillas suffered hardships in the winter months through lack of blankets and warm clothing. Much of this could have been purchased locally, had the Maquis formations had the money. This, however, had to be sent to them from a central fund in Paris, but the distance, coupled with the hazards of the journey, resulted in very little actually reaching the Maquis in the remote south-east.

The situation found by 'UNION' in their area of responsibility was representative of the conditions prevailing at the time throughout the mountain valleys and plateaux of south-eastern France.

A redistribution of existing wireless sets to allow Department HQs direct links to London and Algiers did much to improve control and co-ordination, though the Maquis still suffered from the conflict of personalities and individual aims of the various commanders. In the minds of some, the 'Plan Vidal' was still very much alive, particularly in the case of the leader in the Vercors plateau area.

*The Vercors Plateau*

This plateau, which is triangular in shape, lies with its apex to the west of Grenoble. It is some 10 miles broad at its base from east to west and is about 30 miles long from north to south. 1,000 to 2,000 metres high, it rises sheer from the plain and access to it is limited to eight roads which cut up into the plateau. It was relatively rich in foodstuffs and the population was patriotic and courageous.

It was thus an excellent locality for Maquis camps, and these steadily increased in numbers and strength throughout 1943. By the spring of 1944 the plateau was being prepared for protracted defence, despite counter-proposals by 'UNION' to plan for a more suitable guerilla rôle.

The Germans appear to have shown little interest in the Maquis development of the Vercors and up to June records show only two half-hearted attempts to penetrate on to the plateau, the first by Italian troops and the second by a small German force. It was not until later, in July 1944, that the Vercors redoubt was seriously challenged by the Germans with results that are described later in this chapter.

In the meantime, however, the Germans made determined efforts to repress the Maquis further north. The latter had little difficulty in evading capture and in so doing inflicted casualties on the Germans. Savage reprisals on the population followed, particularly in the Ain. These caused great bitterness and an ever-growing determination amongst the Maquis to fight it out. Eventually a force of some 700 turned on the Germans. Actions lasting some 72 hours took place on a plateau somewhat resembling the Vercors. This the Maquis attempted to hold, but it was a forlorn hope as with light weapons only they had no chance against the eventual attack by a German force of some four infantry battalions and supporting artillery. The final result was some 100 Maquis killed and 150 taken prisoner. The remainder were lucky enough to escape, but in the subsequent German reprisals parts of the country were devastated, and between February and May some 1,500 farms were burnt down in Jura, Ain and Haute Savoie.

*Development of supply technique*

Despite this set-back the spring of 1944 was a period of steady progress in the development and organisation of Maquis guerillas in the south-east. Funds were now being received direct from base; some decentralisation of control had been achieved within the Maquis and the necessary communication links to the United Kingdom and North Africa had been set up.

As already mentioned, the volume of air supply increased rapidly. As early as March, 17 aircraft, carrying 231 containers and 74 packages, flew into Haute Savoie, while on the same night 12 aircraft dropped 178 containers and 72 packages in the area of 'UNION'.

The reception of such quantities called for comprehensive arrangements in the field. For the organisation of the dropping zone each area normally had its own specialised reception committee, but in addition a large number of men were required to collect and remove the supplies dropped. Protective units had also to be deployed to cover the approaches until the DZ was cleared.

One advantage of these large supply drops was the fact that each drop was sufficient to supply the Maquis over a wide area. Thus once the DZ had been cleared it did not matter if it became known to the enemy, as it would not be required again for some considerable time.

But rapid clearance of the DZ was still essential, and this was no easy matter when some hundreds of heavy containers had first to be found and then removed, often across difficult country, to their hiding places.

In an attempt to ease the task of the field, certain developments in air supply took place and this seems an appropriate place to include an outline of these, in so far as they affected the French guerillas.

In the earlier stages supplies for the field were made up in loads on the basis of individual requirements, but, as the various main requirements became better known, a method of standardisation was evolved. Certain standard loads were then made up for specific needs. Thus, for example, containers for the Maquis included a preponderance of small arms, while those for sabotage organisations had more explosives and demolition stores. Standard medical panniers were also produced.

Eventually three standard sets of containers were prepared: one for the initial equipping of a hundred men; another for their re-supply; and a third designed to provide them with a complete load of ammunition.

Descriptions of the various standard containers and a list of contents were sent to the field. Thus not only could demands be simplified but reception committee organisers in the field were able to recognise what they had received without the need for complete unpacking.

Money was included, when necessary, in one of the cells of the standard containers; the cell being sealed and marked 'chef d'operation'. Whenever possible money was sent in on operations where personnel were also being dropped, and the latter could then immediately warn reception organisers. In addition to these precautions further warning was sent over the BBC.

A great deal of wasted time and effort and, in consequence, added danger was caused to the field when loads dropped to them did not correspond to the totals originally stated. Last minute changes at base were often unavoidable, however, and to overcome this problem, labels showing the total number of containers and packages being dropped were fixed to every container as soon as it was known definitely how many were being carried to a given DZ. By these and other similar drills the supply problem was simplified both at base and in the field.

*Co-ordination of operations by the Maquis*

So much for the supply arrangements by which the Maquis guerillas were, by the end of May 1944, beginning to be reasonably well-armed.

There was still, however, no co-ordinated plan between the various Maquis guerilla organisations for their operations in support of 'OVERLORD' and 'ANVIL'. One commander had a 'Plan Vidal', another was already attacking pylons, another was doing nothing. There appear to have been two main reasons for this lack of co-ordination. The first was rivalry and a certain amount of bickering between the French Resistance hierarchy. The second reason was the series of contradictory and incomplete instructions which still reached the field from London and Algiers: this seems to have been largely due to the many and various headquarters who still retained a finger in the French Resistance pie.

In June 1944 General Koenig was appointed Commander, under General Eisenhower, of all French Forces of the Interior, and an integrated French, British and American HQ was formed to combine all the staff functions (EMFFI or Etat Major des Forces Françaises de l'Intérieur). This did much to simplify matters. In the first place, the FFI throughout France came under General Koenig, but their control must have still remained complicated by the fact that a somewhat similar headquarters to EMFFI was already in being in Algiers. SPOC (Special Projects Operation Centre), as it was called, was manned by officers from SOE and its American equivalent OSS. Their task was the implementation of AFHQ's directives for the use of French Resistance to support Operation 'ANVIL'.

Shortly before 'ANVIL' took place, however, areas of control were divided between SHAEF in the north and AFHQ in the south, and General Cochet was appointed to command the FFI in the AFHQ Zone. The dividing line between the two areas of responsibility was approximately Geneva–Lyons–Vichy–River Dordogne.

*'OVERLORD', 6th June 1944*

Meanwhile 'OVERLORD' had begun on the 6th June. On that and the previous day the BBC broadcast the phrases that were to start FFI's attacks against roads, rails and telecommunications. In conjunction with the Allied Air offensive these tasks were most adequately carried out and caused the hoped-for delay in the movement of enemy reserves towards the Allied bridgehead in Normandy.

But such was the enthusiasm throughout France that what had been planned as a mainly clandestine phase of resistance developed in many areas into one of open insurrection against the occupying forces. In the south-east the Allied intention had been to hold the main Resistance effort in check until the launching of 'ANVIL' in August. Within a short time of the Normandy landings, however, many Maquis from the Jura southwards had taken possession of villages and areas where German and Vichy control was weak.

A liaison mission, sent in mid-June from Algiers to Vercors, found 'Plan Vidal' in full swing, with the Maquis organising for protracted defence and the Tricolor flying over every village on the plateau. Frenchmen flocked to the Maquis and missions clamoured for weapons and equipment to arm the swollen formations. On 25th June, as part of the programme to satisfy these needs, three Groups, each of 36 Flying Fortresses, dropped supplies in daylight for the first time into Jura, Ain and the Vercors. Similar operations were taking place over other parts of France, for the plight of those who had come into the open too prematurely was by now serious. The Germans had recovered from their initial shock and had turned on the lightly-armed Maquis, causing them heavy casualties.

*German Assault on the Vercors Plateau*

It was not until 13th July, however, that the first serious German attempt to penetrate on to the Vercors was made. It was repulsed, and on the following day a second and larger daylight supply drop took place, as a result of which the Vercors Maquis received 860 containers of badly-needed weapons and equipment. Some 3,000 were now armed, and the plateau had been organised with outer perimeter defences and an 'inner defence'. There was internal telephone communication and the Maquis had some transport. There now followed a week of increasing German pressure, during which the Maquis were steadily driven back, losing equipment and men as they went, for by now tanks and artillery were being used against them. By the 21st, those of the Maquis who remained were behind their inner defences, whereupon the enemy launched their final ground offensive, which was combined with an airborne landing in the Maquis rear. Tired, short of ammunition, and without reserves the Maquis broke, and those who could dispersed into the mountains to the east. Some 700 Maquis were killed but it was the civilians of the Vercors that suffered most, for there were horrible reprisals in the mountain villages. As a result of this action the Maquis of this area were unable to reorganise in time to provide any support for 'ANVIL'. On the credit side, however, the destruction of the Vercors had caused the Germans to employ elements of an armoured and an infantry division (some 11,000 men), airborne troops and aircraft, all of which could ill be spared at that time. German losses must also have been substantial. There was thus some diversion and dispersal of German forces but it occurred too early to have much effect on 'ANVIL'. Its strategic importance seems therefore very doubtful and in no way commensurate with the losses suffered by the Maquis.

In spite of this serious set-back and of increased German activity in other areas, planning and preparation for the campaign in the south continued.

For some months the Resistance leaders in southern France had been convinced that a rapid advance up the Route Napoléon towards Grenoble, by-passing the main Rhone valley routes, was a feasible proposition in view of the strength of resistance in the mountainous areas through which this route passes. This project was eventually agreed and formed part of the 'ANVIL' plan.

The guerillas' tasks were, first, the dislocation of enemy troop movements and telecommunications while the Allied bridgehead was being secured; secondly, flank protection of the Allied force during its race along the Route Napoléon to Grenoble; and finally, in conjunction with this Allied force, the cutting of the enemy's escape routes into Germany.

*Operation 'ANVIL', August 1944*

On the evening of 14th August 1944 the pre-arranged BBC warning messages were broadcast and the Allied landings in the south followed the next day.

Compared with the north, the Germans were thin on the ground and the fighting never became stable. Opportunities for guerilla operations were therefore numerous. In the first phase, Maquis from the nearby mountains successfully cut the Rhone Valley railway and harassed enemy convoys on the roads. In the Alpes Maritimes they destroyed an important RDF station and blocked the mountain passes into Italy. In the second phase, they facilitated the move of the small regular force up the Route Napoléon to Grenoble which it entered on 23rd July. Further to the north, German convoys were ambushed and a number of the garrisons were contained until the arrival of regular troops. As soon as it became clear that there would be no German stand in the south the final task materialised, that of cutting off the fleeing enemy forces from the south and south-east. As one report puts it 'this was the time of gallant and crazy incidents—the liberation by the French of Lyons, Toulouse, of Bordeaux and of countless towns and villages.' But the FFI could not hold regular troops for long, and those German formations which kept their morale and discipline were able to get back, although much reduced in numbers and stripped of their heavy equipment. The toll of arms and stores captured was enormous and the enemy losses in men heavy, though these cannot be accurately assessed. Many were killed in ambushes, and the FFI in the south claimed 42,000 prisoners.

With the German forces from the south through the Belfort Gap and the campaign in the north now approaching the Rhine, the rôle of the Maquis in the south-east as a guerilla force came to an end.

*Assessment of results*

It is impossible to assess the military value of the guerila operations of the Maquis in south-east France independently from the results of French resistance as a whole. All branches—Secret Army, saboteurs, and guerilla force—played their part, probably in that order of priority. The military value of French resistance as a whole can best be gathered from the appreciation on

the subject prepared by SHAEF and SACMED (Supreme Allied Commander, Mediterranean Area) in which their broad conclusions were that French resistance helped the main operation of the Allied armies as follows:
- (*a*) by sapping the enemy's confidence of his own security and flexibility of internal movement;
- (*b*) by diverting enemy troops to internal security duties and keeping troops thus employed dispersed;
- (*c*) by enabling Allied formations to advance with greater speed through being able to dispense with many normal military precautions, e.g. flank protection and mopping up;
- (*d*) by providing military intelligence.

In addition there must also have been the considerable psychological effect on the enemy forces of being constantly harried and having to operate in a country openly at war, where practically every man, woman and child was set against them.

As on the military side so with the political. The effect of the Maquis guerillas cannot be gauged separately from that of Resistance as a whole. For the latter it is fair to say that post-war France was built upon the achievements of the French Forces of the Interior.

From the Allied viewpoint the cost of their maintenance over the last year of occupation was the continuous activity of five or six squadrons of aircraft and the loss of some 100 with their crews; light weapons, explosives and ammunition were delivered to the field for at least 50,000 men to be scantily armed; between 500 and 700 highly trained Allied personnel kept from operations elsewhere and a very large sum of paper money spent. French losses both in lives and property were heavy, however, not only as the direct result of FFI action but through reprisals by the Germans against the local population in the areas where Resistance forces operated.

## (d) Other European Countries

*Norway*

At first glance it might seem that Norway, with its tangled mountain masses and extended lines of communication, would offer considerable opportunities for guerila operations, but in fact none, in their true sense, took place during the Second World War. The reasons for this are the lack of adequate cover and the climate.

The mountains offer little, if any, natural cover and thus concealment of any large bands of guerillas, difficult enough in summer, would have been well-nigh impossible in winter, when even one man moving across country ran the risk of being tracked in the snow. Shelter from the very severe winters was also lacking for any but small parties which could, if they were fortunate, operate from one of the isolated ski-huts high up in the mountains. Food, also, was non-existent in the mountain regions and had to come either from the valleys or from abroad. The valleys were thinly populated and any unusual activity was easily checked by the occupying forces, while supplies from abroad had to come almost entirely by air operations. Weather conditions over Norway made air supply difficult and uncertain at all times: between May and September it was impracticable owing to the very short nights.

Although guerilla forces could not exist under these circumstances, a number of individuals and small parties lived and operated successfully in the mountains. It was a tough existence and those who did so were mainly *coup de main* parties who were parachuted in or came from elsewhere in Norway to carry out some specific task, and then returned whence they came. Such parties did notable work, probably the best-known being the attack on the Heavy Water Plant at Vemork. Other Norwegian clandestine sabotage organisations also played their part, and in the last phase of the war a Norwegian Secret Army successfully came into action.

From the aspect of guerilla warfare, a number of interesting points emerge from these activities for Norwegian Resistance was almost unique in its combination of solid commonsense and political maturity. These points can best be recorded in a series of negatives.

First, Norway was not rent by divisions between Left and Right, home and exile, and thus her efforts to arm the Resistance did not degenerate into rival preparations for a political coup. This admirable state of affairs was due mainly to the lack of any extreme political feelings within the country and to the fact that throughout the war the exiled King and Government remained the main rallying point and controlling influence for all Norwegians.

Secondly, the Norwegian Resistance did not refuse to accept strategic direction from the Allies. How much the rational approach of Allied strategy to Norwegian Resistance was the direct result of the Norwegian Government's say in the matter is difficult to assess. The fact remains, however, that this was no pauper government, living on the bounty of the Western Allies, as were for example the Jugoslavs. It was a government not only representative of occupied Norway but one having a strong bargaining counter in the form of the Norwegian merchant fleet which played an important part in the Allied war effort.

Thirdly, Norwegian Resistance was not trapped into suicidal paramilitary operations in unsuitable country, nor did its Secret Army take the field prematurely, as happened with such dire results in so many other instances.

*The Low Countries*

Denmark, Holland and most of Belgium are in direct contrast to Norway, for they are thickly populated, flat and quite unsuitable for protracted guerilla operations. Luckily none were attempted or even thought of, except in Belgium where in the Vosges to the south-west small guerilla forces came into being, but played little part in the Resistance until the final phase of the

German retreat eastwards. This was as well, for the Vosges are too limited in area and interspersed with too many roads to offer safe areas for guerilla forces against determined counter-measures.

*Poland*

It is difficult to obtain a clear and comprehensive picture of the part guerilla operations played in Polish resistance, as there were no British witnesses and the Poles themselves appear to have cared little for detailed reports.

The country, with its poor communications and large tracts of forest and swamp, was not unsuitable for the development of guerilla forces, while there could be no better human material from which to recruit guerillas than the Poles themselves. Tough, intensely patriotic and with a long tradition of resistance, the nation almost without exception can be said to have enrolled in the forces of liberation. The great problem, as always, was that of supplies. These were inadequate within the country for maintaining any continuous para-military operations on any but the smallest scale. Air operations were the only means of outside support and these were exceptionally difficult—particularly during the earlier stages of the war—owing to the very long ranges both from the Western Allies and the USSR. Allied supplies could thus do little more than satisfy the needs of clandestine sabotage in Poland.

Under these circumstances it seems that there was general agreement for the Polish resistance to work mainly underground by sabotage and other methods, while building up a Secret Army for the final rising and resurrection of Poland. From available reports this policy seems to have been generally followed, and by an endless sequence of small-scale actions, in part passive, in part sabotage, a heavy and constant drain was made upon German manpower and morale.

Guerilla forces, as such, do not appear to have been employed in any but very minor actions. Instead, they were built up in the more inaccessible regions as part of the Secret Army. The operations of the Polish Secret Army, which culminated in the premature and disastrous rising in Warsaw, have been touched upon in Chapter 1. This type of resistance is outside the scope of the present study.

*Czechoslovakia*

The outline of Czechoslovak Resistance in the Second World War is similar to that of Poland, and can add little to this story of guerilla warfare.

Apart from an area in the south-west the country was unsuitable for guerilla operations: air communications with the eastern and western Allies were too tenuous for the maintenance of guerillas, and the people, despite their resolute nature and long tradition of resistance, were more suited to clandestine action than to a guerilla rôle.

Rightly, therefore, Czech Resistance remained clandestine throughout the earlier phases of the war. But with the Russian advance westwards plans were made for open resistance in the puppet state of Slovakia, should the Germans attempt its complete occupation as part of their strategic defence plan. This attempt came in August 1944, as the Russian armies were pushing through the Carpathians and Roumania, and two very weak divisions of the Slovak Army revolted. In conjunction with the so-called partisans they controlled a considerable area of the mountainous country in the south-west, including two airfields.

The Western Allies had consistently made it clear that it would not be possible for them to provide any worthwhile supply operations for this venture, and it was in any case within the Russian Zone of operations. On the 6th September the latter flew in 30 transport aircraft with arms, as well as 700 men of the Czech parachute brigade. They also sent 24 Czech fighter aircraft.

The whole concept of this operation, however, was that the Russian advancing armies would link up with these Czech forces in a comparatively short time. With their failure to do this the partisans were gradually compressed and eventually overwhelmed in November 1944.

In March 1945 there was a second rising, this time in Prague. Here the Resistance were saved by the arrival of Russian forces.

## (e) Soviet Guerilla Operations

*Introduction*

In writing the preceding sections it has been possible to draw on an extensive selection of official histories, personal reports and experiences of actual BLOs who took part in the campaigns concerned. No such data is available on Soviet Guerilla Resistance in the Second World War. Instead it has been necessary to rely to some extent on the works of Soviet authors and, to a larger degree, on the summaries and appreciations of the German High Command and their forces on the Eastern Front. The Soviet authors are suspect for obvious reasons: neither is it easy to get a balanced picture from the Axis documents, for in the earlier days of the campaign the Germans appear to have entirely failed to appreciate the potential dangers of Soviet Resistance, while later their reports give the impression of swaying to the other extreme and exaggerating the strength and capabilities of the guerilla forces.

A certain amount of 'reading between the lines' has therefore been necessary in the production of this Section. A further factor in the form that it has taken is that any detailed study of guerilla operations in the USSR would inevitably include much that was similar to the other successful European campaigns already described.

For these reasons this Section only summarises the sequence of Soviet Resistance and concentrates on a consideration of those aspects that are peculiar to the guerilla campaign on the Eastern front or that have not been discussed in any detail before.

## Main Factors

Of those factors peculiar to the Soviet Guerilla Campaign probably the most important and far reaching was that, unlike in most other countries where guerilla resistance developed, a large part of the country remained unoccupied by the enemy throughout the war. The Soviet Government and High Command in Moscow were thus able to provide unified direction and support for the guerillas throughout the campaign, a situation which greatly benefited morale and also ensured the close integration of guerilla operations with those of the Soviet regular forces. Furthermore, the ceaseless internal conflicts which characterised other guerilla movements during this period—opposing political factions, governments in exile out of touch with local feeling, support from allies whose motives were not always disinterested—all these disruptive influences were avoided in this campaign.

A second factor in favour of the Soviets was that probably in no other Guerilla campaign were operations fought over so wide an area or in one that contained such large tracts of country suitable as safe areas for irregular forces. Added to this, but not particular only to the USSR, was the bravery and stamina of the ordinary man, woman and child. Their frugal habits, their facility for improvisation, combined with a native wilyness and capacity to withstand want and hardship made them ideal material for guerillas, and enabled those remaining in the towns and villages to continue to supply the guerillas and oppose by all means possible the demands and the reprisals of the enemy.

The Axis, for their part, faced by a hostile population, found it impossible to protect their tenuous lines of communication adequately, and completely beyond their means ever to collect sufficient forces to surround and destroy the many Russian bands that operated from the extensive forests and marshes that cover much of the Soviet Union. The constant activity of the Soviet Regular Forces on the main front also had much to do with this German inability to concentrate adequate troops against the Soviet guerillas.

Lastly, in the USSR, unlike in most other countries, preparations were made before the German occupation for the development of Guerilla forces in those regions that might be overrun by the enemy.

These were the main factors peculiar to Soviet Guerilla Resistance. Before considering certain other aspects which are of interest, it is necessary to give a short summary of the Soviet guerilla campaign in order that these aspects can be seen in their correct perspective.

## Outline of events

As already mentioned, certain preparations for guerilla resistance were made before the German onslaught. The scope of these preparations appears to have varied greatly in different areas, but generally they included the earmarking of skeleton guerilla bands, and the dumping of food and other essentials in selected safe areas.

The formation of these embryonic bands was linked up with the local Defence Battalions (the equivalent of the British Home Guard) and a certain amount of elementary training in weapons, demolitions and tactics was given. In general, however, when these bands took to the field on the approach of the German forces they were still raw and poorly equipped. Nevertheless they were a nucleus round which guerilla resistance could grow.

It was during the summer and early autumn of 1941 that the Axis armies swept eastwards through the Soviet Union. From the guerillas' viewpoint this was an advantage, as the swamps and forests in which they took refuge were at this time of year almost impassable without local knowledge, and provided excellent cover both from ground and air.

For their part the enemy were fully occupied following up the retreating Soviet forces and organising their ever-lengthening lines of communication. This Axis preoccupation elsewhere not only gave the guerilla bands an opportunity to organise and develop unhindered, but allowed limited operations, such as the ambushing of small enemy detachments and despatch riders, to be carried out with comparative ease. Thus practical experience was gained, and badly needed weapons and equipment obtained. It was also possible during this period for contact to be maintained between guerillas and their local villages which supplied food, stores and intelligence. During these early months bands appear to have acted independently and without aid or direction from outside enemy-occupied territory. Some did little more than exist, others harassed the enemy as best they could.

With the coming of winter, military operations on the main front slackened and the German Command were able to concentrate more troops against the guerillas. By this time the marshes and many of the rivers were frozen and no longer provided obstacles to enemy movement. Cover from ground and air in the forest was also less, as many of the trees were deciduous, and the movement of any force through the snow could be followed by its tracks. There were two further factors that weighed against the guerillas. The first was a tendency by some units to remain in the areas of their recruitment, chiefly on account of family and other ties, and also because of their dependence on their home regions for food and the other necessities of life. Thus full use was not made of the greater security offered by the larger forests. A second factor was the influx into the guerilla bands of many of the local population escaping Nazi ruthlessness. This increase in numbers seriously affected the guerillas' mobility when they did eventually move.

German counter measures thus began to meet with success, and most of those bands that did not disintegrate were in the end forced into the great tracts of forest that cover so much of the country. The enemy tried to follow, but the forests were so vast that the guerillas had little difficulty in evading capture, although in the process they suffered heavily from exposure, and a general lack of food, clothing and equipment.

The winter of 1941–42 was probably the most testing period of the war for the Soviet guerillas. Their withdrawal from their own areas meant a dislocation of their sources of supply, and these were not easily re-organised in the even more sparsely populated regions to which they withdrew. There are signs that their attempts to requisition food from those living in these new areas and from people unknown to them not only caused the local population hardships but also built up considerable antagonism towards the guerillas, who did not hesitate to use force when supplies were not readily forthcoming.

The Germans failed to use this friction to their own advantage. Instead they continued to follow a ruthless policy of reprisals, transportation and confiscations, which had the effect of steadily forcing the Russian peasants into the arms of the guerillas. So far as the latter were concerned, limited activity continued in some areas but their main efforts were concentrated on mere survival. Casualties were as great from starvation and exposure as from enemy action. A number of the smaller and less efficient bands disintegrated but, if Russian descriptions are in any way to be relied upon, the morale and offensive spirit of those remaining seems to have kept high. This appears to have been due to four main causes: good leadership, the guerillas' inherent toughness, a belief in what they were fighting for, and lastly, the fact that, due to the harshness of Axis policy, they had little or nothing to lose and something to gain by continuing to fight against the enemy.

As 1942 advanced, conditions improved for the guerillas, not only on account of the passing of winter but also as a result of the growing weight of Soviet operations on the main front which forced Germans to slacken their counter-guerilla activities. During the spring and summer of 1942 there was a steady development of air supply to the guerillas, and with this came increasing psychological, as well as material support for those in enemy-occupied territory. At first this air support was limited to the dropping of essential weapons, explosives and supplies, but later landing strips were constructed and two-way traffic, including an exchange of personnel, began. Apart from the importance of this liaison from an operational point of view, the Soviet Government made full use of their air links with the Resistance to build up and spread propaganda throughout enemy-occupied USSR.

In spite of the fact that the Germans seem to have been well informed on the growing scale of Soviet air supply operations, there was little they could do to counter it. There were not enough ground troops to take effective counter measures and the air force was already fully committed in its attempt to support the main effort in the east and to deal with the growing bomber offensive in the west. The whole task was made more difficult by the vast areas that the Soviet supply operations covered.

On the Soviet side there now emerged a definite overall guerilla control organisation and chain of command, although of necessity this was of a rather loose nature. Under Supreme Headquarters in Moscow, enemy-occupied territory was split into various Area Commands, such as the Ukraine. These Areas were in turn divided into Guerilla Districts, each containing a number of independent guerilla units. These units varied greatly in size, and as resistance developed some in the larger forest regions had a strength going into hundreds; others were never more than fifty strong. Units were normally sub-divided into bands of ten to thirty.

The Soviet guerillas steadily developed in their safe areas, despite periodic Axis counter activity. The Germans did nothing to strengthen their position in the country by the increasing savagery of their reprisals and other measures against the local population. No quarter was given by either side.

Guerilla columns now began to operate at ever-increasing distances from their bases. They lived mainly off the land, but were also supplied with explosives and other essentials by air from Soviet-held USSR. One such unit under a General Kovpak claimed to have travelled 8,000 miles in twenty-six months, attacking Axis lines of communication and small enemy detachments and moving on before sufficient forces could be concentrated to surround it. The guerilla unit moved mainly at night, sometimes as much as thirty miles, and deceived the enemy by constant changes of direction. These long-range guerilla sorties were linked with the Red Army counter offensive that started in 1942, and the targets that were attacked were directly in support of these. At the same time the guerillas had a second rôle of spreading propaganda amongst the villages through which they passed. Their passage seems to have been a great incentive to the local population, who were by now wholeheartedly behind the guerillas, not only on account of Axis measures against them but also as the result of growing Soviet successes, as broadcast to them through guerilla channels.

With the opening of the Red Army's major offensive in 1943 the Soviet guerilla movement rapidly reached its peak both in strength and activity. By now their operations were being increasingly co-ordinated with those of the Soviet regular forces, as the latter neared the areas of the various guerilla formations. This close co-operation between the regular and irregular Soviet units was made easier by the dispersed and widespread nature of the front, which allowed small bands to move in and out of enemy-occupied territory almost at will. Regular Army officers were thus allotted to the guerillas to ensure that military requirements were understood and satisfied, while partisans were exfiltrated and given the task of leading Soviet Army units through gaps in the German defences and into the enemy rear areas.

While guerillas were giving this close support and providing intelligence in the tactical battle zones, others were pressing westwards to reinforce the activities of those still operating farther to the enemy's rear. Here again General Kovpak in his book 'Our Partisan Armies' gives an example of this deep harassing of the enemy's administrative areas, when he describes how he led his unit into the Carpathians to sabotage lines of communication and industrial plant, while at the same time attempting to increase local resistance against the Axis.

As these tactical and strategic operations continued to be carried out behind the enemy's lines, other guerilla units which had linked up with the advancing Red Armies took over the task of clearing up pockets of enemy resistance left in the wake of the regular formations. Thus there seems no doubt that, in the later stages of the Russian campaign, the Soviet High Command were able to use the guerillas as an auxiliary and comparatively closely integrated arm of their regular military forces. The guerilla movement was in fact frequently referred to as 'The Red Army in the enemy's rear.'

*Organisation and composition*

With this 'Outline of Events' as a background there are certain aspects of Soviet guerilla resistance which are worth studying in more detail. The first of these is the organisation and composition of the movement.

Undoubtedly the pre-war preparations that were made were of considerable importance if only because, despite their limited scope, they did at least bring into existence small guerilla cadres at an early date after the German occupation. It was not, however, until after enemy occupation that the bands developed, and then only spasmodically.

Many of the older generation had taken an active part in the 1917 Revolution and thus had some practical experience of irregular warfare. It was from these that a large proportion of the original guerilla leaders were drawn. They came from many walks of life and as the war progressed and practical experience against the invaders counted for more than past experience, the variety of occupations of those who obtained command became even greater.

The growth of one particular band in the Ukraine is probably typical of many others during the early stages of the German campaign. This band consisted of some four dozen men, mainly civilians but with a sprinkling of Red Army personnel who had been cut off from their units during the retreat. As in most other bands there was a proportion of women, who in the early part of the war were employed mainly as nurses, scouts and cooks. They were, however, armed and as the ruthlessness of the campaign increased and hatred of the Germans mounted these women and girls took an active part in the actual fighting. There are reports of their showing great fortitude both in battle and under interrogation when captured. In the early days, when the Germans neither appreciated the growth of resistance nor had available adequate security forces, contact between the bands in their safe areas and the nearby villages and farms was maintained by women and even children, who at this time were able to move with comparative freedom in enemy-occupied territory.

An acute shortage of weapons and explosives was the greatest problem in the early days, and in the case of the band under consideration there are descriptions of individuals travelling many miles in search of abandoned arms and equipment. The weapons collected were few and of many types. As the war progressed and more and more of the second-line Axis security troops were in turn armed with captured Allied weapons from the Western front, the miscellany of weapons used by the Soviet guerillas increased even more. The ammunition supply problem is self-evident.

A second serious shortage described in the account of the Kovpak band was the lack of technical knowledge. At the beginning there was only one person trained in demolitions. In other bands containing people from industrial, as opposed to agricultural areas, this lack of technicians was not so acute.

It is difficult to generalise on the development of Soviet guerilla units. Some appear to have retained their independence and remained mere bands both in numbers and efficiency. Others, amongst them those that were driven into the larger forest areas by enemy operations in the winter of 1941-42, amalgamated with larger formations, building up their own comprehensive base installations hidden deep in the forests. A description of one such base states that it included a log encampment, with flour mills, vats for soap-making, forges and home-made lathes for the repair and alteration of weapons. In addition to a wireless transmitting and receiving station, there was the inevitable printing works for the production of propaganda material and news sheets.

The higher organisation and control of the Soviet guerillas has already been described. Within the formations and units the Communist Party, as was to be expected, had complete control. The commanders were appointed by the Party, while political commissars were allotted to each detachment. In many bands, if not all, the guerillas had to swear allegiance to the Communist Party.

*Co-operation with local population*

One of the outstanding features of the guerilla campaign in Russia was the degree of co-operation actually reached between the partisans and the civilian population. In fact, it is not too much to say that the Germans must have found the one indistinguishable from the other: for it appears that most men, women and children were either potential or actual partisans. The help given by the local population included food, horses (for transport), clothing and day-to-day intelligence. In addition, villagers frequently provided shelter and concealment for a guerilla although they well knew that it would mean certain death if caught.

This high degree of co-operation did not always exist for, as already mentioned, guerilla requisitioning in the early days caused bitterness and resentment. Later, however, the partisans changed their tactics and seem to have done what they could to distribute food supplies to the starving population. From then on, the relationship between the guerillas and the civil population became increasingly close, a situation which was clearly regarded by the Soviet High Command as of great importance and to be fostered by every possible means. Stalin himself said: 'The most important thing is to maintain even closer links with the people.' Thus an exceptional degree of unity and cohesion was developed between the guerillas, the Red Army and the local population, and this factor undoubtedly contributed very greatly towards the success of the partisans in this campaign.

*Intelligence*

It was as a result of this close relationship with the civilian population that the Soviet guerillas were able to build up what became an exceptionally efficient and widespread intelligence system. With the whole population on their side it was possible for the partisans to get ample warning of intended operations against them, women and children being extensively used to carry messages and obtain information. Certain Soviet technicians had still to be employed by the Germans and these provided a fund of valuable intelligence on enemy rail movements and the like. As the war went on and the rôle of the guerillas in co-operation with the Red Army became more important, so the demand for military intelligence increased. In fact, the obtaining of intelligence for the Red Army formed a major part of their rôle. By this time, the guerillas had W/T sets and qualified operators, and there can be little doubt of the general success achieved. One German corps report expresses amazement because 'the enemy is incredibly well-informed of our troop movements.' German captured documents tell little of the guerillas' intelligence work, but it is fairly certain that the Russian attacks were mounted in those areas which guerilla reports had previously indicated as being vulnerable. Thus the Red Army had the immense advantage of an active intelligence service behind the enemy's front line and in his rear areas.

*Propaganda*

By western standards, probably one of the most remarkable aspects of the guerilla campaign in Russia was the amount of time and effort devoted by the partisans to political propaganda. The unique position of the guerillas in the occupied areas was soon recognised, and exploited by the Communist Party leaders with considerable skill. The partisans were given responsibility for the political education of the people and were directed to transmit news of the Soviet war effort on all fronts as well as instructions from the High Command. Thus the guerillas took on the status of a recognised, responsible army of loyal fighter-propagandists with the right—indeed the duty—to carry the news and instructions of the Communist Party to the population. All reports show that the guerillas carried out this duty well; leaflets and pamphlets were published and distributed on an enormous scale, printing presses were seized and used for propaganda purposes, even the teaching in the schools seems to have been a partisan responsibility. The results of this effort were shown in various ways: in the first place, the Germans were prevented from gaining even a psychological advantage over the Russians; secondly, the unity and loyalty of the guerillas was assured by vesting them with high responsibility and an acknowledged position in the Soviet war effort; and thirdly, the Soviets laid firm foundations for an even closer political integration within the Communist Party after the war.

*Results*

As in so many guerilla campaigns, it is not easy to make an accurate assessment of the results achieved by the Soviet partisans. In this case, the task is made even more difficult by the fact that both Russian and German reports are likely to have been exaggerated, albeit for different reasons. Nevertheless, a good idea of the scale on which partisan operations took place can be gained from these reports. The Russians themselves assert that at one time 1,500,000 partisans were in action, and Lieutenant-General Ponomarenko in his book 'Behind the Front Lines' stated that 'in two years of guerilla warfare in the rear of the German invaders Soviet partisans annihilated more than 300,000 invaders, of whom 30 were generals, 6,336 officers and 1,520 airmen. During the same period 3,000 enemy trains were derailed, and 3,263 rail and road bridges, 1,191 tanks and armoured cars, 476 aeroplanes, 378 guns, 618 staff cars, 4,027 lorries and 895 dumps and warehouses were destroyed.' These figures cannot be checked from German sources but Field-Marshal von Manstein at his court-martial said that he recalled a period in 1944 when nearly a thousand guerilla raids took place during the course of seven hours.

Reading between the lines it is clear that most of these raids were directed against the very long and highly-vulnerable German lines of communication—an ideal target for guerilla operations. German alarm at these continual harassing attacks is clearly reflected in one of Hitler's orders (6th September 1942) where he declared that 'the bands in the east have become an unbearable menace during the last few months and are seriously threatening the supply to the front.'

As already discussed, invaluable assistance was also given to the regular forces by the intelligence which the partisans provided to an increasing degree as the campaign went on. Apart from the physical destruction caused, it is clear that the guerillas severely disrupted the German plans for control of the occupied areas by preventing the local population from collaborating with or working for the Germans. As German reprisals increased, so fuel was given to the Soviet propaganda machine and finally the Germans found themselves with the whole population ranged against them. Indeed the situation of a German soldier, perhaps in an isolated unit in the rear areas under the bitterest of weather conditions, must have been terrifying and it is scarcely surprising that morale suffered greatly.

The Soviet guerilla campaign is noteworthy in that it was fought under almost ideal conditions for that type of warfare. In the first place, the

Russian people were temperamentally and, above all, physically well-suited to the rigours of partisan operations. Secondly, the vast area over which the campaign was fought gave every opportunity for surprise attacks against the German lines of communications, as well as ample space for guerilla manoeuvre and dispersal. Thirdly, the forests and marshes provided excellent cover for the partisans, enabling them to operate from relatively 'firm bases'. Fourthly, the German forces were numerically stretched to the limit and thus were never able to deploy in real strength against the guerillas. Finally—and this is a supremely important factor—the guerillas were united politically and acted throughout in full accordance with the military strategy and political directives of the Soviet High Command.

## Chapter 5

# FAR EAST:
# SECOND WORLD WAR

## (a) Outline of Guerilla Resistance in South-East Asia, 1941–45

*Action before Japanese Invasion*

In May 1941 an SOE Mission arrived in Singapore to aid the local authorities in the build-up of general Resistance against Japanese expansion in the Far East.

As described later in this Chapter, proposals were put forward by this Mission to earmark, train and arm a nucleus of resistance in Malaya as well as certain of the hill tribes in Burma, but both projects were opposed by the local Political Military authorities. Their reasons are given in the relevant Sections which follow.

With the Japanese landings in North Malaya and their rapid drive southwards, SOE were given a freer hand, but time was now too short to do more than sow a few seeds of resistance in Malaya. In Burma, which was not invaded for a further few weeks, more tangible but very limited results were achieved.

By the middle of 1941, the last British troops had withdrawn from Burma, the Chinese had fallen back into Yunnan and beyond, and the Japanese were on the Indian frontier. With resources now stretched to the limit and a Japanese attempt to invade India imminent, there was no thought of any Allied offensive for some time to come, while the chance of any material support for Resistance forces was negligible. It was under these conditions that SOE, by this time concentrated in India, started to plan for the future.

*Factors affecting development of Guerilla Forces*

In doing so the following factors appear to have played an important part. Because of the comparatively undeveloped state of the people of South-East Asia and of the absence of any strong national feelings, it was considered that European leaders for the Guerilla forces would be essential. There was also the possibility of post-war complications, particularly in British territory, if large sections of the populace were armed and trained as partisans. To avoid this risk as much as possible, it was decided that guerillas would only be raised in areas which were well placed to attack worthwhile targets, and even in these regions any organisation would be kept comparatively small. Furthermore, the European leaders should as far as possible be drawn from the future administrators and residents of the country.

As regards the supply of arms and equipment, it was felt that if the full scale was supplied some time in advance the Japanese would suspect the existence of resistance forces, either because of the increased air of activity or because of premature action by the guerillas. As this might result in severe reprisals and the eventual collapse of the movement, it was decided that, except for the small quantities required for training, the bulk of arms and equipment should not be introduced until shortly before active operations were due to start.

*Potential Guerilla organisation*

As a guide for more detailed planning it was visualised that guerilla areas would be divided into zones. Each zone would have a European commander who would control up to five sub-units, each of these comprising some 100 guerillas, trained and led by a BLO. The rôle of these forces would be the dislocation of the Japanese lines of communication by attack on telecommunications, railways, roads and airfields, and the timing of their operations would be closely co-ordinated with the reoccupation of the country concerned by the regular military forces.

*Factors affecting implementation*

The implementation of these plans was affected by two main factors. First, all contact with embryonic Resistance Movements had been lost with the British withdrawal to India. Secondly, not only did the Far East remain for many months low on the list for Allied material aid, but within this theatre SOE does not appear to have enjoyed any priority—perhaps rightly.

In the acute competition for available men and equipment, SOE were at a disadvantage in that they could show no results, while there seems to have been a general ignorance amongst the Military Commanders as to SOE's problems, capabilities and limitations. This in turn appears to have been due to the ultra secrecy with which SOE seems to have shrouded itself at this time. As a result, there was not only a lack of understanding of SOE but also a tendency to distrust its intentions. Records show that General Slim, the Commander of the Fourteenth Army which subsequently reoccupied Burma, was originally amongst those who doubted the value of SOE. That in the end he changed his view and placed considerable reliance on the Burmese guerillas seems largely due to a discussion in January 1945 when SOE's potentials and limitations were explained to him, apparently for the first time.

*Growth of co-ordination*

In the initial phases of the Allied offensive in the Far East one of the greatest needs of South-East Asia Command was intelligence. Much of this was provided by intelligence teams operating from guerilla areas, which provided them with the necessary protection. With this growing contribution by SOE's organisations, appreciation of the latter's value seems to have increased correspondingly. This was particularly so in Burma where, in the later stages of the campaign, the co-ordination between the Army, the Air Forces and the guerillas seems to have been excellent, and the support given to the guerillas by the Armed Services impressive.

The reconquest of Burma, which was completed by the late summer of 1945, coincided with the Japanese surrender. Burma was thus the only country in South-East Asia in which the guerillas fought offensively in their main rôle of supporting the Allied armed forces in their reoccupation of the country. But even though the Malayan guerillas were not put to the final test, their development, organisation and actions during the withdrawal of the Japanese, and during their own disbandment is worth studying. Such a study is also of value as a background against which to consider the post-war activities of the Malayan Communists. For this reason a description of the Malayan Guerilla Movement is given in Section B of this Chapter. Section C covers the story of the guerillas in Burma, and Section D contains a brief description of the SOE organisation that controlled and supplied these forces from India.

## (b) Malaya, 1941–45

(*See Map 11 opposite page 131*)

*Geography*

Malaya is a little larger than England without Wales, and rather smaller than the State of New York. In the centre of the country mountains and hills rise in places to 7,000 feet, and these are surrounded by low-lying ground which extends to the coast. On the west this low-lying belt averages 30 to 40 miles in width for some three-quarters of the peninsula's length. As will be seen from Map 11 some fourfifths of the country is forested. Movement through the greater part of this is possible but slow. It does, however, provide almost complete cover from the air. In the low-lying regions below the foothills there are areas of fresh-water swamp forest that are unhealthy and difficult to penetrate, but nearer the coast it is a healthier zone, in places intensively cultivated and dotted throughout with farming and fishing settlements, particularly on the western seaboard.

The rubber plantations are mainly along the jungle edge and in the foothills, but apart from occasional Malay settlements there were few people in the interior before 1942, except for the shy and retiring Sakai tribes who eked out a meagre existence from small vegetable plantations and by hunting. Particularly in the forests, conditions are enervating, and humidity is high throughout the year. The climate is equatorial and there is little seasonal change in temperature while at any time of the year torrential rain is to be expected; one inch in an hour and fifteen in a day is not uncommon.

## The People

At the time of the Japanese invasion the total population of Malaya was about five and a half million, and of these the two main races were the Malays and the Chinese.

The Malay has been described as the 'Gentleman of the East.' Generally polite, reserved and with a sense of humour, he is easy-going and not particularly interested in money or work.

The Chinese formed by far the most virile and enterprising section of the population, but the majority retained their Chinese character, attended their own schools and still regarded China as their mother country. As the Chinese were the backbone of the subsequent Malayan Guerilla Movement it is worth considering their political history in some detail.

## The political parties (Chinese)

In the years preceding the Second World War the two main Chinese political parties were the Kuomintang (KMT) and the Communists. At first the KMT was all-powerful amongst the Malayan Chinese, but with the drastic purge that took place within the party both in China and Malaya in 1928 and 1929 the more radical elements formed a left wing movement which in time developed into the Malayan Communist Party. Although well organised it was, up to 1937, small and played little part in Chinese Malayan affairs, but the Sino-Japanese war gave it the opportunity to weld all the small left wing factions into a Malayan-wide organisation, with its main political platform the boycotting of Japanese goods and the sending of relief to China. This party emerged as the 'Anti-Enemy Backing-Up Society' (AEBUS), but despite its innocuous title it remained in fact the Communist party, and as such illegal. Nevertheless, it was estimated that by 1940 a good three-quarters of the Chinese in Malaya were at least sympathetic to its aspirations. The old KMT party had by now only a small following. Up to the time of Russia's attack on Finland the activities of AEBUS caused the Government little concern, but with the Russian-Finnish war it became strongly anti-British, and later organised strikes and other means to sabotage the war effort. But when Germany invaded Russia and the Communists in many countries did a rapid *volte-face*, AEBUS was amongst them. It threw its weight on the side of Britain, and offered to recruit volunteers to fight for the Allied cause.

## Invasion preparations and activities

For some time before this, SOE in Singapore had been pressing for permission to build up a stay-behind network in Malaya, and in August 1941 submitted a plan to the C-in-C, Far East, for the organisation of parties of Asians, led by British officers with Malayan experience. In the event of invasion these parties would operate in occupied territory, harassing the enemy's lines of communication, acting as nuclei for raiding parties sent in from unoccupied areas, and providing intelligence for the forces in the field.

The scheme was turned down on the grounds that, apart from the drain on European manpower, Europeans would be unable to operate freely in occupied territory, while the very fact of admitting the possibility of an enemy invasion of the country would have a bad psychological effect on the local inhabitants.

No radical change took place in this policy until after the Japanese had established themselves in Malaya. By then AEBUS had, as already mentioned, offered to recruit volunteers from their members to fight the invader, and in the middle of December it was eventually agreed that a proportion of these should be trained by SOE. They were to be selected by the Central Committee of AEBUS and trained as junior leaders, so that they could be infiltrated into the jungle, with adequate supplies of explosives, arms and food, and each would then form a party of ten to fifteen in their local operational area. During the month of January 1942, one hundred and sixty-five of these Communists were trained by SOE.

The original plan was that they should be sent to selected areas in the Peninsula where Malayan Communist Party support was known to be strong, and with this in view dumps of weapons, demolition equipment and food were hidden in the jungle. But as a result of the speed of the Japanese advance many of the trainees had to be infiltrated well south of their dumps. To find a hidden dump at any time is no easy matter, but under the conditions then existing, coupled with the fact that the average Malayan guerilla had little idea of finding direction, most of the dumps were never recovered. There was, however, no dearth of volunteers in the selected areas and the small parties of ten to fifteen, which it was hoped could be raised, were formed without difficulty. These became the framework on which the future guerilla movement in Malaya was eventually built.

In addition to the above, preparations were hastily made for the tasks intended in the original SOE scheme for British led Asian parties to be carried out by British personnel only. Arms, stores and demolitions were dumped in four areas still held by the British but due to lack of time and other reasons only one party under Major Chapman ever went into action. For the two weeks preceding the fall of Singapore Chapman and his two companions operated in North Selangor against the Japanese lines of communication with very considerable success. That this could be achieved by a solitary party, without casualties to themselves, shows what might have been accomplished with adequate numbers properly trained and equipped. With the fall of Singapore and the end of all organised resistance in Malaya further harassing of enemy communications became useless and Chapman's party joined the Communist bands in the jungle.

*Early SOE difficulties*

To SOE, who had by now withdrawn to India, the fate of Chapman and conditions within enemy occupied Malaya remained for many months a closed book, as Chapman's wireless set was wrecked beyond repair and the

Malayan guerillas had none. On the assumption, however, that a guerilla movement was now in being with the Malayan Communist Party as its framework, efforts were made to form teams to infiltrate into Malaya and regain contact. It was decided that these teams should consist of British officers and Chinese. With considerable difficulty a limited number of British officers with Malayan experience were made available, but exhaustive search in India, the United Kingdom and even farther afield failed to find suitable Chinese. Eventually a number of KMT Chinese had to be recruited through the Central Chinese Government, despite their anti-Communist views. They came on the understanding that they were prepared to contact any guerilla force in Malaya that was resisting the Japanese. The disadvantages of such a compromise were obvious but there appears to have been no alternative. As it was, the first team did not start training in India until November 1942, some nine months after the fall of Singapore.

*Methods of infiltration considered*

The transportation of these teams also raised major problems, and a number of alternative methods were explored. Overland through Burma and down the coast by local craft had to be ruled out on account of the presence in the party of BLOs, while a proposal to infiltrate them through the Netherlands East Indies was finally considered to be too uncertain. Aircraft and flying boats with the necessary range were at this time practically unobtainable.

There only remained submarines, of which there were very few and all were fully employed, not only on their normal duties but also in satisfying the demands of other organisations requiring personnel to be moved to and from enemy-occupied territories. There were other reasons why the Royal Navy was understandably most reluctant to provide submarines for SOE's nefarious tasks, for, in order to make room for SOE personnel and stores they were often forced to carry a reduced number of torpedoes. Furthermore, they were unable to attack shipping on the way to the RV and in addition took a grave risk in coming close inshore along the shallow west coast of Malaya. A further complication was the fact that, owing to condensation of moisture in the submarine, the outboard motors used to ferry the long distances from craft to shore invariably failed to start.

From SOE's viewpoint also this method of transport had its disadvantages. The long voyage under trying conditions was exhausting to agents and even after a successful landing there was still the long, difficult and dangerous journey inland. Lastly, only a few men and limited quantities of equipment could be carried by this means.

*First contact, May 1943*

Despite these disadvantages it was from a Dutch submarine that the first party of one BLO (Captain Davis), five Chinese and a wireless were landed on the Perak coast in May 1943. The set had to be dumped but the party successfully crossed the coastal belt and established contact with the

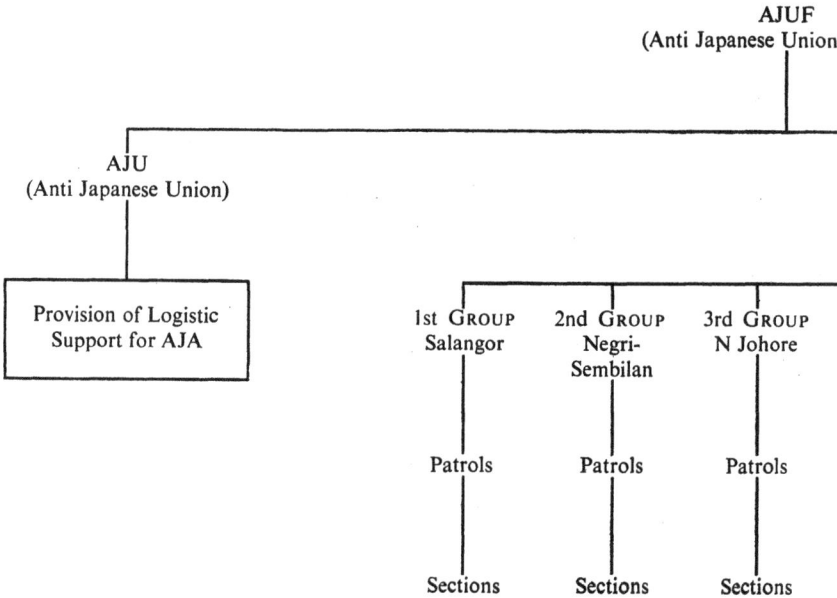

uring the Second World War

Forces)

```
                              AJA
                       (Anti Japanese Army)
                              |
  ┌───────────┬───────────┬───────────┬───────────┬───────────┐
th GROUP   5th GROUP   6th GROUP   7th GROUP   8th GROUP
S Johore    Perak      W Pahang    E Pahang    Kedah
   |          |           |           |           |
Patrols    Patrols     Patrols     Patrols     Patrols
   |          |           |           |           |
Sections   Sections    Sections    Sections    Sections
```

guerillas in the jungle. A month later in accordance with arrangements made before the party left for Malaya, Davis and one Chinese were brought back by submarine to report on the situation. This report gave the first reliable news from Malaya since its evacuation in February 1942.

*Malayan Guerilla organisation (see Table 3 opposite)*

During the year and a half that had elapsed the various anti-Japanese factions in Malaya had, with the exception of the KMT, united under the leadership of the Malayan Communist Party, and had become known as the Anti-Japanese Union and Forces (AJUF). As the AJUF developed it formed two main branches, the Anti-Japanese Union (AJU) and the Anti-Japanese Army (AJA). The AJU consisted of Chinese who, although not taking up arms openly against the Japanese, were prepared to aid the AJA with supplies and food. The AJA grew up round SOE trained Communists and their original small parties. These formed camps in the jungle and became the guerilla forces of the AJUF. Placed geographically between the AJA in the jungle and the AJU outside, were numbers of Chinese who lived in the settlements on the jungle edge and acted as the liaison link between AJA and AJU, and were also used by the AJA as a warning screen.

Following normal Communist practice AJA was strictly controlled by a Central Executive Committee under whom it was organised into eight Regional Groups, each with its own Headquarters.\* The Groups themselves were split into a number of camps hidden in the jungle. In each camp there was normally one patrol, varying from 50 to 100 men; the patrols in turn were divided into sections of some ten men each.

*AJA control and composition*

All policy matters had to be referred to the Central Executive Committee and even on other questions, such as liaison between Groups, the Group Headquarters were allowed little latitude, while the Patrol HQs had none. There was a general tendency to avoid taking independent action. The shortcomings of this extreme centralisation were increased, first because the Central Executive seldom met as a Committee, and secondly through the slowness and inefficiency of communications. These depended entirely on runners, and as patrols were days, and Groups weeks and sometimes months, apart, authority seldom reached those concerned in time to be of use, even if it ever started. Chapman and other British officers, who joined the guerillas when it became useless to continue their isolated attacks against the Japanese, found this particularly galling as none of the patrols or groups with whom they worked would take any initiative without authority from above.

Both Group and Patrol Headquarters had much the same composition. The four main characters were: the political head, whose power was

---

\* See Map 11 opposite page 133.

absolute, and who was a full Party Member; the military commander, who in fact had only limited authority and was not always a Member; the administrative head; and lastly an individual who generally combined the duties of propaganda and instruction. The latter appears to have been in many cases a narrow but clever and fanatical Communist. In addition to his other tasks he produced the various news sheets and propaganda literature both for the camps and outside, as throughout the war there was an insidious and in some cases successful Communist approach to all with whom they came in contact.

The proportion of actual Communist Party members with AJA was said to be small, possibly 10–15 per cent. Some 95 per cent. of the men in AJA were coolies and labourers from the rubber plantations, the mines and the vegetable gardens, and were of low intelligence. There was thus an acute shortage of junior leaders.

The forest camps in which the AJA lived consisted of a number of bamboo shelters built near running water and in an inaccessible part of the jungle, some two to three hours' march from the nearest settlement. They were usually in high, broken country, well sited for defence, with an ill-marked, difficult and steep approach. Down this, and some fifteen minutes from the camp area, a section was normally sited to provide sufficient warning for the patrol to disperse into the jungle with the more important items of camp equipment.

*Administrative problems*

Food was scarce and monotonous. It consisted mainly of rice or substitutes, with an occasional meal of meat or fish when all went well. Most of their supplies had to be provided from outside by AJU. This required an extensive organisation whereby the supplies were collected from the various sources, centralised and carried into the jungle by AJU workers. Here they were dumped, and collected for the final stage to the camp by the guerillas themselves.

Such an organisation took time to build up and thus, although the guerillas and most of their equipment usually escaped capture, any attack which necessitated a change of their camp area was a severe blow, as their supply lines were broken. Until new ones could be organised they were forced to fall back on what limited reserves they might be able to save and on the meagre supplies that the Sakai could give them. As time passed, anything but the bare necessities of life became increasingly hard to obtain in Malaya, and prices soared. Thus the money raised from the camps by AJU, mainly through countless small subscriptions from the coolie class, could buy little, even if the goods were available.

Lack of medicines was another serious matter for quinine, aspirin, iodine and the like became unobtainable. Many of the guerillas, however, were knowledgeable in the medicinal use of jungle leaves and roots and these became their main standby. There was on an average one Chinese doctor to each group, and most patrols were in touch with one outside the jungle. Fevers and poisoned wounds were common, with the British personnel as the chief sufferers. Amongst the latter constant bouts of malaria and the effects of blood poisoning, combined with under-nourishment and a lowering of morale, took their toll and only the physically and mentally strong lived to tell the tale.

*Morale and propaganda*

Despite these hardships, and the absence of offensive action, the morale of the guerillas in the camps remained high. Most of them were young and everyone concerned reported that there was no question as to their courage and constant cheerfulness. Their high morale seems due in large measure to the fact that they were kept fully employed, and in most cases were receiving what they had never received before, a free education, albeit tainted with Communism. From 5.30 in the morning until 8.30 or later in the evening, they were kept constantly employed either physically or mentally. Much of this time was used for direct and indirect Communist indoctrination, but training, language classes in Mandarin, general education and games were also included.

The Communist propaganda within the camps was extremely efficient. Apart from continually confronting the men with slogans and subjecting them to a flow of political lectures and pep talks, a fortnightly paper was published with articles and colour drawings by the various leaders. Singing and plays were also extensively used as a vehicle for propaganda. As no wireless receivers were available, outside news was unobtainable, except for the wildly distorted claims of the Japanese papers. The news service was therefore poor and did little to put the Western Allies on the map, although the might of Soviet arms was constantly vaunted. The men, with no educational background and nothing to lose by Communism, inevitably accepted what they were told, but BLOs who lived with them considered that the majority would have been content to return to their families and to security and easier living conditions under whatever Government would provide these. AJA hatred of the Japanese was intense and the cold-blooded massacres carried out by the latter in their attempts to obtain information about the location of camps merely accentuated this.

*Training and discipline*

So far as training was concerned there was, in the early days, an almost universal ignorance of even the most elementary subjects. The exceptions were the SOE trained guerillas, but very few of these were capable of passing on their knowledge. It thus fell to Chapman and the other British who took refuge with the guerillas to try to bridge this gap, and most of their long sojourn with AJA was spent moving from camp to camp, training. Their constant ill-health was not the least of their difficulties. Lack of weapons was another, for with many of the SOE dumps still undiscovered and others raided before AJA could make use of them, they had to rely on abandoned British arms and many of these, when found, were almost useless. Possibly their greatest problem was the Chinese fear of losing face, and Chapman has described the absurd picture of the leaders in one camp being surreptitiously trained by him in the dead of night, when their men were in bed, for fear that the latter might think that their officers were ignorant.

In all camps which had good and effective communications with Group Headquarters, and came under their control, the discipline was severe. It followed normal Communist lines. All orders were discussed. Any man could bring a charge against another; the matter would then be debated in session and the sentence decided by majority vote, though this could be overridden by Headquarters. With the acute shortage of leaders these methods not only resulted in failure to take action but made junior and sometimes senior leaders frightened of giving definite orders. While punishments for minor offences ranged from cutting down rations to depriving a man of his weapons, the death penalty was passed for what, by non-Communist standards, would appear to be comparatively minor crimes. These included stealing AJUF property or that of outside helpers, and in one case a man was sentenced to death for selling an AJA bicycle. Despite these characteristics, the discipline was, according to reports, well-suited to the AJA rank and file, who were described as having the outlook of Boy Scouts rather than that of an adult community.

Although morale was generally good a number of AJA personnel did become disillusioned over the months and then deserted. Some of these became informers, but owing to the strict security imposed on all ranks their knowledge was generally limited to that of their own camps. Few of the officers, even at Group Headquarters, knew the location of Central Headquarters, while the rank and file seldom knew the situation of other Groups and camps. Runners were normally kept to one specific route for security reasons, and discussions of other unit locations was forbidden. In order to deal with those deserters who escaped the retribution of their own patrols, traitor-killing bands were set up, whose task was to track down and kill anyone known to be helping the Japanese against the AJUF.

On the other hand there never appears to have been a dearth of recruits, and men and women of all callings offered to join the guerillas, particularly when Japanese atrocities became excessive or living conditions outside deteriorated. Few but Chinese were accepted for either AJA or AJU.

*Attempts to contact AJA, 1943–1944*

This then was the general position when in June 1943 Davis provided the first contact with the AJA since the fall of Malaya in February 1942.

In August 1943 Davis returned to Malaya and in the following month a second BLO followed, but the latter's trans-shipment was so hurried owing to the submarine commander's keenness to chase an enemy convoy, that much of the equipment was left on board the submarine. After a hazardous crossing of the plain both officers eventually reached the AJA, but without any wireless. Neither were they able to get to the coast again on account of Japanese activity. Thus none of the monthly RVs with submarines, which had previously been arranged, could be kept.

The RV was, in fact, compromised and on one occasion the submarine was heavily attacked. Without contact with AJA and with no means of finding out Davis's fate, SOE had no alternative but to abandon further attempts to infiltrate personnel by submarine, at any rate for the time being.

There now followed a gap of a year during which SOE tried unsuccessfully to regain contact.

*Events in Malaya, 1943–1944*

Meanwhile much happened to Davis and his companions in Perak. One of the former's main tasks was to draw up some co-ordinated plan of action with the Central Committee of the AJUF. It was not, however, until December 1943 that he achieved a meeting with this Committee, but an agreement was then signed by Davis as the representative of Supreme Allied Commander South-East Asia (SACSEA) and a representative of the Central Committee.

By this agreement AJA agreed to accept the orders and instructions of SACSEA, through BLOs who would be dropped to the various Groups. In return AJA would be supplied with arms, ammunition and explosives on an agreed scale; with foodstuffs when the airlift would permit, and with a subsidy amounting to the equivalent of some £3,000 a month. This agreement was to remain valid during the period of hostilities and until the end of military occupation.

There was no way of getting news of this agreement to India as Japanese activity in the coastal belt still made it impossible to get the wireless sets up to the jungle, or the BLOs to the coast. The Japanese also found one of the dumps on the coast and with the help of informers turned their attention on to the Perak patrols. For the next few months they harried these from camp to camp, while the British officers, now short of European foods and medicine, were constantly ill. Amongst other misfortunes that befell Davis was the capture by the Japanese of his generator and batteries, just after these with the greatest difficulty had been smuggled across the western plain. Months of searching for substitute equipment followed.

*Improved position, 1944*

In October 1944, however, a party which had been sent by way of Australia was successfully put ashore on the South-East coast of Johore, and having joined the Fourth Group of the AJA made contact some ten days later with SOE Headquarters. It was then learnt that Davis, Chapman and the other BLOs were alive and with the Fifth Group in Perak.

Another major step forward at this time was the allotment of a squadron of Liberators with the necessary range from India to Malaya and back. As preparations were being made to drop in a party blind to contact Davis, the latter came on the air. By improvisation, pilfering batteries from the Japanese and by great perseverance they had made their set work. After five days of transmitting, his signals were picked up by SOE, who, at first suspicious, were eventually satisfied by a series of improvised security checks that Davis and his companions were free agents.

*Development of Policy and Plans*

With the re-opening of communications between SOE and Davis's party it became possible for the first time to start practical planning for the build-up of the Malayan Guerilla Movement, in the knowledge that the latter were willing to support the Allied landings for the re-occupation of Malaya.

The immediate military advantages in pressing forward the equipment of the AJA were great. On the other hand there was always the risk that the arms obtained would be used later for political ends. Because of these two conflicting factors the policy decided upon, after considerable discussion between the military and political authorities, was to arm certain of the guerillas, but at the same time to ensure that all possible safeguards were taken for the return of the weapons at the end of hostilities. In addition, the Chiefs of Staff stressed the importance of encouraging Malay-manned resistance units as much as possible in order to avoid creating the impression that HMG was supporting the Chinese alone.

In the light of this policy it was decided to send Liaison Teams to certain selected AJA and Malay units, as well as to some KMT bands which were operating in the north. These Liaison Teams consisted of British officers and the nationals concerned, together with the necessary wireless equipment and operators. Their tasks were to help train and organise the various groups, to control the supply of arms and equipment to them, and to keep SACSEA informed of their development. In addition, the British officers were to take over command whenever possible.

The initial build-up plan for the guerillas was based on the date of readiness being the end of November 1945, and envisaged only the minimum of arms and ammunition necessary for training purposes being delivered until the two months before the invasion. From the first it was doubtful whether the RAF would have the resources to deal with the greatly increased airlift this would entail during October and November, but in any case the whole plan had to be radically altered when the date of readiness was advanced to the middle of August.

This meant a great acceleration in the packing of stores and the procurement of personnel: the latter, particularly wireless operators, being SOE's greatest problem. It also became obvious that the comparatively modest aim of training and arming 3,500 guerillas by the new date of readiness would not be attained with the existing airlift. Accordingly, two squadrons of heavy bombers, which were to provide support for the Malayan invasion from bases in the Cocos Islands, were now used on the guerilla airlift in addition to their mining and bombing duties.

The setting up of yet another loading base for these bombers caused further difficulties but, once in action, they were cited as having carried out some of the most accurate drops that took place in Malaya. All reports speak of the whole-hearted efforts of the RAF to meet this radical change in the airlift required. Their greatest difficulty was the extreme ranges at which they had to operate, for flights varied between 2,500 and 3,500 miles. At first their loads were limited, but these and the distances flown were gradually increased and the safety margin of petrol reduced, until a record was achieved of a twenty-four and a half hour flight at the end of which the aircraft landed at base with approximately fifty gallons of petrol in its tanks. There was little enemy air activity, and it was thus possible to drop at last light, risking a daylight approach but using darkness for the return trip. This avoided dependence on the moon and greatly increased the number of sorties that could be flown.

*Guerilla Development, 1945*

The build-up of the AJA developed steadily but slowly. By the end of July Liaison Teams of one or more BLOs, a wireless operator and an interpreter had been dropped to seven Group and twenty-seven Patrol Headquarters. Some 2,000 weapons, together with grenades, explosives and stores had also been flown in, together with three Gurkha Support Groups.

These Gurkha Support Groups had originally been formed early in 1944 so that they could be infiltrated into Malaya with the object of locating the large numbers of Gurkha prisoners of war who were believed to exist, and if possible to release and form these into guerilla units. Since this original conception they had been formed into twelve support groups, each consisting of one officer and sixteen Gurkhas, with a wireless operator. These support groups, who were dropped to the AJA in Perak and Kedah—and later elsewhere—provided small, highly trained and disciplined units which were of considerable value, not only as an operational and training reinforcement, but also as a controlling influence over the guerillas. Their relations with the Chinese appear to have been universally good.

One major complication had not been foreseen during the planning stage. Previously AJA had been able to provide its own food—a task which was achieved by employing large numbers from each patrol on the supply lines, on foraging duties, or on the actual growing of food. But with everyone fully committed to training, AJA could no longer remain self-supporting and therefore, in the airlift to many patrols, food had to be substituted for arms and equipment.

Progress varied considerably in different groups, the main factors being their varying distances from base, the dates on which British Liaison Teams reached them, and the degree of organisation within the patrols at the time of the BLO's arrival and the opening up of air supply. By August 1945 it was estimated that there were in all some 4,000 to 4,500 AJA under arms in Malaya. With a few exceptions relations between them and the Liaison

Teams remained good throughout the period of preparation. Nevertheless, the question of their own status and the general post-war Allied policy in Malaya was by now one of AJA's chief concerns, and the inability of the BLOs to provide an answer tended to cast doubts on British post-war intentions. For reasons outside the scope of this history no declaration of policy was available. In order to provide some answer for the BLOs, they were directed to point out that their rôle was purely military—that of training, arming and equipping the AJA—and that politics did not come within their charter.

In addition to the AJA units, contact had also been made with KMT guerillas in North Malaya and these were being organised and equipped on similar lines to the AJA. The policy of these KMT bands appears to have been to fight the Japanese, when the chance occurred, and the AJA wherever their interests clashed. Small groups of Malays, with BLO teams, were also now organised in North Perak and Kedah, but these were considered more suited for an intelligence than a guerilla rôle. Finally, throughout Malaya there were numerous small bandit gangs armed with weapons collected during the Malayan campaign. Although these bandits occasionally clashed with the Japanese their main concern was loot and robbery. Some are said to have joined the AJA, but the majority continued to exist on their own, claiming to be AJA or KMT as suited them best. From reports they seem to have been excellent guerilla material, tough, efficient with their weapons, ruthless but cheerful. A BLO was attached to one such gang in Northern Perak, with the unenviable task of guiding its activities into operations against the Japanese.

*Guerilla tasks*

These, then, were the guerilla forces which were available to support the Allied Task Force in its reoccupation of Malaya. During the preparatory phase their main rôle was limited to the provision of intelligence on enemy movements, orders of battle and dispositions. From D-day onwards their task was to support the Allied operations, primarily by attacking Japanese communications.

So far as their task of providing intelligence was concerned, AJA had all the shortcomings noted in guerilla forces in other countries. Not only had they no idea of what constituted good military intelligence, but they showed little interest in obtaining any information that did not directly concern themselves. But despite their limited value as a source of intelligence, they proved of use as protection for other organisations sent into the country for its collection. An example of this was the operation of an Observation Post from an AJA-held area overlooking the Straits of Johore, which produced a mass of valuable information on enemy shipping.

In the initial planning for the invasion of Malaya the D-day tasks and subsequent commitments of the guerillas were limited to mobile operations against the enemy's communications and rear areas. These tasks were well suited to AJA's capabilities and to the country in which they would be operating, but with the approach of D-day and the preparation of detailed plans, demands were made by the Army for the guerillas to carry out a number of anti-scorch operations. Many of these operations were in towns and other populated areas on the coast which it would have been impossible for AJA units to reach, far less to defend against regular Japanese troops.

*The guerillas' value*

AJA were never put to the full test as Japan surrendered before D-day; but some idea can be gained as to the possible value of the guerillas' support from the following factors. First, the Japanese had been led to believe that the Allied main landings would take place on the Kedah coast and had concentrated their forces there. In fact the Allied bridgehead was to be made much further to the south.

Between these two areas there was one main road and one railway, both of which were in range of the best-trained and best-equipped AJA Group, the Fifth. In addition to this, other AJA units were well placed on all other main communications down the length of the Malayan Peninsula. Secondly, as had already been proved by Chapman in 1942, the country itself was ideal for attacks by small bands against troops moving along the restricted main routes from north to south. Thirdly, determined efforts by the Japanese to wipe out the AJA in Perak and South Johore had already failed, while AJA morale was as high as that of the Japanese was low. Lastly, the successes of these same guerillas against the British some years later testify to their capabilities.

So it would seem that, had the Allies been forced to fight their way back into Malaya, the guerillas' contribution would have been well worth the men, aircraft and supplies that were switched from other tasks to build this movement into a reasonable fighting force. Some idea of that effort can be gained from the following figures. Up to June 1945 some 76 tons of weapons, explosives, equipment and other supplies were dropped into Malaya. On the personnel side 102 BLOs, 56 British other ranks, 134 Gurkhas, some 70 Asians and approximately 50 wireless stations had been infiltrated by various means, up to the time of the Japanese surrender. Further statistics as to the effort required at Base are given in Section D of this Chapter.

*After the surrender, August 1945*

The 'Cease Fire' became effective on 17th August 1945 but, although the Japanese as a nation had officially surrendered, it was not known what the reactions of their troops in Malaya would be, particularly since the Japanese commander in Singapore had announced over the radio that he would fight. So in order to avoid clashes and unnecessary bloodshed, BLOs were instructed to do everything possible to keep the guerillas out of all towns and districts where Japanese were present, until the arrival of Allied troops.

There was also the risk that in the vacuum before a Military Administration, backed by an Allied force could take over, AJUF would take the law into their own hands and usurp the function of Government themselves. Matters were made more difficult, both for SEAC and the BLOs in the field during this transitional period, by the fact that it was still not possible to make known the Allied policy for the future of Malaya, nor even the line that should be followed regarding AJUF and its Communist associations. With so little guidance the BLOs with AJA cannot have had an easy time but, as a general rule, the guerillas seem to have shown considerable forebearance during this period of uncertainty.

By the beginning of September AJA units had, wherever possible, come under the local Allied Force Commanders and were being maintained, paid and rationed by them. The Military Administration was also beginning to function, and the delicate period between the Japanese surrender and the start of Allied control had passed. There were, however, a number of guerilla units still at large. Some were AJA patrols with which SOE officers had not made contact, others were merely bandits, but whatever their complexion there was the risk that some or all would take to the jungle, or at least hide their arms. In an attempt to entice these under British control, it was declared that any alleged guerilla who produced an effective firearm would, if he applied before the day of disbandment, be accepted into any guerilla patrol that was under British command. By doing this he would receive clothing, food and 30 dollars per month in pay. Results appear to have been satisfactory.

The date of disbandment was fixed for the 1st December 1945. By making it some months in advance it was hoped that those concerned would have a better chance of finding suitable civilian employment, assisted where possible by the British Military Administration.

In the meantime AJA continued to carry out various military duties, and during this period there were instances of friction between them and the Military and Civil Administration. In the main this discord seems to have been due to misunderstandings and to a tendency on the part of the Allies to expect normal military discipline from the guerillas, although there were instances where extremist elements did attempt to create disturbances and organise strikes and demonstrations.

*Disbandment of guerilla forces*

For disbandment all patrols were concentrated at the main towns in their Group Areas. Here on the 1st December the main event was a ceremonial parade before the local senior Allied Commander. On the ensuing days arms were handed in and each man then received his documents, a final gratuity of (Straits) $350, and was dispatched to his home.

As regards the surrender of arms, some check was available as BLOs were supposed to have kept a written record of those weapons that had been issued through British Liaison Teams. It was against this register that the arms now surrendered were checked. The result on paper was satisfactory, as a greater total was handed in than the number of weapons originally issued by BLOs, but no account could be taken of the large number of abandoned British arms collected by AJA and others during and after the British retreat in 1942. There were also those arms that had been dropped in wrong areas during air supply operations, of which the BLOs could have no record. Many of these were retained, as later events showed. The disbandment itself was completed without any major incidents except that some 100 KMT guerillas absconded, with their arms, across the Thailand border.

Many of the guerillas were young men who had little education and therefore had no background knowledge with which to counter the Communist doctrines and teaching given them during their time with the AJA. There was the further risk that, left to their own resources, they would find it difficult to obtain suitable occupations. This proved to be the case and combined with their previous Communist instruction, made them ripe material for the political agitators who, even at this early period, were becoming active.

## (c) Burma 1942–1945

(*See Map 12 opposite*)

*Guerilla Operations, 1942*

It was not until December 1941 that SOE officers arrived in Burma and set about the task of raising a Guerilla Force. That same month Malaya was invaded and by February, not only had Singapore fallen but the Japanese drive into Burma, across the Thai border, had flung the British forces to the west of the Sittang River. As a result, there had been little time and still less equipment for organising resistance by the local Burmese people.

Some 1,500 Karens had been partially armed and trained in the hills to the east of Sittang, and these gave a good account of themselves during the British retreat. They provided information and some security for the Army's left flank, and also delayed the Japanese advance eastwards towards Toungoo for some 48 hours. But with the retreat of the Chinese forces up the Salween River into Yunnan and the British retreat north-westwards towards the Chindwin River, it was obvious that they could be given no further support. They were, therefore, instructed to bury their arms, lie low and await the return of the Allies, while their SOE officers were told to withdraw northwards.

North-east of the Karens, in the mountains near Kengtong, another small guerilla band had been raised from among the Shan tribes. They continued to carry out pin-prick raids on the Japanese until their only BLO was killed in October 1942. In the extreme north—in the Katchin Hills—other guerilla units were partially organised and helped to cover the withdrawal of the last elements of the Army and civilian refugees from north-west Burma. They also damaged three bridges on the main Japanese line of advance towards Fort Hertz.

By the end of April, however, the British Army had withdrawn over the Indian frontier towards Imphal and, with no prospect of Allied help for some time to come, further guerilla activity was considered useless. Although it had been impossible to achieve much in the short time and with the limited resources available, events had shown that a number of the hill tribes were suitable and willing to fight the Japanese, provided they were given equipment and were well led.

*The people and country*

These tribes inhabited the semi-circle of jungle-clad hills and mountains that curve from just north-east of the Irrawaddy delta around Burma's northern borders and to the south as far as Moulmein.

Taking these hill tribes in a clockwise direction, the first are the Chins, in the north-west, a physically well-developed people who had for many years before the war been considered good material for the Burma Army. From an Allied viewpoint their main disadvantage was the wide variety of languages and dialects spoken. Living in very hilly and heavily forested country they were expert in jungle-craft and readily took to modern weapons. The next group of note were the Katchins in the northern apex of Burma, on the border of Tibet, and extending down the China frontier to Lashio. Unlike the Chins they had one common language. Their past history was one of feuds and fighting, and they had readily taken up arms again.

Both the Chins and the Katchins originally came from the cold and arid lands of Tibet, but the Shans who lay to their south were mainly of Thai origin. Their country, the Shan plateau, is much less forested and more agricultural. These facts probably account for their softer and less warlike disposition, for they are a friendly and easy-going people who, although hunters and used to firearms, were never previously regarded as good fighting material.

As with the Chins the term Shan embraced a number of sub-tribes, all with their different dialects.

The last large hill group, the Karens, also came from the east and are of Thai/Chinese origin. Even though their previous record for strife did not compare with that of the warlike Katchins, they had always been regarded as good soldiers on account of their ready acceptance of discipline and comparatively high standard of intelligence and education. Their resistance to the Japanese in the opening stages of the British withdrawal had enhanced their reputation. Furthermore, they lay astride the Japanese main lines of communication from Thailand.

There was little or no interest in politics amongst the hill tribes. Simple and in many ways backward, they willingly acknowledged a loyalty to their chiefs and through them to Britain and the King-Emperor. This loyalty was no doubt tinged with self-interest, as they knew that they were minority communities whose lot would be uncertain if left to the mercies of the plains-dwelling Burmans. Christianity had made considerable strides amongst all but the Chins, and there were numerous Protestant and Catholic Missions working among the hill tribes. Because of these trends not only were there strong ties between the people and Britain as the Paramount Power, but there had also been a strengthening of character and a marked educational development. This growth was most evident amongst the Karens.

As a rough estimate of numbers the Chins totalled some 50,000, the Katchins about 150,000, the Shans 1,000,000 and the Karens rather more. Of the latter, however, nearly half lived in the Central basin on the lower reaches of the Irrawaddy.

This wide Central basin, which is drained by the Irrawaddy and Sittang Rivers, covers the whole of Central Burma from the coast in the south to as far north as Katha. Its central area is open country but to the south and on its other fringes there are areas of jungle, the largest of which is the Pegu Yomas between the Sittang and Irrawaddy, north of Rangoon.

The chief inhabitants of this Central basin are the Burmans, numbering about 10 millions. Although of Tibetan descent their long sojourn in the plains had sapped what original energy they may have possessed. They were in general neither so vigorous nor so simple-minded as the hill tribes. Through the influence of the Buddhist priests literacy had always been high, and commerce with the West had left its mark. Many relished politics and amongst the more vociferous there was a constant demand for independence from Britain. The more extreme were prepared to support Japanese intervention, believing that this would in the end lead to Burma's independence. These extremists went by the name of the Thakin party, a number of whom had in 1941 been trained in Thailand by the Japanese. These returned with the occupation forces and actively assisted in the expulsion of the Allies from Burma.

*The difficult period, 1943–1944*

With the withdrawal of the Allies from Burma contact with the loyal hill tribes was temporarily lost, as SOE recalled their BLOs. This was done as it was felt that they could do little good until a clear-cut plan for the development and employment of Burmese Resistance could be put into effect. It was also considered that the presence of Europeans would soon become known to the enemy and would bring down reprisals on the local and very poorly-armed inhabitants, while much of the country itself was malarial and unhealthy for Europeans to live in for any length of time, particularly under the conditions forced upon BLOs.

The earliest comprehensive plan for the development of Burmese Resistance is dated August 1942. It envisaged a number of bases, specially selected as suitable for BLOs, in the forested hills around Burma's perimeter. From these British staffed centres, native officers and men would infiltrate into the surrounding areas in order to expand and build up the guerilla forces.

The strategic importance of the Karen hills has already been touched upon. This was in fact the most favourable area in Burma for guerilla operations. First, as a base against communications, these hills overlooked the main road and rail communications between Rangoon and Mandalay; they were astride the roads from Toungoo and up the Salween Valley to the north-east and they commanded a number of the routes into Thailand. Secondly, the country itself was very hilly and difficult of access, while, thirdly, it contained a race that had already shown its willingness and suitability for guerilla operations.

To start organising a guerilla force in this area a Karen officer and a small team were landed by parachute in the hills east of Toungoo during February 1943. It was intended that their W/T set would follow a few days later when they had formed some sort of reception committee. Subsequently BLOs and other W/T stations were to be dropped in. But despite constant attempts during each moon period the original W/T set had still not been delivered by September, seven months later.

The chief cause for this failure was the weather, combined with the difficulty of recognising the dropping zone, which was typical of the DZs in most of the jungle-clad hill areas. They were mainly small patches of paddy, seldom more than 800 yards by 400 yards and generally in narrow valleys with hills as high as 400 ft. on each side. In the dry season the ground and the climate combined to produce a ground mist after dark, while in May, when the monsoon broke, the hills were shrouded in clouds for days on end. These conditions continued till the end of the monsoon in September or October.

During this long drawn-out failure to get in touch with the Karens by air, plans were started to build up a clandestine land route to them and, with this in view, contact was successfully established with the Katchins—in the spring of 1943—by one of their own officers. From then until September 1944 liaison with these tribes, who remained loyal throughout, was steadily expanded. No effort was made to operate offensively during this period as it was considered that this safe area was of more value as a source of intelligence and as the first link in the clandestine route to the Karens.

The second obvious link in this overland route was the Shan tribal area to the south of the Katchins. Here, however, the country is less suitable for guerilla operations, as the Shan plateau, which stretches from Lashio in the north to the Karen hills in the south, is mostly composed of open rolling country where the road system is relatively well developed. Further, the Shans as a whole were not considered good guerilla material on account of their somewhat pliable and easy-going nature. For these reasons no effort was made during 1943 and 1944 to make contact with the Shans themselves, although a forward base was established in their area on the Burma-China border north of Kengtung. The object of this base was twofold: first, to provide the link in the Karen route and, secondly, to be the springboard from which to renew contact with the tougher North Shan sub-tribes, who had continued to fight the Japanese until their BLO was killed in October 1942.

In the west two other bases were set up, one in the Chin hills, and the other further north near Tamu, in the Naga Hills south-east of Imphal. Through these it was hoped, with the help of the friendly Burmese, to build up an alternative route to the Karen Hills and Thailand across the Central basin of Burma. The base near Tamu is of interest, as an operational training centre was developed here. Some 100 to 200 Burmese were trained by a BLO in extended overland patrols into enemy-held territory under actual operational conditions. From this beginning was born the idea of Special Groups which later operated in the country.

These Special Groups were normally composed of two officers—at least one of whom had to know Burmese—two W/T operators and sixteen other ranks who were natives of Burma and usually from the same tribe. Their rôle was sabotage in basically unfriendly areas. They were to rely on their superior jungle-craft to avoid actions with Japanese troops and were therefore only lightly armed with automatic weapons. The first Special Groups were launched in October 1944, but results appear to have been disappointing, for their few successes were achieved not in basically unfriendly country but in areas where the locals were passively or actively friendly.

It was mentioned earlier that there was a large Karen community in the Irrawaddy Delta. Its members were generally of a higher educational standard than the hill Karens, and there never appears to have been any doubt as to their loyalty to the British. For these reasons early plans had been made to establish contact with them so that they could be organised into a guerilla force. It is difficult to see the soundness of this enterprise, for the Karen community was interspersed with Burman villages whose inhabitants were hostile at that time, both to the Allies and the Karens. The Burmans had, in fact, fought a murderous communal war with the latter in 1942, in which the Burmans had been the victors. The Japanese, who knew of the pro-British sympathies of the Karens, made full use of this enmity between the Burmans and the Karens to build up an effective informant organisation in the area. It is, therefore, not surprising that all attempts to raise this guerilla force failed.

Let us return to the attempts to regain touch with the hill Karens. At long last a BLO and a W/T set were successfully dropped in October. It was then learnt that the Karens were eagerly awaiting the return of the British. Further teams went in, but each in turn was either captured or killed by the Japanese until finally in February 1944, there was compete silence from the whole of the Karen hill areas.

After this serious set-back it was decided that BLOs could only be put in for comparatively short periods, and that no further effort should be made to develop the Karen movement until an Allied offensive into Burma was imminent.

Nor were the attempts to set up an overland route successful. Movement through the forests and hills was extremely slow and tiring, not only because of the lie of the land and the thickness of the jungle, but also because of the climate. As already related, this was generally malarial, while in the monsoon months from May to October when torrential rain falls, it is hot and muggy with sudden drops in temperature. Added to these natural difficulties was the fact that movement through certain areas proved impossible because of Japanese counter-measures. The overland route had therefore to be abandoned, but the bases set up were to prove of inestimable value later, when the build-up of the guerillas began in earnest with the impending reconquest of the country.

*The main problems*

Until that time it was a period of frustration and setbacks, which were not helped by a number of teething troubles, chief amongst which was the maintenance of wireless equipment, in the hot muggy climate of Burma. Two other serious problems during these early years were the acute shortage of certain personnel and of all forms of equipment, including aircraft.

In the early days it was considered that only officers who knew Burma and the Burmese language could justifiably be employed operationally. The field for recruitment was, therefore, very small and competition for the officers available was intense. Thus, through force of circumstances, it was recognised that officers would have to be used who did not know Burma, its people or its language. This principle was first put into effect in the Special Groups already mentioned, which included one Burmese-speaking officer, one non-Burmese-speaking officer and at least one English-speaking native. Shortage of W/T operators was another vital problem that was never solved.

In the general fight for what little equipment there was available in India at this time, SOE's claims were weakened by the fact that they had little or nothing to show in the way of results. In December 1944 the situation was as follows: there were two W/T stations and two BLOs in Arakan; one W/T and an officer in an isolated part of the Shan States; and two other small groups which were just beginning to produce intelligence. In addition there were four W/T stations, and a good intelligence set-up in the Katchin hills, but this was an American theatre and did not serve very well to impress British commanders.

The build-up of the Katchins was, in fact, the most successful operation that had so far been undertaken. Apart from the intelligence the Katchins produced, they also actively assisted the long-range penetration columns of General Wingate when these operated against the Japanese rear areas in North-West Burma. Similar aid was given to an American marauding column under Colonel Merrill, which was working in support of General Stillwell's Chinese Army.

There were considerable complications, however, in the development and control of the Katchin area as both SOE and its American counterpart (OSS) were working in this territory independently. Attempts to divide it into two spheres of responsibility failed, and there was further friction on account of the different methods employed by the two organisations, both as regards security and the recruitment of the local population. The trouble sprang from the fact that the Karen area came into the sphere of General Stillwell who was operating independently and in no way under GHQ India. He had given OSS the rôle of providing a forward screen, both intelligence and operational, for all his ground forces. As these moved southwards so this screen advanced, with the inevitable result that OSS moved into areas nursed and developed by SOE. It was not until the appointment of a Supreme Commander, South-East Asia Command, that these difficulties were solved by the Karen guerillas, now some 2,000 strong, being placed under OSS control. This was in the autumn of 1944.

*Plans for the 1945 offensive*

By then the Japanese attempt to invade India had failed. Instead they had been soundly defeated at Imphal and Kohima, had suffered heavy casualties in Arakan and found their communications and administrative system badly over-strained. The Allies now went over to the offensive, their strategy being an advance into Burma on three main axes: the British from the west, General Stillwell's Chinese from the north and a second Chinese force from the north-east. The main British thrust was to be made by the Fourteenth Army from Imphal towards Mandalay and then southwards on Rangoon. A subsidiary offensive was to take place in Arakan.

In support of General Stillwell and to a lesser degree of the second Chinese force moving in from Yunnan, the Katchin guerillas operated against the enemy's lines of communication, while some 600 North Shans, under BLOs, also harassed the enemy's rear for a short time. Both these operations were, however, short term as they were soon overrun by the advancing Chinese. Neither was there any guerila activity of note in the Arakan Sector.

It was in support of the Fourteenth Army's thrust through Central Burma to Rangoon that the main local forces of the country were concentrated. In the last phase of this advance from Mandalay to Rangoon the air lift required to supply the Fourteenth Army was such that it could only be maintained for a limited period, and that only during the dry season. It was therefore vital that this final bound to Rangoon should be rapid, and also that the port of Rangoon itself should be in British control before the rains started.

To lessen the chance of protracted Japanese resistance during this critical phase, it was essential to prevent reinforcements moving in from the east and to dislocate the enemy L of C and rear. This was to be done, firstly by raising guerilla forces on a large scale in the Karen Hills, and secondly by organising what amounted to a Secret Army in the area of Rangoon and to the north. 'CHARACTER' was the name given to the Karen operation; 'NATION' to the Burmese Secret Army.

*Operation* 'CHARACTER'

To prevent Japanese reinforcements moving into Southern Burma from the east it was necessary to organise guerilla areas down the length of the Karen Hills, but with particular strength astride the main road that ran south-westwards to Toungoo.

It was therefore planned that initially three Liaison Teams should be dropped in simultaneously, one to the north of the Toungoo road, one astride it, and the third some 50 miles to the south. These would have to go in 'blind', as there had been no contact with the Karens since the loss of the BLO teams with them early in 1944. Existing conditions could only be guessed, but it could reasonably be assumed that the people were still loyal, although probably cowed by the severe reprisals taken against them when the presence of the earlier BLOs became known to the Japanese.

February 1945 was chosen for these first parachute drops, as it was calculated that this would just give the necessary time to raise the Karens and carry out the task allotted. The crux was whether they could establish themselves firmly before the Japanese realised the implications and were able to take effective counter-measures.

The first set-back was caused by all three liaison teams having to be parachuted on to the same DZ, to the south of the Toungoo road.

Because of the difficult country and the need to avoid any knowledge of their presence becoming known to the enemy, the progress of the northern team to its allotted area was extremely slow. It was soon, in fact, evident that it would be too late to complete the build-up in the Northern area in time. Another team was therefore dropped to the North to take over this task.

The Karen region was then divided into four areas, one to the north of the Toungoo road, one astride it and two to the south. Each area was commanded by a BLO and each area HQ had direct links to SOE Calcutta and the SOE Tactical Headquarters with Fourteenth Army. The original intention had been to unify the four areas into one command, but this was dropped when it became obvious that the Commander would have no hope of visiting his areas owing to the immense difficulties of travel.

A number of sub-units, led by BLOs and consisting of approximately 100 men, were organised within each area. Control and co-ordination of these sub-units was made particularly difficult by the complicated nature of the signal communications. This was due largely to improvisation and arrangements which resulted in some sub-stations having direct links to SOE Calcutta, some to the SOE element with Fourteenth Army HQ and some with area HQs only.

There was little or no Japanese interference until mid-April 1945, by which time some 6,700 arms had been supplied to the field. By then the forward elements of the Fourteenth Army were in the vicinity of Pyinmana, while a Japanese Division, the Fifteenth, was moving south-westwards to reinforce Toungoo. There seemed every chance of this being achieved before the arrival of British forces, unless the Karen guerillas could delay the Japanese division.

The northernmost area was still in the early stages of its build-up, as a result of the late arrival of the British team, and did little to check them. The guerillas in the area astride the main Toungoo road, however, succeeded in stopping the leading elements of the Fifteenth Division by ambushes and blown bridges. Instead of attempting to drive on to Toungoo the enemy turned his forces against the guerillas, whose predicament in the two northern areas became precarious, but it gave the Fourteenth Army time to reach Toungoo and effectively block the exits from the Karen hills. This allowed the Fourteenth Army to achieve its objective of opening up the port of Rangoon before the arrival of the monsoon.

Rangoon was in fact captured in May, but there were still some 20,000 Japanese troops to the west of the Sittang and another 50,000 in the Karen hills. All these made widespread but unco-ordinated efforts to break through to Moulmein. They were in poor shape but their numbers were such as to cause a serious situation for the guerillas, whose supply problem was becoming acute owing to the arrival of the monsoon and to the fact that their supplies were still having to be flown in from India.

To relieve this situation standard loads of food and ammunition were eventually dropped to them by Fourteenth Army Dakotas, based on Toungoo. With this very short flight it was possible to drop a total of 1,300 tons in to the Karens in less than two months. (The scale of this support in comparison to what had been possible from Indian bases can be appreciated by the fact that for the whole of 1945 only 614 tons were dropped into Burma by aircraft based in India.) In addition, single engined aircraft, based on Rangoon, could now carry out small emergency drops and pick-ups. With this greatly increased support the Karens inflicted very considerable damage and casualties on the retreating Japanese.

By August 1945 the war was over and 'CHARACTER' at an end. Originally it had been hoped to raise 3,000 or possibly 5,000 Karen guerillas: in fact 12,000 had been armed before the end of hostilities. That this was accomplished virtually from scratch in the four months between March and the end of June, despite the many other major commitments of SEAC and India, is a noteworthy effort. It paid a good dividend, for apart from the vital delay imposed on the Japanese Fifteenth Division, it is claimed that the Karen guerillas killed some 12,590 Japanese and were indirectly responsible for the death of many more.

*Operation* 'NATION'

The second clandestine activity in support of the reconquest of Burma, Operation 'NATION', which it will be remembered was the development of a Burman Secret Army, is outside the scope of this study. It is, therefore, sufficient to relate here that despite many difficulties, not the least being the fickleness of the Burmans, and the divergence of British military and political opinion as to the advisability of arming them, an organisation was eventually built up. This provided some 80 per cent. of all the intelligence received from Japanese-occupied Burma, and played a worth while part in mopping up enemy units left behind in the rapid advance of the Fourteenth Army. It also welded together two potentially dangerous groups in Burma —the Anti-Fascist organisation and the Burma Defence Army—and by doing so enabled the Allied Command to maintain some measure of control in the difficult period of change from war to peace.

*Comparison of efforts and results*

In assessing the value of Burmese Resistance to the Allies the following few statistics may be of interest. From the beginning of 1943 to the end of 1944 less than 55 tons of stores and equipment were dropped to the various resistance organisations, as compared with just under 2,000 tons in 1945. Included in the latter tonnage were 18,574 weapons of various types. At the peak of the campaign some 120 BLOs and 40 British NCOs were operating with resistance forces in the field: of these 17 were killed.

As already related the greater proportion of the intelligence obtained from enemy-occupied Burma came from Operation 'NATION', while at a critical period in the advance of the Fourteenth Army the guerillas successfully delayed the arrival of Japanese reinforcements. In addition, the resistance forces not only caused further considerable dislocation to the enemy's war effort but, it is estimated, killed over 18,000 of them. Even should the latter figure be exaggerated, which there is no reason from records to believe is the case, the results achieved at such small cost and comparatively small effort are still astonishing.

It is, however, improbable that any such success could have been gained, had not the Japanese resources already been stretched to near breaking-point by the Allied air offensive and the advancing British and Chinese Armies. Burma, in fact, provides an excellent example of the successful and close co-operation of guerilla resistance with the strategy of the main regular forces in the field.

## (d) S.O.E. Organisation in India by 1945

The aim of this Section is to set out in general terms the SOE organisation that had been developed in India by 1945 in order to control, develop and support Resistance Movements in the areas of South-East Asia Command. The territory included Burma, Malaya, Siam, French Indo-China and the Dutch East Indies.

*Table 4*

## SOE Basic Organisation, South-East

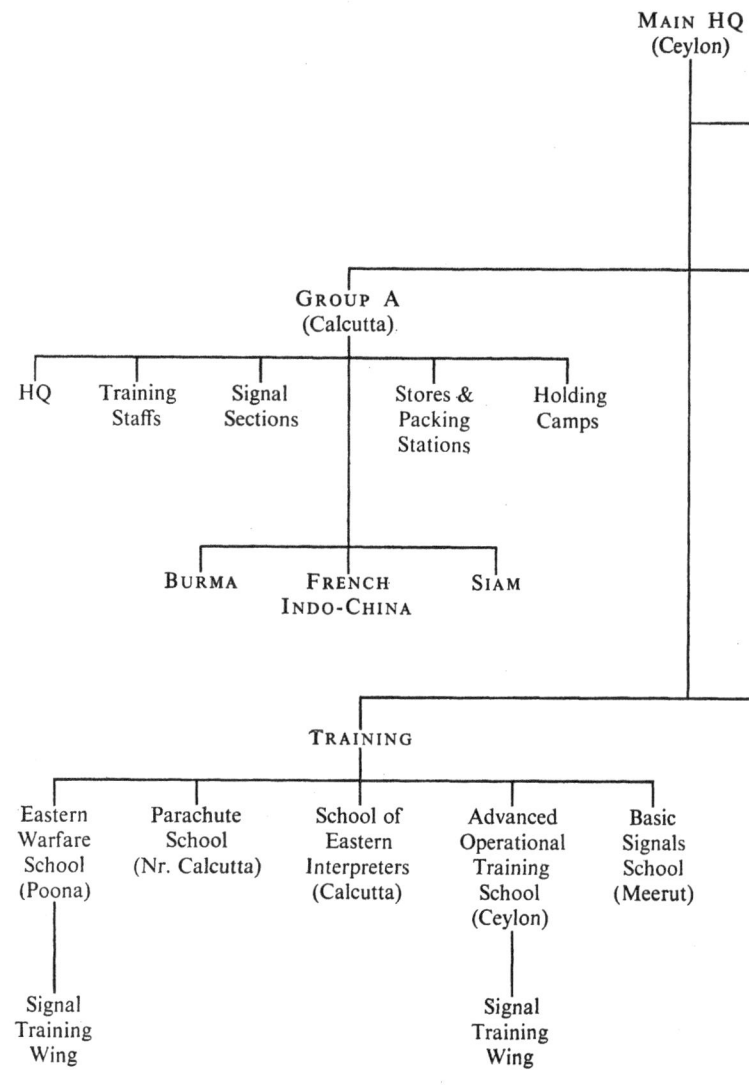

...sia Command, 1945

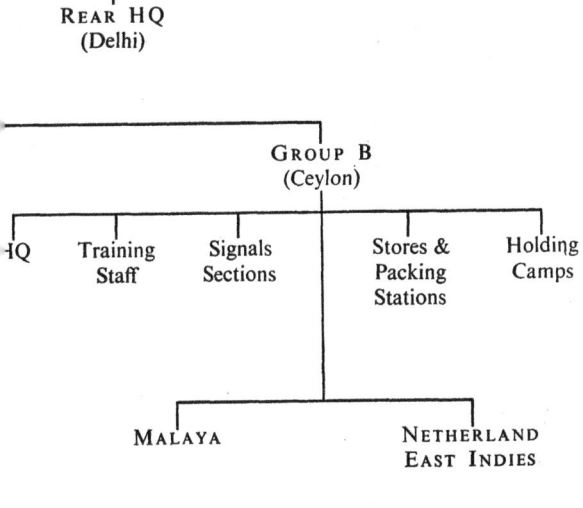

# S.O.E. ORGANISATION

*Outline Organisation (see Table 4—opposite)*

Broadly speaking, SOE India was by 1945 organised into:
  Main Headquarters in Ceylon
  Rear Headquarters in Delhi
  Group A Headquarters in Calcutta
  Group B Headquarters in Ceylon

Under these various Headquarters were the necessary administrative and training establishments, signals stations and staff for the mounting and supplying of all SOE operations in the field. The overall lay-out is shown in diagrammatic form opposite and the following paragraphs are in amplification of this 'family tree'.

*Main HQ*

Main Headquarters at Kandy, in Ceylon, formed part of the Supreme Allied Commander's Staff. Based on directives from SACSEA it commanded and controlled all SOE organisations and operations within South-East Asia Command. It consisted of the normal General Staff, Naval and Air Liaison Sections, Security, Psychological Welfare, and Signals, together with Q (Operations), Adjutant General's, Finance and Medical Branches.

*Rear HQ*

Until 1944 SOE Main Headquarters had been in India at Meerut, where it was in close touch with GHQ India and the Indian Government, both at Delhi. With the formation of SEAC and its subsequent move to Ceylon, a Rear Headquarters had to be left in Delhi to continue to maintain contact there, as many administrative matters still had to be dealt with through GHQ India and the Government.

*Groups A and B HQs*

Group A Headquarters in Calcutta was responsible for the detailed planning and mounting of operations into Burma, Siam and French Indo-China, while Group B in Colombo had the same task in Malaya and the Netherlands East Indies. The location of these two Group Headquarters and the division of responsibilities between them was due initially to the fact that Group A's first operations (into Burma) could be carried out by air, whereas those of Group B (to Malaya) had at that time to rely on submarines from Trincomalee, as the distance was beyond the range of the aircraft then available.

Both Groups contained the same branches as Main Headquarters with, in addition, Country Section staffs to deal in detail with each of the countries for which the Group was responsible. Attached to each Group were the necessary Stores and Packing Stations, Holding Camps, Signal Stations and Training elements. The Stores and Packing Stations received supplies, weapons and equipment from the various Base Storage Depots (shown under 'SUPPLY' on the diagram), broke these down and repacked and loaded them for the particular operations concerned. The Holding Camps were used to house either personnel waiting to be infiltrated into enemy-occupied country or those who had just returned. At these Holding Camps a certain amount of final and 'refresher' training was carried out; hence the small training cadre allotted to each Group.

*Training*

The main bulk of the training was centralised at the schools shown on the diagram. Their various functions are best explained by following the training of a new intake from the time he joined SOE until his despatch to the field.

Having passed a Filter and Selection Board in order to determine his suitability for employment and to ascertain the type of operational rôle for which he would be best suited, an individual was normally posted to the Eastern Warfare School at Poona. Here he was given basic military training and, if necessary, he attended a W/T course. These two courses normally lasted 6 to 13 weeks respectively. Before leaving this school he might also receive jungle, marine or industrial sabotage training, depending on his future operational rôle.

After these basic courses and before advanced operational training, he attended a week's parachute course at the Parachute Training School near Calcutta. He then moved on to the Advanced Operational Training School, where personnel were pooled and the various teams for specific operations were selected. Instructions here included the latest intelligence on Japanese forces and conditions in the field, and culminated in team exercises under field conditions. Courses at the Advanced Operational Training School lasted from six to eight weeks. Lastly, if the individual required Specialist training in any particular subject such as photography, he would go to a Specialist School in Calcutta. The final briefing and training for particular conditions was done under arrangements made by the Country Section at the Group Headquarters concerned.

For unavoidable reasons, such as the need for suitable country, the various Training Schools were scattered over a wide area from near Bombay in the west to Calcutta in the east and Ceylon in the south. A great deal of time was, therefore, wasted and considerable discomfort caused to students and staff by having to travel long distances. This was aggravated by the slowness and difficulty of communications. Neither was this limited to training personnel, as liaison between SOE Headquarters and Establishments suffered equally. For example, it generally took one and a half days by air and about five by train to get from Delhi to Ceylon, and from Delhi to Calcutta six hours by air and thirty by rail. Moreover, air priority was difficult to obtain, as the demand for air transportation greatly exceeded that available.

Two other factors had an adverse effect on training generally. The first was the Asian fear of losing face, and as a result their unwillingness to admit failure to understand any of their instruction. This increased the difficulties of training and the length of courses, as the only method of discovering how much Asian students had learnt was to give them tests. The second was the lack of individuals back from the field, who could provide the practical experience so essential to good training.

The following numbers of students trained at the various schools during the first six months of 1945 give an indication of SOE's training commitment:

| | |
|---|---|
| Eastern Warfare School | 301 |
| Parachute School | 794 |
| Advanced Operational Training School | 839 |
| School of Eastern Interpreters | 145 |

Two factors which made the commitment larger than is at first apparent from these figures were that instruction had to be given in some eleven different languages, while many of the individuals and parties had to be segregated throughout their training for security reasons. It was thus not possible to concentrate trainees into the normal squads and classes. During the same six months 785 individuals were given signals courses of varying types.

*Signals*

Signals had, in addition to a large Main Line Signal Network in India, 125 W/T Stations in the field in July 1945. For security reasons the great majority of these worked direct to Base and not laterally between each other. Thus, for example, an area commander with the Karens in Burma would not get in touch with one of his Liaison Officers direct but would do so via Calcutta. Calcutta would then pass his signal to the BLO concerned. Finally, on the Signals side there was, at Meerut, a Central Stores and Workshop which tested and packed all W/T equipment for SOE before its despatch. A representative figure of its output is that for May 1945, when some 450 tons of equipment passed through this unit; this included 219 W/T sets tested and repaired, and 462 batteries initially charged.

*Supplies*

The Supply Organisation has already been touched on in discussing the rôles of the Stores and Packing Stations attached to Groups A and B. These were supplied with the necessary stores, weapons and equipment by the two Base Depots at Kirkee and Jubbulpore. Kirkee was the Depot to which all bulk stores from GHQ India Depots and RAF Maintenance Units were sent, while Jubbulpore received and 'broke down' SOE stores coming into India from the United Kingdom and the Middle East through Bombay. The SOE Shipping Staff, Bombay, which is shown on the diagram, was employed in the collection and despatch of these stores to Jubbulpore.

The following statistics give an indication of the volume of supplies handled and delivered to the field. They all refer to the first six months of 1945. During this period the two Depots at Kirkee and Jubbulpore received a total of 7,400 tons of bulk stores and issued a total tonnage of 5,270: some 38,700 containers and packages were prepared as aircraft loads, while the following deliveries were made to the field:

    25,036 personal small arms (rifles, etc.)
    57,743 grenades
     1,280 Group small arms (Brens, etc.)
       27·2 tons of explosives
      654·3 tons of equipment, W/T, food and miscellaneous items

If given as a total weight this is the equivalent of just over 1,149 short tons.

*Air Support*

These deliveries were flown in by Liberators and Dakotas of five RAF Squadrons which were earmarked for special duties. Although these Squadrons also had to provide the aircraft for other clandestine operations, by far their greatest commitment was that of supplying the guerilla forces. At various times additional RAF squadrons were switched as a temporary measure to supporting the guerillas: the two best examples being the temporary air lift to the Karens in Burma from Toungoo by Dakotas working with the Fourteenth Army, and the employment of the bomber squadrons from the Cocos Islands to drop stores and weapons into Malaya at the peak period when the Allied invasion of that country was imminent.

*Naval Support*

There was also a small para-naval section, which consisted in 1945 of two schooners and one motor mine sweeper. Amongst other tasks this section ferried stores to the Cocos Islands for the air lift from there to Malaya. Reference has already been made to the employment of submarines on SOE tasks, and the difficulties in making them available.

*Manpower*

The War Establishment for SOE India in 1945 allowed for 2,500 British all ranks and 2,500 Indians. The latter included non-combatants, such as cooks and water-carriers. In July 1945 SOE strength was, in fact, just under 2,000 British and 1,300 Indians. The main reason for the under-establishment in British personnel was the extreme difficulty of obtaining suitable officers and other ranks at this period of universal expansion. They were certainly badly needed in the field, and in an attempt to cut to a minimum those kept at HQs, women were at this time being recruited for certain appointments in signals and finance, and also as secretaries and clerks.

*Conclusion*

This comprehensive organisation did, however, take three years to develop, and was only achieved in the final phase of the war in the Far East and at a time when Allied war production had reached its peak. In the lean years before, SOE operations were of necessity based on *ad hoc* arrangements and improvisation. A similar period of difficulty, shortage and frustration seems probable at the beginning of any similar war of the future, but it is hoped that the above description gives some idea of the extensive base organisations required in a theatre the size of SEAC, in order to develop and support guerilla forces of the type that were raised in Burma and Malaya.

# Chapter 6

# MALAYA: POST 1945

(*See Map 11 opposite page 131*)

*Preliminary Events*

As already described in the previous Chapter on Malaya, the Communist-controlled Malayan Peoples' Anti-Japanese Army (AJA) was officially disbanded during December 1945. The Malayan Communist Party (MCP) remained, however, and through a newly-formed ex-Comrades Association retained control over many of the old AJA. Ostensibly this Association was formed to look after the interests of the guerillas in their retirement; in fact it did its best to make the Government's fulfilment of its promises of rehabilitation for the AJA as difficult as possible, and at the same time waged a violent anti-British propaganda campaign. It was also used, clandestinely, to organise and train the future resistance forces of the MCP.

In other fields the MCP outwardly co-operated with the authorities, and it seems probable that at this period they hoped to attain their aims by political means, or had temporarily at least abandoned the idea of force. The Government, for their part, did not enforce the 'Societies Ordinance' and thus tacitly allowed the MCP a legal status.

The steady post-war recovery of the country, however, provided increasingly unfavourable conditions for the growth of Communism, and by the end of 1947 the MCP had changed to a more aggressive policy. Growing labour unrest, with Communist-inspired strikes, was followed in the Spring of 1947 by armed robbery, arson and murders. Large quantities of rubber were stolen, estate offices burnt down, individuals murdered and communications disrupted. On the 18th June 1947 a State of Emergency was proclaimed in Malaya, and the following month the Malayan Communist Party was declared illegal.

*The MCP Plan*

Captured documents show that the Communist Central Committee visualised their campaign of aggression being carried out in three main phases. Phase one was to be a preparatory period of limited guerilla operations, with the twofold object of wearing down the Government's strength and of building up the MCP, both militarily and politically. Phase two was to be one of expansion, with an intensification of attacks on communications, while some of the smaller towns and villages would be occupied by Communist troops. The third and last phase was the control by the MCP of areas abandoned by the Security Forces, the establishment of permanent bases and the conversion of the guerilla forces into a regular army. It is not clear whether the Communists drew up this ambitious scheme on the assumption of outside help, but in fact throughout their operations they had to rely almost entirely on local resources and their own efforts. Nevertheless during the ensuing three years there was mounting guerilla activity and sabotage, with a steady increase in the dislocation of the country's economy.

*MCP Organisation*

During this period the MCP consisted of two main branches: the Malayan Races Liberation Army (MRLA) and the Min Yuen. The MRLA, successor to the wartime AJA, contained the guerilla bands which were operating in the jungle. They were organised on a regional basis, with the country divided into some eleven Regimental Areas. In theory each Regiment consisted of three battalions, each of three companies. In practice the operational unit was seldom stronger than thirty to forty men, these units or patrols themselves working from separate base camps, deep in the jungle. Attempts were made to operate in larger formations, particularly in Johore, but these were abandoned mainly on account of the difficulty of finding sufficient supplies. In any case, from a tactical point of view the employment of bands of platoon strength would have seemed to be the ideal size for the rôle of MRLA units at this time.

In the first months of the campaign the strength of the MRLA was estimated at about 4,000, of whom some 90 per cent. were Chinese. There was no dearth of recruits, for many Chinese joined MRLA in order to avoid conscription under the Government's Manpower Regulations. MRLA's main strength was derived from the labouring classes and there was as a result a shortage of leaders, as had also been the case in the AJA. Arms and ammunition, however, were the main factor that limited the size of the MRLA. For these they were at first almost entirely dependent on those collected and retained by AJA during and after the Japanese campaign, but with the opening of guerilla operations in 1948 further supplies were captured from police detachments and other security forces. These additional weapons went some way towards replacing MRLA wastage, but there seems no doubt that further arms and ammunition were smuggled to them across the Thai border.

The MRLA's administrative needs and intelligence were provided by the Min Yuen, which in turn was merely the war-time 'Anti-Japanese Union' under another name. The Min Yuen was a network of clandestine workers, living in the more cultivated and populous areas outside the jungle, who were responsible for supplying the MRLA with food, money and clothing, and at the same time acting as the latter's main source of intelligence. It was also MRLA's recruiting agency and reserve of manpower. In addition to its rôle in direct support of the MRLA, the Min Yuen carried out acts of sabotage and disseminated propaganda. It was estimated to have some 11,000 active members, of whom between 3,500 and 4,000 were thought to be armed, the latter being mainly employed on sabotage and on intimidating the large numbers of individuals who were forced to help in the provision of MRLA's requirements.

*The Population*

Only a comparatively small minority of the population were wholeheartedly prepared to aid the MCP, and these were mainly Chinese. Of the latter there had been a very great increase in Malaya during the post-war years, when some quarter of a million refugees had moved south from China. These spread over the country, eventually settling in the more sparsely-populated areas on the fringes of the jungle, where they caused a communal problem to the Government and aroused considerable enmity amongst the non-Chinese sections of the community. These 'squatters', as they became known, had no ties in Malaya, were uncertain as to their future under British rule and had racial sympathies with the preponderantly Chinese MCP. It is therefore not surprising that they proved a source of strength to the latter for, although not openly opposing the Government, they provided help and cover for the Min Yuen and intelligence for the MRLA. The remainder of the population were governed more by fear of MCP reprisals and the inability of the Government to protect them than by political considerations.

*Early Government Difficulties*

As a result there was a general unwillingness to help the Government and its forces, either with active support or even with information. This failure to obtain intelligence from the people was made worse by the fact that the Police Force was inadequate and out of touch with the community. On account of this lack of information the Security Forces, already inadequate for the task of stamping out the guerillas and protecting the people, could make little impression on the MRLA in the early days of the campaign. The guerillas for their part were well served by the Min Yuen, the 'squatters', and their own intelligence network, both as regards target data and security force movements and intentions. While the MRLA maintained the initiative and the Government failed to protect the people adequately, this state of affairs continued.

In addition to lacking intelligence, the Army was hampered in its counter-guerilla operations by the fact that its many commitments made it difficult to concentrate a reserve either to follow up initial contacts or to carry out large-scale operations. A second adverse factor was the dual military and civilian control under which they operated when employed in aid of the civil power. This frequently proved a slow and complicated channel of command, which, combined with the efficiency of the MRLA warning system, meant that surprise would be lost—a situation that dogged most military actions in these early days. The whole Government machinery had in fact to be geared up and streamlined before being capable of dealing with a major rebellion, and it was many months before the necessary adjustments and reorganisations were made.

## Events, 1948-51

In the meantime the MCP, and in particular MRLA, carried out an increasingly successful campaign of terrorism and destruction. The MRLA used much the same tactics as did Chapman and his companions in their successful operations against the Japanese early in the Malayan Campaign. Operating in small parties from camps in the jungle, they made the most of their mobility and superior intelligence. Small, isolated police detachments were raided for their arms and equipment, transport was ambushed, the rubber trees slashed and the labourers driven off the plantations. The jungle remained ideal for such tip-and-run tactics, for despite the use of helicopters in an attempt to locate the guerillas, there was still ample cover both from air and ground. The helicopters seem to have been of little help, and MRLA's guerilla operations continued to show results out of all proportion to their effort and the numbers of men employed. This situation lasted throughout 1949, 1950 and the early part of 1951.

## Government counter-measures, 1951

By the Spring of 1951, however, there were signs that the Government's drastic counter-measures were beginning to take effect. These not only included a great expansion of the Security Forces—the police, for example, to eight times its original strength—but also entailed the resettlement of many thousands of the population. The object of this resettlement was twofold; first, to ensure better protection for those in isolated areas, while at the same time limiting the number of Security Forces required to guard them; and secondly, to remove the Chinese 'squatters' from Min Yuen control and out of the areas from which they could supply the MRLA. Some idea of the magnitude of this resettlement task can be gained from the fact that by April 1951 some 67,000 individuals had been resettled in 59 different areas in South Johore alone, while it was estimated that over 300,000 more remained to be dealt with. Apart from the transfer of population—which in itself placed a major administrative commitment on the Government—the new areas had to be defended, and for this garrisons and equipment such as barbed wire had to be provided. Besides those moved to resettlement areas, some thousands of the more undesirable were repatriated to China.

## Effect on MRLA

The resettlement scheme proved a growing embarrassment to the Communists, for it seriously dislocated the MRLA system of supply, which was similar to that used by AJA during the Japanese occupation, as already described. At best it was a complicated organisation, comprising a number of collecting agencies and carriers, which took time to build up and which disintegrated with the removal of the local population to the resettlement areas. Furthermore, the deportation of undesirables on the one hand, and the added protection afforded in the resettlement areas on the other, caused a hardening in Chinese anti-Communist feeling.

Guerilla activities, however, still showed no signs of decreasing, and captured documents during the early months of 1951 showed a determination on the part of the Communists to step up their attacks in an effort to slow down the Government's counter-measures. The MRLA continued to concentrate on the disruption of the country's economy by attacks on communications, rubber estates and tin mines, by ambushing Security Force patrols, and by attacks on police posts, the last two mainly with the object of obtaining arms and ammunition.

On the Government side there were still great difficulties to overcome. The Resettlement Scheme called for many more security detachments and, despite the rapid expansion already mentioned, these were still far from adequate. In the police there was a great shortage of gazetted officers and police lieutenants, while the standard of efficiency and training still left much to be desired, as was only to be expected with such rapid expansion. There were thus more opportunities for the capture of arms by the guerillas, while the Home Guard and other local units were penetrated by the Communists. Despite a growing confidence there was still a lack of information, and many abortive actions were carried out by regular and irregular units alike.

*Events, 1951*

Nevertheless, MRLA's difficulties steadily increased during the summer of 1951, and this was largely owing to the resettlement scheme, for by August some 280,000 people had been moved. The resettlement also had repercussions on the Min Yuen organisation, for its supply system to the MRLA was dislocated, and a number of its executives, who were themselves resettled, either failed to get in touch with the MCP again or absconded. In a number of areas, therefore, the MRLA patrols were no longer able to obtain their supplies through Min Yuen channels, but were forced to deal direct with the local population, with the resultant security risk. Guerilla casualties and surrenders were also on the increase, while more information was being given to the Government as a result of growing confidence in the latter's ability to protect the people. With more information came more success for the Security Forces.

There is evidence that the Johore Communist Party had intended during 1951 to pass from the First to the Second Phase of the Central Committee's Strategy Directive (*see* page 163), that is from the period of limited guerilla actions to that of wholesale attacks on communications and the occupation of certain areas. In a written document they give as reasons for their failure to do so, first, insufficient strength and a falling off of recruits for MRLA, and secondly, a shortage of supplies and ammunition. The situation in Johore was probably very similar to that in other MRLA Regimental areas, for at no time did any of these areas progress to Phase Two, with the exception of North Perak, Pahang and Kelantan, where MRLA units claimed to have 'liberated' certain of the more isolated villages. But these gains were only temporary and of slight propaganda value. They had little effect on the course of operations as a whole.

Despite these difficulties it is thought that MRLA strength remained constant throughout 1951 at somewhere near 7,000. Limited quantities of arms and ammunition continued to be smuggled into the country, while the MRLA themselves in the first ten months of the year captured more weapons than they lost. With these it was estimated that they were able to keep all 7,000 armed, albeit with a mixed armoury ranging from rifles to shot guns, and with an average of 50 rounds of ammunition per man.

In an attempt to overcome their failure to provide for MRLA needs, the Min Yuen made determined efforts to reorganise cells within the resettlement areas. In part they succeeded, and a limited quantity of supplies and money passed to the MRLA. Another source successfully tapped by Min Yuen was the newly-formed Home Guard. In the creation of this force the Government had taken a calculated risk, for a large proportion of Chinese had been recruited into it with the object of making them protect their own properties and at the same time of giving them more responsibility in the life of the community. This and other methods of giving the people an increasing part in the administration of the country in the end played an important part in building up support for the Government.

*MRLA aspects*

The flow of supplies from the resettlement area was, however, insufficient for MRLA needs and they had to turn to other sources. To a growing extent they now relied on cash purchases direct from the local population, and so long as they were able to pay well, in some cases as much as ten times normal wholesale prices, they had little difficulty in obtaining supplies from the Malay farmers, many of whom remained outside the resettlement areas.

At first there seem to have been ample funds available within MRLA to meet these demands, but their finances depended mainly on extortion and thus their continuation in the event of MRLA setbacks was uncertain. The accounts of one district, for example, showed that only 8 per cent. of its income was derived from members' subscriptions, 63 per cent. being obtained by intimidation from property owners, and the remaining 29 per cent. coming from the same source but by 'special donations'. There was also for a time a considerable income in many areas from the sale of stolen rubber.

The morale of the hard Communist core of the MRLA remained high throughout the varying fortunes of this period, but there were signs that Security Force successes in some areas were beginning to have an effect. According to some of those who surrendered, Government propaganda was also causing some uncertainty and distrust amongst the rank and file.

The fortunes of the MRLA continued to vary throughout the remainder of 1951, but as early as June the Communist Executive Committee predicted great difficulties during the coming year and warned the MRLA that Phase One, that of unco-ordinated guerilla actions, would have to continue. The emphasis was to remain on ambushes in order to capture arms, on the creation of as many incidents as possible including sabotage, and on the development of more Min Yuen cells.

By October 1951 the Communists' situation had further deteriorated, for a document entitled 'The Party's Achievements and Mistakes' set out, amongst other points, the failure to develop an effective supply organisation and the error in not striking a correct balance between revolutionary aims and the interests of the 'masses'. It went on to point out the need to ensure the support of all sections of the population, and in particular the Malays.

From this stocktaking there emerged two important changes in MCP policy: first, the Min Yuen's chief rôle became the development of a clandestine Resistance Movement amongst the masses, instead of supporting the MRLA as before. Secondly, in order not to alienate the masses further, operations that were likely to clash with their interests were to be avoided.

This meant a marked change for the MRLA, for in effect it relegated guerilla operations to second priority. Furthermore, whereas up to now their aim had been to dislocate the economy of the country regardless of the effect on the population, their attacks were henceforth to be selective and therefore limited. Also whereas MRLA's administrative needs had been till now theoretically supplied by the Min Yuen, MRLA had now to supply themselves in those areas where Min Yuen was responsible for the development of resistance.

Some months passed before this change in policy percolated through the various committees and along the tenuous courier communication system to patrol level, and by then the march of events had in any case forced the MRLA into largely fending for themselves.

But meanwhile there was no slackening in guerilla activity and the months of October and November 1951 were probably, from the MRLA point of view, the most successful period of any throughout the emergency. Early in October Sir Henry Gurney, the High Commissioner, was killed in a road ambush; raids and attacks on security detachments and communication targets, road and rail, increased; while damage to rubber plantations was greater than ever before.

*Comparison of effort*

Up to this time there is little doubt that the dislocation, uncertainty and wasted effort caused by the activities and threat of the MRLA and Min Yuen paid a dividend out of all proportion to the numbers employed by the Communists, as can be seen from the following summary.

On the economic and social side mention has already been made of the vast resettlement scheme that had to be carried out, entailing the transfer of some 450,000 people, the organisation of protected areas, and the provision of supplies and equipment for them; all at a total cost, up to July 1951 only, of $21,500,000. There was also the disruption caused to the economy of the country by this transfer of manpower. Damage to rubber estates between July 1950 and November 1951 was in the region of $27,500,000.

The great expansion of the Security Forces was equally marked. From a total strength before the Emergency of 9,000, the strength of the Police Force had risen by November 1951 to 83,750 regulars, auxiliaries and special constables: a Home Guard of 60,000 had been raised: the Army in Malaya had been reinforced and now included over twenty-five units of battalion strength, together with administrative troops. Supporting them was an Air Arm of some ten squadrons of close support, transport and intercommunication aircraft, together with a squadron of helicopters. Even with these forces there are constant references to a shortage of troops and the subsequent inability of the Security Forces to press home an initial advantage.

The cause of this expenditure of effort and resources was estimated to be between 4,000 and 7,000 MRLA guerilas, supported by a Min Yuen still with some 11,000 active members and relying almost entirely on local resources and their own efforts for arms, ammunition and all the necessities of life. Since the beginning of the emergency MCP casualties had amounted to 2,697 killed, 856 captured and 658 surrendered, but intelligence reports as late as November 1951 continued to stress that the MRLA were still able to keep their armed strength up to 4,000, while during the preceding year their tactical and technical efficiency had improved.

There was at this time a marked drop in the confidence of the population, while reports show considerable uneasiness over the situation in Government circles in Malaya. In December 1951 the then Secretary of State, Mr. Oliver Lyttleton, visited Singapore and in a speech there reviewed the measures that had been or were being taken to deal with the emergency. These included the unified direction of the Military and Civil forces; the reorganisation of the Police; improved education for all; the formation of a Home Guard in towns and resettlement areas; the review of terms of service and recruitment standards for the Civil Service, and the supply of armoured cars for civil use. He also stressed the reliance that was being placed in the loyal Chinese and their recruitment in large numbers into the Home Guard.

When General Templer became High Commissioner in February 1952 he also stressed the Government's intention of political advancement for the Federation, and himself followed a vigorous policy of giving more responsibility to the people, while at the same time dealing firmly with those who assisted the MCP and with the MCP themselves. The Security Forces continued to expand and improve in efficiency. All these were factors in restoring confidence within the country.

*Events, 1952 onwards*

MRLA in the meantime had failed to maintain their 1951 pressure and from the beginning of 1952 there was a slow but steady decrease in their activity. This decrease continued until by mid-1953 the MCP campaign was mainly underground, with MRLA playing a very subsidiary rôle in support of the Min Yuen. During the previous year and a half the efforts of the MRLA units became increasingly concentrated on obtaining supplies for themselves, with operations more and more restricted to targets which could provide them with arms and ammunition.

The curtailment of MRLA's operations may possibly have been due in part to the MCP change in policy during October 1951, as already mentioned. By the middle of 1952, however, Security Forces, helped by better intelligence and a more sympathetic population, were driving the MRLA patrols deeper into the jungle. By now the former regimental and company organisation of the MRLA patrols had been abolished, and most—if not all—were operating under direct control of the MCP State Committees.

With the rise in Government successes and prestige, MRLA difficulties multiplied. Greatest amongst these was that of providing food. Supplies from resettlement areas were a mere trickle, now that security arrangements had been improved and there was a hardening of anti-Communist feelings. Local purchases could still be made, but by 1952 MRLA funds appear to have begun to run low, as demands upon their contributors were as much as 100 per cent. above those of the previous year. Thus, as MRLA's situation deteriorated, so the quantity of supplies from their supporters lessened: for force could not be used in view of existing MCP policy not to antagonise the people.

As a result, more and more emphasis was being placed on jungle cultivation, and by 1953 large numbers were being employed on this at the expense of operations. Communist directives captured during the summer of 1953 showed that the bulk of the MRLA and Min Yuen 'comrades' in Johore, Negri Sembilan and Selangor were to be employed on cultivation. The directives stated that their whole energy must be devoted to this important task, and that any consequent reduction in aggressive operations and work among the masses would have to be accepted as inevitable. One of the essentials to the success of this cultivation was some permanency in one area, but in those areas not too deep in the jungle the MRLA units were now being kept on the move by the presence of Security Forces and by the fact that their areas were now being constantly reported. Neither were the clearings deep in the jungle safe, for these were spotted by helicopters and sprayed with weed killer. The surprising fact is that despite this concentrated attack on the MRLA's supplies—truly their 'Achilles Heel'—they still continued to operate and remained a threat to the economy of the country, albeit on a reduced scale.

With the decline in operations, the increase in hardships and the lack of food, it was inevitable that the morale of the rank and file should suffer, as was proved by the increased number of surrenders to the Security Forces during 1953. The Government did their best to exploit this possible weakness by a psychological warfare campaign which included encouragement to surrender, details of other surrenders and casualties, and the defeat of Communism in other parts of the world. Other incentives were monetary awards and the promise of a new lease of life. Broadcasting from aircraft, pamphlets and a periodical News-sheet were amongst the methods used. But the main factors influencing MRLA's morale continued to be the pressure of the Security Forces and the shortage of food. In an attempt to counter these threats to morale, efforts were made to pay more attention to health and welfare, and the privileges of rank, financial and otherwise, which had come into being, were abolished. At the same time, party discipline was tightened and an increasing amount of publicity and propaganda was given to the achievements of the Chinese Communist Party and international Communism in general.

Possibly with the view of restoring morale, a directive issued by the South Johore Committee in October 1953 laid down a more aggressive policy. It stated that MRLA was to spend less time on jungle cultivation and return to more aggressive tactics, with less concern for their repercussion on the 'masses', while Min Yuen were once more to be responsible for feeding MRLA. This reversion to the pre-October 1951 policy was reported as being put into effect not only in Johore but wherever the pressure of the Security Forces allowed.

In fact this change in policy had little effect, for, as a guerilla force the MRLA had shot its bolt and its activities after 1953 provide little of value to this particular study.

*Summary*

Even so it says much for MRLA morale and endurance that they operated without outside aid, but with marked success for three years as a guerilla force, and at the end of a further year and a half were still a threat to the stability of Malaya.

From their success three main points emerge. Firstly, it proves what can be achieved in the way of dislocation to a country's administration and economy by guerilla methods, at comparatively small cost in resources and manpower, provided the country is suitable for such operations. Secondly, it shows how important it is to guerillas to have a friendly or at least neutral population. Thirdly, it demonstrates the weakness of having an inflexible supply organisation. Lastly, there is the controversial question of the soundness of supporting, to the extent we did, a movement politically opposed to our colonial policy, in order to strengthen our war effort. It is easy to be wise after the event but any post mortem here would be of little value. Suffice it to say, therefore, that this is yet another example of the need to balance most carefully short-term military needs against possible long-term political repercussions.

## Chapter 7
# SUMMARY OF GUERILLA WARFARE

*Introduction*

In the introduction to this book it was stated that its aim was to provide, on the basis of lessons drawn from previous guerilla campaigns, sufficient information to enable a reader to form a balanced understanding of the scope and limitations of guerillas, the main principles involved and the political factors with which this type of warfare is inevitably complicated.

It is hoped that by now the reader will have obtained a general picture of the many complex problems with which guerilla campaigns have in the past been surrounded, particularly in so far as the United Kingdom, or any other nation is concerned when that nation is attempting to develop support or control a foreign guerilla movement in enemy occupied territory.

It now remains to study the lessons that can be learnt from the past, and how best these lessons can be applied to the future. But before any such consideration can take place, it is necessary to have some appreciation of the conditions under which guerilla forces are likely to have to operate in the foreseeable future.

Obviously the greatest new factor is the advent of nuclear weapons. Their availability to both potential contestants means that humanity is at last faced with the real possibility of self-annihilation. At the moment neither political, military, nor, above all, ethical thoughts have kept pace with this new concept and, as a result, this is a period of transition, when ideas, policies and plans are constantly changing.

Under these conditions it is extremely difficult to define the shape of wars to come, but in an attempt to provide the necessary background four possible eventualities are considered:

(i) War between East and West, introduced by an 'exchange' of nuclear weapons on such a scale and over such an area that the major civilised areas of the world are so destroyed or contaminated by 'fall-out' that the only remaining problem will be in the form of an individual struggle for survival.

(ii) War between East and West, introduced by a comparatively brief exchange of nuclear or atomic weapons, causing great devastation in the main industrial areas and centres of population but leaving vast expanses of country relatively undamaged. This preliminary nuclear stage might be followed or accompanied by sweeping Communist invasions.

(iii) War between East and West on a world-wide scale, but in which the universal fear of nuclear or atomic retaliation is so great that only 'conventional' weapons are employed.

(iv) Wars between nations, but on a limited scale, in which nuclear/ atomic weapons may or may not be used.

The first eventuality means virtual world annihilation and, even if such destruction were possible, which at the time of writing is doubtful, it would seem that many months and possibly years might elapse before the survivors would be in any position even to think of further aggression. Such a concept has little or no bearing on this study of guerilla warfare.

The second eventuality, in which nuclear or atomic weapons are used on a more restricted scale, is one which enters the field of possibility, or even probability. While for many millions of people the result is likely to be unpleasantly final, many more millions will remain, in varying degrees, alive. Many of the more industrial and developed areas will have been obliterated, while the regular military forces that are still in being are likely to be disrupted and dispersed. Thus, in Europe for example, even assuming that the Soviets have succeeded in occupying countries in Western Europe, their control will be limited, and their resources dispersed. This dispersal, which is one of the characteristics of nuclear warfare, means that a great additional burden will be placed on communications, a target system which has been repeatedly shown as particularly suitable for attack by guerilla forces. Furthermore, this dispersion will inevitably stretch the enemy's security force, and thus make the tasks of guerilla bands the easier. A last point is that the type of country suitable for guerillas is also the type of country most likely to escape the devastation and contamination caused by the initial nuclear bombardment, which will have been chiefly concentrated on the more highly developed areas. Thus good guerilla country will become a synonym for 'safe living country' to which multitudes of homeless and despairing people will at least try to make their way. This movement of the national population may make it even more possible than in the past for the guerilla movement to become a rallying point for resistance to the invader. But the development of a guerilla movement under these conditions is likely to be even slower than in the past, for the period of inertia that had generally followed an enemy occupation is likely to be much more prolonged by the fact that for some time mere survival will be the predominant aim of the majority. While appreciating that the course of any nuclear war is largely unpredictable it would seem, therefore, that on the scale of nuclear bombardment that appears at the moment most probable, there will be very considerable scope for guerilla forces, but that they are likely to develop slowly.

Should the third eventuality—a war of conventional weapons—materialise, it is fair to assume that conditions would not be greatly dissimilar to World War II. The probability, therefore, is that the potential and basic principles and characteristics of guerilla warfare in the past will be little, if at all, changed.

The last eventuality is that of limited wars between nations. Depending on whether atomic weapons are used, or not, it is felt that the points mentioned above for nuclear and conventional wars apply equally to limited wars, so far as guerilla operations are concerned.

With this short appreciation of the possible shape of wars to come, added to the background of the various campaigns described in the preceding chapters, the paragraphs that follow summarise the main characteristics and capabilities of guerilla forces, together with those aspects that are likely to effect a nation supporting a foreign guerilla movement in enemy occupied territory.

*Guerilla rôles*

From the guerilla campaigns already described, it will be seen that their main contribution in the past has been their ability to tie down considerable enemy forces, who would otherwise have been employed on the main battle fronts. This the guerillas generally achieved by operations—or the threat of operations—against enemy lines of communication. As events proved, few economic and industrial targets were attacked by guerilla forces, and this failure to destroy what in many instances were vital sources of supply for the enemy was largely due to the fact that most of these targets were in the more developed areas, and these in turn were seldom regions suitable for guerilla activities.

The threat of widespread devastation from nuclear bombardment may well in the future force industries to be dispersed and be sited in less developed country. This in turn will afford more opportunities for guerilla forces to attack them, while, as already mentioned, communications themselves may well become more tenuous and more difficult to guard.

In addition to forcing the occupying power to deploy forces for the protection of his communications, guerilla attacks on these communications in a number of instances prevented the enemy from making full use of the country's economy, as happened in the USSR in World War II. For some time to come air transport will only be able to lift a comparatively small part of these loads, and much will have to continue to be moved overland. A second rôle of guerilla forces is, therefore, the prevention of enemy exploitation of the country's resources.

A third rôle of guerilla forces has been to provide safe areas from which other organisations can operate with comparative security. The intelligence unit that, from the security of a Malayan guerilla controlled area, provided valuable information on Japanese ship movement through the Straits of Malacca is one example. The launching of the British *coup-de-main* attack on the Asopos viaduct from a Greek guerilla safe area, and the use of an advanced landing ground for air strikes, protected by guerillas at another time in Greece, show other uses which can be made of guerilla controlled zones; while escape organisations also may site their staging posts under guerilla protection.

Fourthly, as in France in World War II, guerilla forces can play an important part in maintaining the morale of the local population, and forming a rallying point for all those willing to resist the invader.

Lastly, there is the value of organised guerilla forces in maintaining law and order in the period of vacuum immediately after liberation, and before local governments or military administration have moved in and taken over control. Not always, however, were guerilla movements of such assistance in the past, for where their motives did not coincide with those of the Allies, there was always the danger of friction and even open hostilities, as occurred in Greece at the end of World War II.

There seems every likelihood that in any future war these rôles will be equally suitable to guerilla movements.

It has in the past been consistently proved that guerilla forces cannot wage regular military operations against the forces of an occupying power, except under very exceptional conditions. These conditions normally only occur shortly before the reoccupation of the country by Allied armies, or when the enemy is on the point of collapse. Where such military operations have been attempted prematurely, the guerillas have usually been so badly mauled as to be incapable of any further contribution to the Allied war effort. The attempt of the French guerillas to hold the Vercors, in South Eastern France in 1944, is a case in point. This inability to fight pitched battles with regular troops will always be a basic characteristic of guerillas, as the mobility on which the latter must largely depend for survival in turn precludes them being armed with the more powerful and heavy weapons of regular field units.

*Extent of reliability*

If history is any guide, it will by now be clear that it is unwise to place too much reliance on guerilla forces carrying out to the letter tasks allotted to them by an ally, even though those tasks are well within the guerillas' capacity. There are many factors that may affect the outcome, but all these stem from the guerillas limited view of the war as a whole, his natural concentration on those events that most obviously are to his direct advantage, and his general antagonism towards any form of foreign coercion. To mention only two widely different examples from World War II, there was the Jugoslav unwillingness to destroy communications, the destruction of which was an essential part of the Allied plan to dislocate German movement northwards, and there was the case of an Italian guerilla unit failing to attack the enemy in order to conserve its ammunition for use against a rival political organisation.

Where the guerillas are mainly dependent upon the Allies for supplies, there is more chance of guiding their activities along the lines required by the Allies. Even so, considerable uncertainty is likely to overshadow the actions of many guerilla movements, and it would seem wise policy, from a military view-point, to look on the guerilla operations more as a possible bonus than as a major contribution to the Allied war effort, anyway in the early stages of the guerillas' development. Where the guerillas are fighting in close co-operation with their own national forces, as for example was the case in the USSR, and are not dependent on a foreign Ally, their reliability is likely to be far greater.

*Political Considerations*

So much for the purely military possibilities of guerilla movements: let us now consider these in conjunction with the political aspect, for in nearly every instance in the past military aims have been affected to a greater or lesser extent by politics.

In the Second World War Britain, with her back to the wall, first concentrated, understandably, on obtaining all possible military assistance from anywhere that she could, and the possible political repercussions were left to take care of themselves. With the progress of the war, political problems assumed major proportions, and Foreign Office policy became increasingly opposed to the purely military concept of all-out aid to whoever was prepared to fight the Axis. We thus, as in the case of Greece and to a lesser extent Malaya, find the military authorities tending to press for maximum aid to the guerilla movements for the furtherance of military strategy, and the politicians attempting to limit this support for post-war political reasons.

A further complication that may face a nation supporting a guerilla movement from outside is the presence in its country of an exiled Government, to whom it has pledged its support, but who is opposed to the political hue of the resistance in its own country. Such was the case, it will be remembered, in Greece.

In a future war the chances are that the political problems and complications will be lessened, as it will be a conflict between two basic ideologies, the Western way of life and Communism. Nevertheless the difficulty of reconciling long-term political and short-term military aims may well recur, even though in a less acute form. In finding the answer to this vexed problem accurate, up-to-date and detailed intelligence on the country, prevailing conditions and the resistance movements concerned, is a vital necessity from the outset.

In order to obtain this information at the right time, it will be necessary to establish or maintain a comprehensive intelligence network in peace time, which can give an accurate picture of the political scene, the strength and characteristics of possible resistance movements and current conditions within the country concerned. At a later stage, the contribution of BLOs through their wireless links will be invaluable, but in addition every effort must be made to bring liaison officers out of the country to make a full, personal report. The value of two-way personal contact cannot be overstressed, and in World War II a failure to obtain direct personal reports in time, from either Jugoslavia or Greece, appears to have been one of the main causes of the series of wrong appreciations made by Cairo and London on guerilla forces in these two countries.

## Strategic considerations

Another aspect of guerilla warfare—which affects both the military and political spheres—will be the relationship between guerilla operations in the area concerned and the war effort as a whole. In the early days of a future war, quite apart from the devastation that would be caused if nuclear weapons were used, there will presumably be the usual shortage of men and supplies, coupled with the inevitable conflict of priorities between one area and another. In assessing the military advantage of giving support to a guerilla movement, such factors as the time likely to elapse before the guerillas can show positive results, as well as their location in relation to targets, will have to be considered. In some cases, these and other factors may rule out the possibility of Allied support for a guerilla movement until a much later stage: in others resistance forces unlikely to produce much in the way of results may have to be supported for political or morale reasons. But even where support has to be deferred, the time need not be wasted: in the first place, as already discussed, every effort must be made to obtain up-to-date, reliable political and military information from the country. Secondly, skilful propaganda can be used to build up the morale of the guerillas so that they do not feel they are being left entirely alone. An explanation of the reasons why help cannot be given at the time is better than no explanation at all, and can perhaps be linked with firm promises of support in the future.

## The country

As a generalisation, it is fair to say that the potential of any area for guerilla warfare can be gauged by the type of country and the people, in that order, for guerilla forces can seldom exist in war, however good the human material, if the terrain is unsuitable. An interesting example of this fact can be seen in the case of Norway, during World War II, where a brave, tough and united people, temperamentally well-suited to guerilla warfare, were unable to form a movement of this type because of unsuitable terrain and climate. There was an almost complete lack of cover in the mountains, the ski-tracks of relatively large groups moving across the snow would have been all but impossible to conceal, while the absence of shelter on the high ground made the bitter Arctic winters an even greater adversary than the Germans.

The essentials of good guerilla country include adequate cover both from ground and air observation, sufficient space for manoeuvre—so that the guerillas can exploit to the full their inherent mobility—and finally, the absence of a well developed road network. Good road communications make it impossible to maintain safe bases, even for a limited time, owing to the ease with which the enemy can encircle the guerillas and destroy them. Generally, good guerilla country consists of woods and mountains or jungle and swamp, but it must be remembered that no country, however wild, will prevent a determined enemy in sufficient strength from reaching the guerilla base.

The area of operations must afford the guerillas much, if not all, of the food they need. For this reason they may have to range far and wide in order to provide themselves with supplies throughout the year. This is not necessarily a disadvantage, since the very existence of the guerillas depends on continued mobility, and the necessity for foraging expeditions may ensure that this mobility is maintained. The more usual method of obtaining food will be by local purchase, a procedure which may necessitate an extensive organisation for liaison with the civil population, with its adverse effect on the guerillas' mobility, as happened in Malaya to the Communist guerillas both during World War II and after. Another method, which the reader will recall was also used at one time in Malaya, is for the guerillas to develop an organisation for growing their own food, but this system not only reduces the fighting strength of the movement, it also turns the guerilla base into a static camp, the disadvantages of which are obvious. In some areas the most difficult problem will be that of survival through a winter, a situation which, in the early days of the Soviet guerilla campaign, for example, reflected itself by the partisans taking all they could from the local population. Excessive commandeering of this nature may have the effect of alienating an otherwise friendly people. Thus the question of food supply may be one of the chief difficulties facing a guerilla band during the whole of its existence and might well influence both the development and the offensive tactics of the force.

*The people*

During the initial development of guerilla movements in the past, the hard core has been provided by the people who lived in the regions suitable for guerilla warfare. Most had a long tradition of resistance, and all had certain common characteristics. Accustomed to hardship and want, simple, independent and tough, they made excellent guerilla rank and file, but few were suitable as leaders.

As life in enemy occupied areas became more difficult, there was an ever increasing influx into the guerilla bands of a wide variety of individuals, with many different incentives for being there. Thus the political refugee might be fighting alongside the criminal fugitive, while the genuine patriot might join the same band as the careerist, who was out for himself alone or for any loot that might come his way. Many others joined for a chance to revenge themselves against the occupying power. The pattern varied in different parts of the world, but many of those who joined lacked the qualifications required of an ideal partisan.

To be a good guerilla, a man—or indeed a woman for that matter—must be, in the first place, physically and mentally tough, courageous and resolute. Much of the necessary resolution will spring from the cause for which the particular individual is fighting, and this aspect is discussed later. But, in addition to toughness and bravery, the efficient guerilla needs what may be described as aptitude, the most important manifestation of which is an ability to appreciate the use of ground. Within this broad expression are included such matters as cover, protection, lines of approach, natural camouflage and all those other things that the countryman understands so well, but which many townsmen find so hard to learn. A willingness to accept discipline is essential, and the extremely strict discipline successfully imposed by the Communist guerillas, both in Jugoslavia and Malaya during World War II, was an important feature in both these movements.

Unfortunately, however, there seems every reason to think that in the future, guerilla movements will draw on much the same human material as in the past and will thus have similar shortcomings. To weld so many different individuals into a cohesive whole two things are essential, and these are a 'cause' and good leadership, both of which are considered later.

Equally important, but extremely difficult, is the maintenance of morale for, unlike the regular soldier, a guerilla can seldom gauge the success of his efforts by a definite advance or the occupation of ground. Often on the retreat and always avoiding pitched battles against a stronger enemy, he has little idea as to the course the war, or even his own operations are taking. He therefore tends to believe the wildest rumours and this, combined with the constant strain under which he lives, can cause his morale to vary with astonishing rapidity. He is prone to magnify the importance of his own small corner of the war, and this in turn leads to dissatisfaction with the support that he receives from outside sources and a general distrust of all those not immediately connected with his own faction.

*Propaganda*

The guerilla is therefore an easy prey to propaganda, and the Communists were—and are—more alert to this than the West appear to be. The efficiency of the former's propaganda and its value has already been mentioned in the review of the Soviet guerilla campaign in World War II. Here the Communists devoted an exceptional amount of time and trouble to the production of leaflets, news sheets and pictures in order that the people in the occupied areas were kept fully informed of the Soviet war effort. In Jugoslavia, on the other hand, Allied propaganda was sadly mishandled and the broadcasting of inaccurate, badly-timed statements and reports caused immeasurable harm. From a study of our shortcomings and successes in the propaganda field in the past, the following main lessons emerge.

The main theme of propaganda in support of a guerilla campaign should reflect faith in Allied victory and sympathy for the guerilla cause, coupled with hostility towards the mutual enemy and the discrediting of his policies. In so far as broadcasting is concerned, propaganda will be based on two main categories of events; first, those incidents affecting the course of the war as a whole and covering matters outside the guerillas' knowledge and area of operations, and secondly, those events related directly to the activities of the guerillas themselves. The first type of broadcast propaganda—

that based on world-wide events—is easy to provide and, in fact, was carried out during World War II via the BBC with considerable success. It is the second type—that arising from purely local events—that presents so many difficulties, although it is likely to have a far greater effect on the guerillas. Anything put over must not only touch their day-to-day activities but must be based on comprehensive, accurate and up-to-date information. Clearly this is extremely difficult to manage from outside enemy-occupied territory, and this places the occupying power at a considerable advantage. Thus the supreme necessity for building up and maintaining a first-class intelligence network in peacetime is, once again, illustrated.

*Discipline*

Good discipline is another factor in the maintenance of morale. The form that it takes will need to be modified to suit the individual races and factions concerned, for obviously the boy-scout approach which proved so successful with the Malayan guerillas would never have suited, for example, the French Maquis. As a generalisation, though, it can be said that discipline in efficient guerilla units will tend to be very strict by normal military standards. In the tense conditions of guerilla life, and given the far-reaching effects of even comparatively small crimes, the need for this severity is understandable.

The ideal is where the guerilla movement is motivated by such strong ideals that discipline is self imposed. This happened in certain of the Jugoslav partisan units in World War II.

*The Cause*

To reach this state of self imposed discipline, or to provide any sufficient and lasting incentive, it is essential that a guerilla movement should have a 'cause', and it is the degree of devotion to this cause which will represent the ultimate strength of the movement. The cause itself may take various forms, ranging from the idealistic to the material. It may include liberation of the country from an occupying enemy, the overthrow of an existing political system or the defence of religious principles. It may even be a cause of desperation, where the people are driven to resist by the excesses of the occupying power and the fact that conditions of life become so bad that they have nothing to lose and possibly something to gain, by forming guerilla bands in the more inaccessible regions and from there fighting back against the invader. Whatever form it may take it is the cause that fuses the mixed collection of individuals who join the guerilla bands into a united force. Its importance is, therefore, paramount.

If the Western Allies are to combat the undoubted theoretical appeal of Communism, the formulation of a clear and vital cause, which will have a universal appeal is essential, for without this the chances of stimulating resistance on a significant scale, and at a time in a future war when that resistance is most required, are remote.

One of the greatest problems in the development of guerilla warfare springs from the conflict of opposing causes and political beliefs. There will always be a tendency for political parties to try and gain control of a guerilla movement, ultimately using it as a weapon to obtain ascendancy for their party after liberation. Indeed it may well be that political parties will form guerilla movements themselves, since in many areas it is these parties which are most alive to the possibilities of resistance work. In World War II, Greece, Albania and Jugoslavia all provide examples of conflicting political causes which, in Greece, eventually erupted into civil war. On the other hand, in Russia, the influence of the Communist Party was so strong that the question of opposing political factions never had the opportunity to arise. This state of affairs enabled co-ordinated plans to be made, simplified every aspect of the guerilla campaign and materially accelerated the defeat of the enemy in that country. Clearly, such a situation represents the ideal which the Western Allies are only likely to achieve by the provision of a burning cause, excellent intelligence, close liaison and effective propaganda. But these alone will not guarantee unity: this can only come from within the country itself.

*Leadership*

Because of their mixed composition and character, guerilla forces are difficult to control, co-ordinate and direct. Much will therefore depend upon the calibre of the leaders and the influence that they can exert upon their followers. Obvious essentials are an ability to handle men and to deal with the idiosyncracies of those under their command. Personal example in battle is an important qualification, particularly amongst junior commanders, but in addition to the normal military attributes, such as courage, endurance, initiative and clear-headedness, a guerilla leader must also have political knowledge and ability, for politics are still likely to play a part in this type of resistance. He must also have a knowledge of tactics, although his technical military training need not extend further than small arms and explosives, since heavier and more intricate equipment should not form part of a guerilla force's armament.

Unfortunately, for reasons already discussed, when considering the type of person who becomes a guerilla, there may well be an acute shortage of leaders amongst those who join in the early days. The situation should improve as individuals gain practical experience and prove their worth under operational conditions.

A possible method of filling the initial vacuum in leaders might be to earmark and train potential guerilla leaders in peace. In this respect it is interesting to note that the successful guerilla leaders of the past have either been well known and distinguished figures long before the guerilla campaign began, or have risen the hard way from very subordinate command at the start of guerilla operations. In no instance, to the writer's knowledge, has a foreigner risen to high command in another country's guerilla movement for although some may consider Lawrence did, he himself stresses in all his writings that his strength lay in remaining in the position of adviser to Feisal and never presuming to command.

*Forms of development*

A guerilla movement may develop in several ways. In Jugoslavia, for example, the two main forces grew out of existing organisations, the Cetniks and the Communists. Thus a considerable degree of cohesion in each movement was achieved from the start. In France, on the other hand, independent Maquis cells mushroomed into existence all over the country and created problems of control and co-ordination that took months to sort out. Palestine, in World War I, was a different case altogether. Here the Arabs were recruited largely by gold, the promise of loot and Feisal's persuasiveness, and little or no cohesion between rival tribes was possible. Thus the method was to use each tribe independently for specific tasks: Lawrence and a cadre of highly trained and specially selected men attaching themselves to the tribe, while the particular operation allotted to the latter was being undertaken.

By whatever means development takes place, there is always the risk of over-recruitment, both in the sense that the numbers become too great for guerilla resources to cope with and lessen the mobility of the force, and also in the sense that the numbers exceed those needed for carrying out the military operations required by the Allies. This over-recruitment may be caused by the ruthlessness of the enemy driving large numbers of people from their homes into the guerilla areas, or it may be as a result of the determination of the guerilas themselves to swell their ranks to gain political ascendency. Examples of the many and major logistic difficulties this situation caused, both to the guerillas and Allies, abound in the campaigns described in this book.

As the reader may remember, an attempt was made by GHQ Middle East to limit the number of Jugoslav partisans by establishing a fixed ceiling beyond which the Allies would not increase supplies. This method was not successful, and the most that can reasonably be said is that the over-development of a guerilla movement is a factor which must be constantly borne in mind and on every possible occasion attempts should be made to keep some control over its size. In this respect, a point not always appreciated by military commanders in the past is that it is well-nigh impossible to disband or lessen the strength of guerilla forces as and when required. The disastrous effects of attempting to do this are well exemplified in the Italian campaign during the winter of 1944–45. Here, the Allies, after having given the guerillas every encouragement to build up their strength, reversed their policy and gave instructions for numbers to be reduced to a minimum. Although this order, from an Allied standpoint, had good reasons behind it—the demands of the 'Second Front' had greatly lessened the allied logistic resources in the Italian theatre—it had serious repercussions on the morale and efficiency of the Italian guerillas, for a disbanded guerilla generally has no alternative but to surrender to the enemy, if only to avoid starvation.

This great difficulty in subsequently cutting down the strength of a guerilla force is yet another reason for making every attempt to control its original development.

*Organisation*

The organisation of guerilla forces cannot be made to conform to any rigid system, since it must depend on a number of factors, such as the number of junior leaders available, the terrain, the size of the force, political issues and problems of supply. In general, however, the guerillas should be organised on semi-military lines, based on a section or party of about ten men. This section should be so armed and equipped that it is highly mobile over the country in which it will operate and has also comparatively great fire power for its numbers. It will thus be well suited to carry out the normal guerilla rôles of ambush and small scale attacks. Usually the military value of the main body of the force will be low, at any rate during the early phases, and it may therefore be best to form special sections for demolitions and operations of particular importance. The nucleus of these sections may well be ex-army NCOs or young civil engineers who have joined the partisans.

The maximum size of the guerilla band or company will be regulated by mobility, which is the basis of all guerilla operations. Much will depend on the nature of the country and its capacity for providing food; an additional factor will be the facilities for control. It will usually be found that the largest manageable body is about one hundred, that is, ten sections of ten men, but this can only be a rough guide.

The higher organisation of the partisan forces should follow normal army lines as far as possible, within the limits imposed by local conditions and enemy activity. The guerilla bands or companies should be organised into brigades, whose strength can be of about two to three hundred men. Guerilla brigades can again be grouped into divisions of perhaps a thousand men, and the division might sometimes be formed into Corps or Zones of two or three divisions.

An important point to bear in mind is that this 'higher organisation' is required mainly to deal with problems of overall control, strategy and logistics. It will be unusual for guerillas ever to operate as a brigade or larger formation and although this did in fact occur in Jugoslavia—for by then the partisans had virtually become a National Army—it should be regarded as exceptional. If guerillas do concentrate in large numbers for some particular operation, then they should do so at the last moment and disperse as soon as possible afterwards.

Because of the distances and difficult country likely to be lying between units, because of the tenuous communications and because of the ever present risk that the command structure may be destroyed by the enemy

# SUMMARY OF GUERILLA WARFARE

(as happened to Tito at Drvar in 1943), decentralisation of control within a guerilla movement remains an essential. Thus considerable latitude will have to be given to junior commanders, whose instructions should be in sufficiently broad terms to allow the latter to adapt their methods to suit the local situation. Under such conditions mutual confidence and understanding between the commander and his subordinates is of great importance.

The last important stage in the development of a guerilla movement occurs when the partisans feel themselves sufficiently successful, and sufficiently strong, to establish the framework of a post-war political regime. Probably the best example of this was in Jugoslavia, when the Communists set up, in November 1942, the Anti-Fascist Council of National Liberation (AVNOJ). AVNOJ not only became the central organ of the new government, it provided the machinery for producing policy statements and it also assumed the task of co-ordinating and controlling the vast network of local and administrative authorities through partisan-controlled territory. Thus the establishment of AVNOJ was the first step in the transition between Partisan resistance and peace-time government. Similar, though smaller, organisations sprang up in other resistance movements, but the degree of control that the Allies can exert on these potential governments will be limited, since the previous efforts and suffering of the guerillas is likely to induce a fiercely nationalistic spirit and any suspicion of pressure from outside will be strongly resented.

*Tactical considerations*

Throughout history the tactics employed by guerillas have remained very much the same and all the successful operations described in this book have been the result of the correct application of three main tactical principles—mobility, surprise and flexibility. Of these probably the most important is mobility, and where this has been sacrificed the guerillas have generally suffered crippling losses. Despite the great changes that have, and are taking place in other spheres of warfare, there seems no reason to think that these basic principles of guerilla tactics will be affected.

Guerilla operations should still, therefore, be carried out as a series of 'pin-prick' or 'tip and run' attacks, each blow being delivered in strength and the guerillas vanishing before the enemy can retaliate. This blow should be followed in a different area, the process being continued with the object of bewildering and disorganising the enemy on an ever growing scale. Throughout these operations the guerillas must make every attempt to retain the initiative as by so doing they will also retain freedom of action.

There are a number of military, and other pamphlets which describe in detail the various tactical methods that are best used by guerillas. It is, therefore, sufficient to mention here that probably the commonest and most successful form of attack for guerillas to employ is the ambush, in which they hold virtually all the advantages.

Despite the fact that it is wrong for guerillas to attempt to hold a particular area against enemy forces, there must be somewhere into which they can withdraw to rest and reorganise. There is no question of these safe areas or bases being of a permanent type, except under very exceptional circumstances (as occurred in the vast forests of the Soviet Union) and, where attempts have been made to develop guerilla bases to this degree, as did the British Military Mission in Albania, disaster has generally followed. Rather should they be on the lines of the Malayan jungle camps which the guerillas aimed to evacuate with all their essential gear in a matter of minutes. If alternative bases have been reconnoitred beforehand, and reserves of food, ammunition and equipment hidden near by, a guerilla force can continue to maintain its mobility and flexibility, even at the height of an enemy counter offensive.

*Enemy counter measures*

Such an offensive is certain to materialise if the guerillas are sufficiently successful in their operations against the occupying power and, in fact, one of the rôles of a guerilla movement is to divert enemy forces from the main front for this very purpose. An enemy counter offensive is likely to be a complicated and expensive undertaking but, if the enemy has enough time, adequate forces and a good knowledge of guerilla methods, he can eventually reduce the guerilla movement to impotence and perhaps annihilate it. Where, however, the guerilla operations are part of a greater conflict, the enemy will seldom possess all these advantages and the inability of the Axis to eliminate the guerillas in the USSR, Albania, Burma and elsewhere in World War II show how difficult it is to destroy a guerilla movement. Postwar British experience in Malaya is a further proof of this fact, if one is needed.

Before an enemy counter drive can begin there will have to be considerable preparation, such as reconnaissance and the movement and concentration of troops. These activities should give the guerillas at least some warning of the enemy's intentions. The employment of airborne troops may well give a considerable initial advantage to the enemy in the form of surprise, but their drop into the broken and rugged country in which the guerillas will be operating is likely to be hazardous and expensive in casualties. Later they will have the inherent disadvantages of all regular troops operating in this type of country against local guerilla units.

Enemy counter operations will probably consist of several phases. First he will attempt to surround the area in which he believes the main guerilla force is at the time located. If he fails to do this and the guerillas find a bolt hole, the attack is doomed from the start. The next phase will be to tighten the ring and prevent the guerillas forcing a way out. This phase will require advances by a number of units to a carefully timed programme—a difficult operation in the type of country concerned, and one which can well be upset by the guerillas themselves. If the ring is not broken and continues to contain the partisans, the third phase will be an attempt to annihilate the guerillas, either by dividing them and attacking them piecemeal, or by driving them against a chosen line on a natural obstacle. No operation of this kind is likely to be completely successful and a proportion of the partisans are certain to escape. The enemy will seek to crush the remainder of the movement by a process of attrition.

The success of any such enemy offensive will largely depend on accurate, up-to-date and comprehensive intelligence. Much of this intelligence must come from the local population, and in his determination to obtain it and stop the people assisting the guerillas, the enemy is likely to go to any extreme. An excessively ruthless policy can, however, be a two-edged weapon, as was shown in Jugoslavia, USSR and Malaya, where the reprisals against the local inhabitants were so excessive and created such hatred and terror, that the populace were driven into the arms of the guerillas. It may well be, therefore, that the occupying power in any future war may attempt, at first anyway, to woo the people away from support of the guerillas, although the past behaviour of our most likely main opponent would make it appear more likely that he will use a mailed fist.

It is also worth remembering that the USSR and Communist Party as a whole are more experienced in conducting guerila warfare and, conversely, of countering it than any previous enemy.

Other methods that may be employed by an occupying power against guerilla forces, in addition to direct military activities, are attempts to liquidate guerilla leaders and attempts to penetrate both the movement itself and the organisations supporting the latter. They will launch a propaganda campaign and undertake subversive activities with, amongst other aims, the belittling of the Allies in the eyes of the guerillas and the playing off of resistance movements, one against the other.

*Intelligence*

Not only to give timely information of enemy activity against them, but also for the success of their own operations against the enemy, one of the first essentials for any guerilla force is to establish an efficient intelligence system. Until the movement has developed into a large and widespread guerilla organisation their main need will be tactical intelligence on such matters as enemy movements, concentrations and intentions, with—from the counter intelligence aspect—warning of enemy attempts to penetrate the guerillas' own organisation. To satisfy these requirements, guerillas must have their own tactical intelligence service but—like the occupying power—they will also have to rely largely on the local populace, who in turn will have to penetrate the enemy's security services to obtain the necessary information.

Conversely, if the enemy are unable to obtain intelligence about the guerillas through the local population, they are themselves very greatly handicapped in their counter-resistance activities. It is, therefore, extremely important that the local population are in active sympathy with the guerillas, and it is interesting to note that in every successful campaign reviewed in this book this local support has been forthcoming.

Later, as the guerilla force expands, it will require strategic intelligence not only for its operations and own security but also as a basis for internal propaganda. This type of information may be provided through national guerila or clandestine sources (as happened in the case of the Jugoslavs receiving details of the plans for the German Fourth Offensive) but is more likely to have to come through Allied channels.

*Communications and control*

One of the difficulties in the past has been to disseminate this intelligence, when received, for communications within guerilla forces have always been elementary and slow, and as late as the end of World War II still relied to a very great extent on couriers and runners. This was mainly due to a shortage of wireless sets, difficulties of maintenance and repair, and, in particular, a dearth of suitable and adequately trained operators. Subsequent technical developments have meant a lightening of wireless equipment, more robustness and greater range, but transmission and receiving still remain comparatively difficult techniques, requiring a certain aptitude and comprehensive training. Therefore, until these techniques can be greatly simplified the shortage of adequately trained operators is likely to remain.

This situation could be ameliorated by the cacheing of sets and the training of operators in peace time, but there are many and obvious difficulties in doing this. Even if undertaken, the numbers so trained are likely to be limited.

It may well, therefore, be some time before there is any alternative but to rely mainly on couriers for inter-communication within a guerilla force, although this will be augmented by a limited wireless network.

*Equipment and weapons*

Because of the vital need for guerillas to remain mobile in the difficult country over which they have to move, a most important consideration in the selection of wireless and all other equipment and stores, is that of weight and portability. Obviously equipment must be cut to a minimum, and what is used must be robust and simple. Delicate items can neither be operated by those likely to be available in the guerilla ranks, nor properly maintained under the conditions prevalent in guerilla warfare. For the same reasons the greater the standardisation achieved in equipment and weapons the better.

The choice of weapons will naturally depend to a certain extent on local conditions, such as the closeness of the country in which the guerillas are operating, but as a general rule a guerilla force's weapons should be limited to those types carried within the normal infantry company of the British Army. In the past guerillas have successfully employed heavier weapons, such as mountain howitzers, but in the early stages of a movement's development the risk to mobility by being tied to such weapons, not to mention inability to handle them, is not commensurate with the possible gain in fire power.

The value of standardisation is as great in weapons as in other equipment, but as the guerillas may well have to be dependent for the greater part of their arms on what they can capture from the enemy, they are likely to amass a heterogeneous collection. As an example from World War II, it may be remembered that the Soviet guerillas were dependent on captures from a German Security force that had been armed with weapons from most of the Allied armies. With such a multiplicity of types the guerillas' problems of training and ammunition supply are obvious.

It may be possible to assist a guerilla movement in its initial and probably most difficult stage of development by cacheing, or otherwise hiding in suitable areas in peace time, arms and other equipment most needed but most difficult to obtain locally. Of the latter the most likely items are demolition stores, medical supplies, communication equipment and, possibly, gold. The chances of this equipment being brought into the country by Allied means at the beginning of any future war must be considered remote, for air and suitable sea craft are likely—as in the past—to be almost impossible to obtain for these purposes, more so if hostilities have opened with nuclear attacks.

It would, therefore, it is felt be quite wrong for any embryonic guerilla movement to rely on anything but the most limited practical outside help in the opening phases of any future war.

*Supplies*

As regards supplies and administration within guerilla formations, it has already been made amply clear that guerillas cannot afford to be tied down to any administrative echelon of the type that forms an integral part of the establishment of regular troops. Instead, a guerilla must carry his immediate needs upon his back and must rely for their replenishment on what he can capture from the enemy or obtain locally. Hidden dumps from which he can draw, when all other sources cease, will greatly relieve his troubles, but in the hand to mouth existence that is the lot of most active guerilla forces, the husbanding of the necessary reserves to stock such dumps may not be possible.

The vital need for food, or even clothing, in the past has often forced guerilla units into carrying out operations against the enemy for the specific purpose of obtaining such supplies, and if at some period the guerillas are required to undertake essential operations as part of Allied strategy it may be necessary to fly in the essential foodstuffs, clothing or whatever is required to the exclusion of more warlike stores.

This occurred, the reader may remember, in Jugoslavia and Malaya, to mention only two examples, but such supplies were extremely bulky and wasteful of storage space. (The development of hydrated foods may, in the future, lessen this disadvantage.)

Nevertheless it will be on local supplies that the guerillas will have to continue to rely and yet again the unlucky local inhabitants are likely to be the main sufferers, on the one hand from the importunities of the guerillas, and on the other from the Security Forces' attempts to prevent these supplies reaching the guerillas, or their retaliation if the supplies do get there.

As failure to obtain the sympathy and assistance of the local inhabitants will almost certainly have serious consequences for the guerillas, it goes without saying that the latter's demands must be kept to a minimum. Some form of compensation for the stores so obtained should be made, and even if the Allies cannot provide the needs of the guerillas themselves, they can assist in this compensation by the provision of gold and other money for repayment—and did so on many occasions in the past.

*Finance*

The various aspects of financing a guerilla movement from outside have already been studied in some detail, as applied to the Albanian Resistance in World War II. While it is indisputable that considerable financial aid may be necessary, especially in the early stages of a force's development, there are considerable dangers in pouring large quantities of gold or currency into an occupied country. By doing so, serious inflation may occur owing to shortage of local supplies, and this in turn may cause great hardship and consequent resentment amongst the civil population. Neither is there any guarantee that the money is used entirely for the purposes for which it was given: there is the difficulty of ensuring that it is received by the Allied representatives intended, and there is the personal danger facing the BLOs when carrying gold in large quantities. It is difficult to conceal, heavy to handle and the BLO or leader who is responsible for it runs a continual risk of being murdered and robbed, as occurred in a number of instances in World War II. For these reasons the supplies of money, be it gold or local currency, should, as far as possible, be kept on a tight rein and efforts made to supply the requirements of the guerillas in kind.

*Outside support*

The dependence of a guerilla force on aid from outside has already been implied in the preceding part of this Chapter, and it is fair to say that such outside support will be essential, if a guerilla movement is to play a continuous and worthwhile part in the defeat of the enemy. In fact, a study of past guerilla campaigns has shown that all those where outside aid was not forthcoming have eventually ended with the defeat of the guerillas.

The possible political repercussions in providing this outside support have already been discussed. There is also almost certain to be a clash of priorities as between the needs of the guerillas and those of the fighting services, for overall shortages, both in supplies and transportation are bound to exist, except in the closing stages of a war. It is essential, therefore, that support to the guerillas is limited to those things that it is impossible for them to get for themselves—hence the continuous need, as stressed throughout this Chapter, for guerillas to rely as much as possible on what they can capture from the enemy or obtain from the local population.

Because of the fluid nature of guerilla warfare and the tenuous lines of communications that are likely to exist between the field and the allied Base, the supply arrangements that are made must be as flexible and simple as possible. This has been achieved in the past, after a great deal of trial and error, by building up the supply organisation on military lines and by standardisation wherever possible, of both stores and equipment and the loads that they are made into.

A detailed description of a base organisation, as used successfully in the last war, has already been given in Chapter V, Section D. This shows a Base at its maximum expansion in World War II, but it should, even so, allow the reader to form a picture of the scope and size of such bases at the various stages of development in the support of guerilla forces.

The advantages of standardisation of guerilla requirements with existing service stores and equipment are obvious. There will, however, be certain items that will have to remain peculiar to the guerillas, but once the latter have developed from the clandestine stage into overt para-military units it should be possible to satisfy the greater proportion of their needs with standard military items. The second aspect, the standardisation of loads, should not become too rigid, as there will always be a percentage of special requirements, but flexibility can be maintained by having an adequate selection of well-balanced loads, each designed for an appropriate number of guerillas. These can then be prepared as standard loads at Base, each with a code letter by which the field can order them. The categories of these loads fell in the past into four groups—weapons and ammunition, communications equipment, demolition stores and medical supplies. A fifth was added in some theatres—for food. These five groups would seem adequate to plan for in any future war.

*Allied Control and Liaison*

When—or possibly before—support of a guerilla movement has been decided upon, it will be necessary to establish a Liaison Link or Links with the guerillas concerned. The size of these Links will depend upon the strength and importance of the guerilla movement, and the conditions under which they are working. As shown in the previous Chapters, these Liaison Links will vary from one BLO and his wireless operator, to a large mission of the type attached to Tito, with MacLean as its Head.

These Missions and BLOs form an essential part of any outside support, as they provide two-way communication between the Allies and the guerillas down which all requests for supplies, equipment, etc., can be passed, and up which the Allies can make known their operational requirements of the guerillas. They are the means of providing technical advice and instruction to the guerillas. They are the Allies' check that the support being given to the guerillas is being used to the best advantage, and that Allied requests for specific activities are being undertaken.

Missions and BLOs can also serve as an important stimulus to the morale of the guerilla force, representing by their presence the interest of the Allies and their intention to help. In World War II this incentive to morale was in some instances partly nullified by the Allies sending in large numbers of BLOs (to check on the capabilities of the guerilla forces concerned) with very little material aid to follow. This was particularly resented in Jugoslavia, where the sardonic comment 'A ton of supplies is better than a ton of BLOs' originated.

The importance of selecting suitable men as liaison officers to guerilla movements, though patently obvious, can hardly be over-stressed; particularly as in World War II this importance does not always seem to have been appreciated.

Essentially, a liaison officer to a guerilla movement is a 'fighting ambassador' of the country sending him, and thus he must have the qualities of both fighter and ambassador: the difficulty will be to find men who can successfully combine these two requirements. Resolute but flexible, firm yet tolerant, understanding and understandable—all these things and more will be necessary. It is desirable that he should have previous knowledge of the country; it is essential that he should know the political background and speak the language. He must be of such an age, rank and personality as will command respect from the guerilla leaders and their men, and he must be able to hold his own as much at the conference table as under the gruelling physical conditions and hardship of guerilla warfare. A sense of humour will help him over many of the petty difficulties with which he will be faced almost continually. But these qualities alone will not enable the liaison officer to make a success of his appointment: he must be given clear political and military guidance, and he must be able to speak with the knowledge of adequate 'backing'. Anything less than this will make his position most difficult and will reduce the confidence of the partisans in their Allies. In World War II, due mainly to shortage of suitable officers and SOE's apparent need for large numbers of BLOs, many sent in were junior Army officers with no background knowledge or experience, other than their military training. They had little or no briefing on the country, the people or their background, were forbidden to discuss politics and were given little or no briefing on the subject. Most of these BLOs were, as a result, of very limited value, some were the cause of complications and resentment, and in one case at least, became the unwitting mouthpiece of the Communist Party.

Some of these repercussions are touched on in the preceding Chapters, but the lesson to learn for the future would seem to be—so far as BLOs are concerned—'Quality rather than quantity'.

*Allied Communications*

Liaison officers, however excellent they may be, cannot function without good communications. These, which will nearly always be W/T back to

Base, must be kept open at all costs and every possible precaution should be taken to ensure that this happens. The complications that follow when a BLO or Mission goes off the air is well demonstrated by the situation that developed when Hudson's W/T in Jugoslavia broke down at the critical period of decision as to whether or not to support Mihailovic. The wasted effort and uncertainty raised by the long silence between the Far East Base and guerilla forces in Burma and Malaya during World War II will also be remembered.

Since those days wireless equipment has become more reliable, robust and portable. Failures should therefore be fewer and the maintaining of reserve sets in the field easier.

If, as in Jugoslavia, Burma and elsewhere in World War II, large numbers of liaison officers are deployed in the field, the problem of wireless control and security will arise.

In the past it appears to have been generally agreed that the most secure method was not to have direct wireless inter-communication between liaison officers in the field, but to route all messages through Base. For obvious reasons this method is more secure than direct wireless contacts between those in enemy territory, while it also means that Base have direct control over all liaison officers. On the other hand, such a procedure has its drawbacks: firstly, there is the risk of the increased traffic causing a bottleneck at Base, with a subsequent delay in the passing of urgent signals between those in the field; secondly, it tends to make the Mission's task of controlling and co-ordinating the activities of their liaison officers more difficult, and both Bailey in Jugoslavia and Myers in Greece complained of this. Which system to use in the field will have to depend on the situation at the time, and what developments may have taken place in the meantime as regards security to wireless transmissions and efficiency in interception.

Wireless communications are, however, no substitute for personal liaison between the field and Base, and except in the early part of a guerilla campaign, when conditions may make it impossible, there should be regular personal visits by senior officers to and from the guerilla area. Without this personal contact, as was proved in World War II, Base gets out of touch with conditions in the field, and—worse still—without visits from the field it is difficult to obtain a comprehensive and balanced picture of the situation prevailing within an occupied country. The results of failing to recall Hudson from Jugoslavia and Myers from Greece have already been noted in the relevant Chapters.

*Responsibility for control of support*

One of the major problems that remained not fully solved at the end of World War II was the question of the control and organisation of Allied supplies to guerilla forces in the field. There were in fact two aspects: firstly, what service or organisation should be responsible for this control and support from the outset of the War and, secondly, if this initial responsibility was for SOE or an equivalent organisation to shoulder, when, if at all, should this responsibility pass to the military.

The reader will remember that initially this control and organisation of support was the task of SOE. In Jugoslavia, however, the commitment became so great as to be completely above SOE's capacity and, somewhat tardily, a tripartite committee (RN, RAF and Army) was formed to take over the control and organisation. The provision of supplies to the field from then on became a military responsibility. As a result there was a marked improvement in support of all Balkan resistance. In Greece, on the other hand, although the circumstances were somewhat similar to Jugoslavia, this change over did not take place. What then are the lessons that can be learnt and what is the correct answer for the future?

When guerilla forces can be supported from within their own country, albeit outside that part occupied by the enemy, as was the case in the USSR during World War II, political differences, if they arise, can be resolved nationally. It is also probable that under the conditions of national crisis prevailing, there will be unity of aim between the guerillas and the regular forces. Finally, conflicting priorities can be decided again nationally, by direct reference to the combined aim. Under such conditions, there appear to be clear and positive reasons for placing the guerillas under the control of the military from the beginning of the campaign. Thus the responsibility for the co-ordination of guerilla operations and the responsibility for all forms of support rests squarely with the armed Services—and, if it is to be one particular Service, then this should be the Army. This principle is strongly supported by Mao-Tse-Tung, the acknowledged Communist expert on guerilla warfare, who repeatedly emphasises the necessity of having guerilla movements controlled and co-ordinated by the regular military forces.

Where a guerilla movement is being supported and, to a varying extent, controlled from outside its own country by a foreign power, the solution is far more difficult. Here, as was so clearly shown during World War II, conflicting political interests and military aims created the most complex problems and, even though in the future this conflict may be much less, there is no guarantee that political policy and military aim will always walk hand in hand, so far as the development of guerilla resistance is concerned. This seems to be one reason why purely military control by the external power would be unsound in the early stages of the war: the responsibility at this period becomes more of a diplomatic than a military matter. Even before the war starts, it should be possible to prepare some of the ground for future guerilla activities: potential leaders may be selected and trained, stores, equipment and arms earmarked and hidden, guerilla bases chosen and plans for development made. Any such preparations in a foreign country would have to be the task of some clandestine organisation; as will also the build-up of the intelligence organisation so essential for the initial build-up of the guerilla movement. Furthermore, in the very early stages of a guerilla movement's development, it may well have to remain underground, and all communication with it will have to be through clandestine channels. For these reasons there seems no doubt that Allied control and support of a foreign guerilla movement during the preparatory stage, its initiation and early development, cannot be a military responsibility as they will not have the necessary resources, technique or knowledge. It should, instead, be the task of SOE or some similar clandestine organisation.

Once, however, the guerilla movement has achieved the strength and status of a reasonably unified fighting force, has been cleared from the political angle, and has freed itself from its covert background, then the clandestine organisation should be relieved of responsibility, as they are neither equipped nor intended to organise and carry out the large-scale supply operations that would then be required. It is at this stage that the military authorities must take over. In order to do so effectively, there must be a really close liaison between the military and clandestine organisation at all stages in the development of a guerilla movement.

It is obviously impossible to lay down any definite period, either in the guerilla movement's development or in the war itself, when this transfer to military control should take place, but the following would seem to be the factors that should be taken into consideration. Firstly, the guerillas must have developed sufficiently for clandestine techniques to be dispensed with: conversely the movement must have developed to such a stage that there is a close relationship between current guerilla and orthodox military operations, for clearly the military authorities cannot be expected to control and support minor activities of the cloak and dagger type. Secondly, there should be political agreement that the change is desirable. It may, for instance, not be possible to admit that HMG is giving support to a guerilla movement, a fact that would immediately become apparent once the regular forces assumed control. Lastly, the change in control should not be allowed to impair the momentum of the guerilla movement. In order to assist in preventing this, the military authorities should take over, as it stands, any BLO network that may have been built up, and they will also probably find it necessary to absorb, if only temporarily, a number of the specialist staff of the clandestine organisation.

# BIBLIOGRAPHY

Much of the information included in this book has been obtained from official sources such as the histories of the British Organisations concerned, reports from the field and Axis appreciations. Considerable use has also been made of various published works and the following is a short list from a mass of literature available on the subject.

This list makes no claim to being comprehensive but will, it is hoped, provide sufficient material for anyone who wishes to obtain a wider historical background than can be given in a book of this size.

## 1. BACKGROUND

(a) *Small Wars. Their Principles and Practice.* By C. C. CALLWELL. HMSO for War Office.

Describes various guerilla campaigns of the nineteenth and early twentieth centuries. Mainly written from an army viewpoint. Is of interest, however, in showing that the characteristics and basic principles of Guerilla Warfare change little through the years.

(b) *Secret Forces.* By F. O. MIKSCHE. Faber and Faber.

Discusses the value of General Resistance as a whole, with examples from the last War, and the author's views of its employment in the future.

(c) *Irregulars, Partisans, Guerillas.* Edited by IRWIN R. BLACKER. Simon & Schuster (New York).

An interesting selection of mostly first-hand accounts by irregulars writing on guerilla warfare. Most aspects of the subject are covered, including politics and strategy, but it is the day-to-day problems and conditions of guerilla warfare which are particularly well illustrated.

(d) *Guerilla Warfare.* By 'YANK' LEVY. Penguin Books.

This small book was written in the early days of the Second World War as an unofficial training manual for the newly-formed and untrained Home Guard. The author discusses the advantages to be gained by irregular warfare methods, cites a number of historical examples, and gives some useful and practical advice on minor tactics.

## 2. PRIOR TO THE FIRST WORLD WAR

(a) *Guerilla Leaders of the World.* By P. C. STANDING. Stanley Paul.

Provides an interesting series of descriptions of Guerilla campaigns in various parts of the world from the time of Napoleon to the Boer War.

(b) *History of the Peninsular War.* By SIR CHARLES OMAN. Clarendon Press.

Although this is a massive work in several volumes it is possible by reference to the index to limit reading to those chapters dealing with the Guerilla aspects of the campaign. These give a well balanced picture of the capabilities and limitations of the Spanish Guerillas in their support of Wellington.

(c) *The Military Exploits, etc., etc., of Don Juan Martin Diez.* (A translation from the Spanish) Printed for Carpenter & Son.

This gives an interesting, although partisan account, of one of the Spanish Guerilla leaders in the Peninsular War. Despite its bias in favour of Martin Diez, it does give a vivid picture of the conditions of life, and the idiosyncracies of the Spanish Guerillas.

(*d*) *Garibaldi and the Thousand.* By G. M. TREVELYAN. Longmans.
   Although a very comprehensive work and dealing with operations that are not truly Guerilla in character, it is of interest in that it paints a clear and detailed picture of Garibaldi who probably had more of the qualities necessary in a great Guerilla leader than anyone before or since.

(*e*) *Handbook of the Boer War.* Author is Anonymous. Gale and Polden.
   Describes the campaign as a whole and the results achieved by the Boers' Guerilla tactics, from the British viewpoint.

(*f*) *With Steyn and de Wet.* By PHILIP PIENAAR. Methuen.
   The Boer commando operations as seen by the author, who took part as a signaller. Of value as shows the shortcomings of the Boers and the conditions under which they operated.

## 3. FIRST WORLD WAR

(*a*) *The Palestine Campaign.* By Field Marshal THE EARL WAVELL. Constable.
   This clear and concise history of the overall military campaign is an excellent background against which to build up an appreciation of Lawrence and the Arab Guerilla operations described in the three books mentioned below.

(*b*) (i) *Revolt in the Desert.* By T. E. Lawrence. J. Cape.
   (ii) *T. E. Lawrence.* By LIDDELL HART. J. Cape.
   (iii) *Lawrence and the Arabs.* By R. GRAVES. J. Cape.
   Describes the operations of the Arabs in support of the Allied Campaign in Palestine. As each deals with the subject from a different angle, a possibly more balanced picture can be obtained by reading all three.

## 4. BETWEEN THE TWO WORLD WARS

(*a*) *The Irish Rebellion of 1916.* By WELLS and MARLOWE. Maunsel.
   In particular Chapter VI shows the type of resistance organisation to be expected in such a country as Ireland.

(*b*) *France, Spain and the Rif.* By WALTER B. HARRIS. Arnold.
   A comprehensive study of the 'Moroccan Problem' from the political, economic and military standpoint. The military difficulties and reverses suffered by the Spanish and, later, the French in conquering the Rifs are described, and the problems experienced by regular troops opposing highly-mobile irregular forces are clearly shown.

(*c*) *English Captain.* By TOM WINTRINGHAM. Faber & Faber.
   An account of the Spanish Civil War, which although not strictly guerilla in type, provides a number of interesting points of value to the student of Guerilla Warfare.

(*d*) *Scorched Earth.* By EDGAR SNOW. Victor Gollancz.
   Although this book is concerned primarily with the political and economic aspects of the Sino-Japanese War, Part 9 covers the strategy and tactical methods employed by the Chinese guerillas against the Japanese.

## 5. JUGOSLAVIA, SECOND WORLD WAR

(*a*) *Eastern Europe, 1918–41.* By H. SETON WATSON. Cambridge University Press.
   Describes the economic and social conditions in Jugoslavia and the Balkans up to the Second World War. Possibly over-accentuates the shortcomings of the ruling class and the hardships of the workers.

(*b*) *Whirlwind.* By STEPHEN CLISSOLD. The Cresset Press.
   Mainly of interest for the description of Tito and Mihailovic, and the motives of both Resistance movements. A live account, but one which

# BIBLIOGRAPHY

perhaps tends to exaggerate the magnitude of the various operations mentioned.

(c) *The Chetniks.* By GEORGE SAVA. Faber & Faber.
A light account of the author's journeys in Jugoslavia before the War, which ends with a short chapter on Cetnik operations.

(d) *Mihailovic and Jugoslav Resistance.* By ALEC BROWN. Bodley Head, London.
Is strongly biased and for that reason the historical accounts of Cetnik operations are of questionable value. Provided the sympathies of the author are borne in mind, the detailed picture of Mihailovic is of interest.

(e) *Miss Fire.* By JASPER ROOTHAM. Chatto & Windus.
A fair, well balanced account of Cetnik operations as seen by one who was with them in the field. Is of particular interest from the human angle, and gives a good insight into conditions with the Partisans as well as Cetniks.

(f) *Eastern Approaches.* By FITZROY McLEAN. Jonathan Cape.
Part 3, 'Balkan War', gives a valuable explanation of Partisan policy and operations from the time the author arrived at Partisan GHQ as Head of the Allied Mission.

(g) *Marshal Tito.* By MICHAEL PADER. Frederick Miller.
This short book fills in some of the gaps in Marshal Tito's earlier life, but otherwise is of rather limited value.

(h) *Partisan Picture.* By BASIL DAVIDSON. Bedford Books.
Operations with the Partisans as seen by a British Liaison Officer.

## 6. GREECE

(a) *Apple of Discord.* By C. M. WOODHOUSE. Hutchinson.
A comprehensive work of reference, dealing with all aspects of the Greek Guerilla Campaign, historical, political and military.

(b) *When Greek Meets Greek.* By SIR REGINALD LEEPER. Chatto & Windus.
An account of particular value from the political point of view in that the author was H.M. Ambassador to the Greek Government in Cairo and later in Athens.

(c) *We Fell among Greeks.* By DENYS HAMSON. Jonathan Cape.
The author was a BLO operating with the Greek Guerillas in the mountains of Western Greece. His story gives an insight into the problems common to most BLOs and provides a good personal picture of conditions within the Greek Guerilla Movement.

(d) *A War of Shadows.* By W. S. MOSS. Boardman.
Chapter 3 deals with the author's experiences in the field with the Macedonian Guerillas, and gives yet another slant on the latter's habits, shortcomings and capabilities.
Chapter 2 gives a personal account of Guerilla action in Crete and clearly shows the limitations imposed on Resistance in that island.

(e) *Ill Met by Moonlight.* By W. S. MOSS. Harrap.
A more detailed description of Guerilla activity in Crete, as seen by the author. It includes the kidnapping of a German Divisional Commander.

(f) *Greek Entanglement.* By E. C. W. MYERS. Rupert Hart-Davis.
An account of the author's experiences and difficulties as head of the Military Mission to the Greek Resistance Movements. The complexities of the political and military factors involved during this campaign are well brought out.

## 7. REMAINDER OF EUROPE: SECOND WORLD WAR

(*a*) (i) *Sons of the Eagle*. By JULIAN AMERY. MacMillan & Co.

(ii) *Illyrian Venture*. (First eight chapters.) By Brigadier E. F. DAVIES. Bodley Head.

These two describe Albanian Guerilla operations as seen from two somewhat different angles, the first by a BLO with considerable background knowledge and practical experience, and the other by an Army Officer sent into the country at short notice in an attempt to co-ordinate the activities of politically opposed factions.

(*b*) *Rossano*. By GORDON LETT. Hodder & Stoughton.

An excellent, well balanced account by a British Officer of his experiences with Italian Resistance. It gives a clear picture of the difficulties facing a BLO who is trying to weld politically opposed groups into a unified resistance movement, and shows the shortcomings common to any such organisation. The human side is also well described.

(*c*) *Winged Dagger*. By ROY FARRAN. Collins.

Book 3 describes the activities of the author when a BLO with the Italian partisans in Italy, operating in direct support of the Allied armies in the Appenines.

Book 2 (Chapter 8) while not directly describing Guerilla operations, is of interest as it deals with the actions of a Special Air Service Unit deep in enemy occupied France, operating in conjunction with the Maquis.

(*d*) (i) *Communist Guerilla Warfare*. By C. A. DIXON and OTTO HEILBRUNN. Allen & Unwin.

Deals with Soviet Guerilla operations against the German forces operating in the USSR. Its aim appears to be to stress the danger to the West of Soviet Guerilla methods and for that reason may possibly credit the Soviet Guerillas in the Second World War with rather more efficiency than they in fact possessed.

(ii) *Behind the Front Line*. By Lt.-Gen. PONSMARENKO. Hutchinson.

(iii) *Our Partisan Course*. By Major-Gen. KOVPAK. Hutchinson.

(iv) *We are Guerillas*. By Soviet War News. Hutchinson.

All three books are written with an eye to propaganda, and the sweeping successes claimed must therefore be suspect. They do, however, between them give an indication of the characteristics of the Soviet Partisans, and of the tactics and conditions under which they operated. In this respect 'Our Partisan Course' is the most interesting and gives the impression of being the most accurate.

(*e*) *Specially Employed*. By M. J. BUCKMASTER. The Batchworth Press.

Although not dealing with guerilla warfare as such, this book, which recounts the story of British aid to the French resistance, is of value in that it illustrates the organisational and communication aspects of 'outside support'.

(*f*) *The Undaunted*. By RONALD SETH. Frederick Muller, London.

Does not deal specifically with guerilla warfare as such, but gives a good account of national resistance throughout Western Europe. The countries dealt with are Norway, Belgium, Denmark, Holland, Luxembourg, France, Greece, Jugoslavia and Italy.

## 8. THE FAR EAST (SECOND WORLD WAR)

(*a*) *The Jungle is Neutral*. By F. SPENCER CHAPMAN. Chatto & Windus.

A good description of conditions in Malaya, of the Guerillas and the problems facing Liaison Officers in that theatre. The author remained in the country throughout most of the period of Japanese occupation, having previously been one of the officers responsible for preparations for Resistance in the Far East.

(b) *Grandfather Longlegs.* By I. MORRISON. Faber & Faber.

Is the story of a BLO who became an almost legendary figure amongst the Karen tribes of Burma, and is of value for its description of the Karens and conditions in South West Burma during the Japanese occupation.

(c) *A War of Shadows.* By W. S. Moss. Boardman.

Chapter 4 gives the author's experiences with guerilla units in Siam, during and after the Second World War.

(d) *We Remained.* By Col. R. W. VOLCKMANN. Norton, New York.

This is the story of an American Army Colonel's activities during three years behind the Japanese lines in the Philippines during the Second World War. The later chapters are of particular value as they show clearly the main factors affecting the build-up of guerilla resistance in the islands and the results achieved.

## 9. POST WORLD WAR II

(a) *Jungle Green.* By ARTHUR CAMPBELL. Allen & Unwin.

This book deals with the campaign in Malaya against the Communist terrorists. Although written from the aspect of the Regular Forces, it illustrates the problems of fighting Communist Guerillas under jungle conditions.

(b) *Menace in Malaya.* By HARRY MILLER. Harrap.

A good account of the development of the Communist threat to Malaya and of the various steps taken by the Government to defeat the terrorists.

*RESTRICTED*

www.ingramcontent.com/pod-product-compliance
Ingram Content Group UK Ltd.
Pitfield, Milton Keynes, MK11 3LW, UK
UKHW021257180426
11947UKWH00011B/817